Carlos A. Segovia

The Quranic Jesus

Judaism, Christianity, and Islam – Tension, Transmission, Transformation

Edited by Patrice Brodeur, Alexandra Cuffel, Assaad Elias Kattan, and Georges Tamer

Volume 5

Carlos A. Segovia

The Quranic Jesus

A New Interpretation

DE GRUYTER

ISBN 978-3-11-059764-6
e-ISBN (PDF) 978-3-11-059968-8
e-ISBN (EPUB) 978-3-11-059896-4
ISSN 2196-405X

Library of Congress Control Number: 2018951346

Bibliografic information published by the Deutsche Nationalbibliothek
The Deutsche Nationalbibliothek lists this publication in the Deutschen Nationalbibliografie; detailed bibliografic data are available on the Internet at http://dnb.dnb.de.

Typesetting: Integra Software Services Pvt. Ltd.
Printing and binding: CPI books GmbH, Leck

MIX
Papier aus verantwortungsvollen Quellen
FSC® C083411

www.degruyter.com

To Sofya

وَإِذَا آمَنَ بِعِيسَى ثُمَّ آمَنَ بِي ، فَلَهُ أَجْرَانِ
صحيح البخاري ٣٤٤٦

Preface

While clearly affirming that God has no partner, and moreover that he is childless,[1] the quranic authors repeatedly encourage their audience to behave like Jesus's disciples, defend Jesus against the Jews, declare him to be the Messiah and the Word of God as well as a spirit from him (a series of titles they never apply to other prophets), make systematic use of a number of crucial Christian rhetorical moves, and quote more or less verbatim the New Testament Apocrypha and the writings of several late-antique Christian authors. Furthermore, they seem to be engaged in intra-Christian controversies just as much as they seem to partake in anti-Christian polemics. Conversely, the apparently pro-Jewish passages that one finds in the Qur'ān often prove tricky, as they are usually placed within, or next to, more or less violent anti-Jewish pericopes that bear the marks of Christian rhetoric despite a few occasional anti-Christian interpolations. And to further complicate the matter, the earliest quranic layers seem to develop a high- yet non-incarnationist Christology of which, interestingly enough, Jesus's name is totally missing.

What, then, can we make out of this puzzle? To what extent may the Qur'ān's highly complex Christology[2] help to decipher not only the intent of various quranic authors – which may well be very different from what has been hitherto taken for granted – but also the likewise complex redactional process characteristic of the document itself? Is it, moreover, possible to inscribe the often – indeed too-often – oversimplified Christology of the Qur'ān within the peripheral religious culture of the 6th-to-7th-century Near East? Is it possible, also, to unearth from it something about the tension carefully – or perhaps not so carefully – buried in the document between a messianic-oriented- and a prophetic-guided religious thought, and to root therein the earliest "Islamic" schism – if speaking of Islam before 'Abd al-Malik's reign in the late 7th century makes any sense, that is? By analysing, first, the typology and the plausible date of the Jesus-texts contained in the Qur'ān (which implies moving far beyond any purely thematic division of the passages in question), and by examining, in the second place, the Qur'ān's earliest Christology vis-à-vis its later (and indeed much better known) Muhamadan *kerygma*, the present study tries to give response to these crucial questions.

1 On the difference between God being "sonless" and "childless," see further Chapter 5.
2 Let this composite term be provisionally understood here in its broadest sense, i.e. as allusive to the treatment that God's Word and Jesus's messiahship receive in the quranic corpus.

https://doi.org/10.1515/9783110599688-201

A few acknowledgements are in order here. I should like to thank Ali Amir-Moezzi and Guillaume Dye for encouraging me to work on *sūra-s* 2 and 3 of the Qur'ān for a collective volume forthcoming at Les Éditions du Cerf, of which I have extracted a few excerpts in Chapter 3; Haggai Mazuz for allowing me to include in it a few paragraphs of a paper of mine upcoming in a volume he is preparing for the Brill Reference Library of Judaism;[3] William Adler, Lorenzo DiTommaso, and Matthias Henze, for permitting me to reproduce there too a few fragments of my recent contribution to Michael Stone's *Festschrift*;[4] Isaac Oliver and Anders Petersen for their helpful feedback on an earlier draft of my analysis of Q 9:30-1, which I have undertaken and reworked in Chapter 4; Manfred Kropp for his valuable insights on the section on Abrəha's Christology included too in it – whose first draft, moreover, he welcomed for publication in *Oriens Christianus* in 2015;[5] Matt Sheddy, for authorising me to incorporate to the Afterword some excerpts of a paper of mine on the Dome of the Rock inscriptions;[6] and Daniel Beck, on whose hermeneutical insights I substantially rely in Chapter 5. I am also grateful to Guillaume Dye, with whom I have had the pleasure to thoroughly discuss many of the views put forward in the pages that follow; Basil Lourié, who without knowing it helped me to make of the study of the Qur'ān my field of specialisation over the past ten years;[7] Emilio González Ferrín, who kindly shared with

3 Carlos A. Segovia, "Friends, Enemies, or Hoped-for New Rulers? Reassessing the Early Jewish Sources Mentioning the Rise of Islam," forthcoming in *Jews and Judaism in Northern Arabia*, ed. Haggai Mazuz (BRLJ; Leiden and Boston: Brill).

4 Carlos A. Segovia, "An Encrypted Adamic Christology in the Qur'ān? New Insights on 15:29; 21:91; 38:72; 66:12," in *The Embroidered Bible: Studies in Biblical Apocrypha and Pseudepigrapha in Honour of Michael E. Stone*, ed. William Adler, Lorenzo DiTommaso, and Matthias Henze (SVTP; Leiden and Boston: Brill, 2018) 913–27.

5 Carlos A. Segovia, "Abraha's Christological Formula *RḤMNN W-MAS¹Ḥ-HW* and Its Relevance for the Study of Islam's Origins," *OC* 98 (2015): 52–63.

6 Carlos A. Segovia, "Identity Politics and the Study of Islamic Origins: The Inscriptions of the Dome of the Rock as a Test Case," forthcoming in *Identity, Politics and the Study of Islam: Current Dilemmas in the Study of Religions*, ed. Matt Sheddy (CESIF; Sheffield, UK, and Bristol, CT: Equinox)

7 For this book, together with my upcoming papers: "Messalianism, Binitarianism, and the East-Syrian Bacground of the Qur'ān" (forthcoming in *Remapping Emergent Islam: Texts, Social Contexts, and Ideological Trajectories*, ed. Carlos A. Segovia [SWLAEMA; Amsterdam: Amsterdam University Press], "Asceticism and the Early Quranic Milieu: A Symptomatic Reading of Q 17:79, 43:36, 73:1–8, 74:43, 76:26, and 108" (forthcoming), and (with Gilles Courtieu) "Bābil, Makka and Ṭā'if, or (always) Ctesiphon(-Seleucia)? New Insights into the Iranian Setting of the Earliest Quranic Milieu" (forthcoming) is my final contribution to the study of Islams origins, since I have recently moved into an altogether different field of research at the crossroads of postcolonial studies, contemporary philosophy, and anthropological theory – after having fulfilled, that is, an ambitious research project whose two principal results I take to be (1) the underlying of the

me his impressions after reading a first draft of this book; my former chair of division at Saint Louis University in Madrid, John Welch, for thoughtfully making possible for me to teach on the quranic Jesus during three consecutive years – an experience from which this book has, I think, consistently benefited; and my students, with whom I have intensely and fruitfully worked month after month on the typological classification ventured in Chapter 3 and the evolution of the Qur'ān's Christology examined in Chapter 5. Above all, however, I should like to express my deepest gratitude to my wife, Sofya, without whose generous inspiration and precious love I would be unable to breathe and think; dedicating this book to her is but a humble sign of my devotedness to whom I feel blessed to live with every day.

---

key role that corresponds to the Jesus-texts for deciphering the threefold (pre-Muhammadan, Muhammadan, and post-Muhammadan) chronology of the quranic corpus, and (2) the establishment of an original Iraqi, rather than Hijazi, setting for the latter's earliest layers. Visibly, a this implies expanding the boundaries of the proto-Islamic milieu (I am reluctant to speak of "Islam" *strictu sensu* before the late 7th century) in both space and time, as also the composition and collection of the Qur'an itself. Yet I am persuaded that we need a new interpretative lens, as well as more sophisticated tools, to study the latter, and that questions of theory and method must be very clear from the outset if we want to get a clear picture of what the quranic corpus originally was – supposing we can still speak in the singular. I moreover take this type of investigation to be of special relevance given the naivety of a field of study that has been, and sadly remains today, excessively dependent on obsolete and purely emic master-narratives. Thus I am persuaded that applying internal, textual criteria to the analysis of the quranic corpus provides far more satisfactory results for a correct understanding of the document's content and setting than the mixture of doctrinal and pseudo-historical interpretation supplied by the Islamic tradition does. More specifically, this book attempts at deciphering some of the document's key redactional layers, periods of composition, and geographical-cultural settings through the examination, and typological classification, of a number of symptomatic textual indices combining group-identity markers, ideological discursive strategies, and (meta)religious concepts. The task can be viewed as recursive and intersectional, for typology is often indicative of context and contextual analysis often serves to trace chronology.

Contents

Abbreviations

AIBL	Académie des Inscriptions et Belles-Lettres
AIG	Arabic Infancy Gospel
ANZM	Administration der Neuen Zeitschrift für Missionswissenschaft
apud	At, in the writings of
Arab.	Arabic
ASA	Ancient South Arabian
ASMEA	Association for the Study of the Middle East and Africa
b.	Babylonian Talmud
BEHE	Bibliothèque de l'École des Hautes Études
BEHESR	Bibliothèque de l'École des Hautes Études Sciences Religieuses
BHMIIS	*Bulletin of Henry Martyn Institute of Islamic Studies*
BJQHS	*Al-Bayān: Journal of Qur'ān and Ḥadīth Studies*
BJRL	*Bulletin of the John Rylands Library*
BRLJ	Brill Reference Library of Judaism
BSOAS	*Bulletin of the School of Oriental and African Studies*
c.	Around (Latin: *circa*)
C1	Christology no. 1
C2	Christology no. 2
C3	Christology no. 3
CCL	Collection Cerfaux-Lefort
CESIF	Cultures on the Edge: Studies in Identity Formation
cf.	Compare (Latin: *confer*)
ch(s).	Chapter(s)
CIH	Corpus Inscriptionum Himyariticarum
contra	In opposition or contrast to
CRSAIBL	Comptes rendus des séances de l'Académie des Inscriptions et Belles-Lettres
CSAI	Corpus of South Arabian Inscriptions
CT	*Cave of Treasures*
CTh	Cahiers théologiques
CUASEC	Catholic University of America Studies in Early Christianity
d.	died
DA	Diskurse der Arabistik
DACS	Dissertations: Ancient Christian Studies
DAI	Deutsches Archäologisches Institut
DHR	Dynamics in the History of Religions
DOP	*Dumbarton Oaks Papers*
DORLC	Dumbarton Oaks Research Library and Collection
DR	*Dublin Review*
DRLAR	Divinations: Rereading Late Ancient Religion
ECCA	Early Christianity in the Context of Antiquity
ECS	Easter Christian Studies
ed(s).	Edited by, editor(s)
e.g.	For example (Latin: *exemplum gratia*)
EI	*Encyclopaedia of Islam*

https://doi.org/10.1515/9783110599688-202

EME	Éditions Modulaires Européens
1 En	1 Enoch
EnIr	*Encyclopaedia Iranica*
esp.	especially
EUS	European University Studies
GDN	Grosser Damm Nord
Gk.	Greek
Heb.	Hebrew
HR	*History of Religions*
HTR	*Harvard Theological Review*
i.e.	That is (Latin: *id est*)
IFD	Institut Français de Damas
IISMM	Institut d'études de l'Islam et des sociétés du monde musulman
IJHCME	*Der Islam: Journal of the History and Culture of the Middle East*
IS	*Iranian Studies*
IVP	InterVarsity Press
JA	*Journal asiatique*
JAOC	Judaïsme ancien et origines du christianisme
JAOS	*Journal of the American Oriental Society*
JCIT	Judaism, Christianity, and Islam – Tension, Transmission, Transformation
JCSSS	Journal of the Canadian Society for Syriac Studies
JESHO	*Journal of the Economic and Social History of the Orient*
JPS	*Journal of Persianate Studies*
JQR	*Jewish Quarterly Review*
JSAI	*Jerusalem Studies n Arabic and Islam*
JSS	*Jewish Social Studies*
KTAH	Key Themes in Ancient History
l(l).	Line(s)
LAE	*Life of Adam and Eve*
LAMINE	Late Antique and Medieval Islamic Near East
lit.	Literarily
LOS	London Oriental Series
MA	*Miscellanea arabica*
MAIBL	Mémoires de l'Académie des inscriptions et belles-lettres
MDCSPCK	Madras Diocesan Committee of the Society for the Promotion of Christian Knowledge
MLR	*Mediterranean Language Review*
MMW	Makers of the Muslim World
MW	*The Muslim World*
n(n).	Note(s)
N1	Narrative no. 1
N2	Narrative no. 2
N3	Narrative no. 3
NAPSPMS	North American Patristics Society Patristic Monograph Series
NNT	Nederlands Theologisch Tijdschrift
NPNF1	*Nicene- and Post-Nicene Fathers*, First Series
NRSM	*Nouvelle Revue deScience Missionaire*
NZM	*Neuen Zeitschrift für Missionswissenschaft*

OC	*Oriens Christianus*
OECS	Oxford Early Christian Studies
OJC	Orientalia Judaica Christiana
OLA	Orientalia Lovaniensia Analecta
OM	Orient et Méditerranée
OSB	Oxford Studies in Byzantium
p(p)	Page(s)
P1	Period no. 1
P2	Period no. 2
pace	With due respect to, but disagreeing with
PHR	Problèmes d'histoire des religions
pl.	Plural
PO	Patrologia Orientalis
POr	*Parole de l'Orient*
PRE	*Pirqê de Rabbî 'Elî*'ezer
PsM	Pseudo-Matthew
Q	Qur'ān
r.	reigned
RA	Religion et Altérité
REB	Revised English Bible
RHR	*Revue de l'histoire des religions*
ROMM	*Revue de l'Occident musulman et de la Méditerranée*
RSQ	Rutledge Studies in the Qur'ān
Sab.	Sabaic
SBEO	Société Belge d'Études Orientales
SBL	Society of Biblical Literature
SBLEJL	Society of Biblical Literature Early Judaism and Its Literature
SCM	Student Christian Movement
SFGMO	Schriften der finnischen Gesellschaft für Missiologie und Ökumenik
sic	Thus (Latin: *sic erat scriptum*)
sing.	Singular
SLAEI	Studies in Late Antiquity and Early Islam
SNT	Studien zum Neuen Testament
SO	*Studia Orientalia*
SSN	Studia Semitica Neerlandica
STDJ	Studies on the Texts of the Desert of Judah
SVTP	Studia in Veteris Testamenti Pseudepigraphica
Syr.	Syriac
SWLAEMA	Social Worlds of Late Antiquity and the Early Middle Ages
TCH	Transformations of the Classical Heritage
TSAJ	Text and Studies in Ancient Judaism
TSQ	Texts and Studies on the Qur'ān
v(v).	Verse(s)
VCS	Variorum Collected Studies
vol(s).	Volume(s)
WBG	Wissenschaftliche Buchgesellschaft
WUNT	Wissenschaftliche Untersuchungen zum Neuen Testament
ZRGG	Zeitschrift für Religions- und Geistesgeschichte

1 Introduction: Traditional Views and New Insights on the Quranic Jesus

Descriptive *vs.* Anti-Christian Theological Texts?

Heretofore the modern study of the quranic Jesus has basically moved in a single direction, as generally scholars have approached the Jesus passages contained in the Qur'ān from a thematic standpoint. Somewhat inoffensively, therefore, they tend to distinguish between the passages in which Jesus's birth is reported, those that mention his mission to Israel (including his teachings and miracles), those relative to his death, those which mention him as a prophet or a righteous among other prophets and righteous, and those that discuss his divine sonship and hence the very basis of mainstream Christian doctrine – which most modern scholars regard as the primary target of the Qur'ān's counter-Christology.

It is this last point, moreover, that has largely overdetermined all modern interpretations of the quranic Jesus.[1] Accordingly, most scholars take the quranic passages allusive to Jesus's birth, life, and death as being merely illustrative of some key episodes of Jesus's "biography" as told in the gospels; in their view, therefore, such passages convey a purely *descriptive* purpose, even if their narratives often draw on apocryphal (i.e. non-canonical) sources, or else display new (i.e. elsewhere unmatched) "data." In contrast, the passages that criticise the notion that Jesus is God's son – and which question, thereby, the cornerstone of any recognisable Christology – are interpreted by them to contain the Qur'ān's own *theological* message about Jesus.

As I hope to prove in this book, things are much more complex than most modern interpreters are willing to assume. It may well be, for example, that some if not all of the alleged descriptive Jesus passages hide more than they seem to offer at first sight; or, to put it in more forceful terms, that they serve an ideological purpose which is anything *but* descriptive. Also, it is not altogether clear how one ought to articulate and interpret the quranic passages that refer to Jesus as God's messiah instead of God's son, those which deny Jesus's divine sonship, those that impugn the Christian trinity, and those which contend that God is

---

1 Two notable exceptions are Peter von Sivers, "Christology and Prophetology in the Umayyad Arab Empire," in *Die Entstehung einer Weltreligion III*, ed. Markus Groß and Karl-Heinz Ohlig (Berlin: Hans Schiler, 2014) 255–85, and Daniel A. Beck *Evolution of the Early Qur'ān: From Anonymous Apocalypse to Charismatic Prophet* (ACDE 2; New York and Bern: Peter Lang, 2018). – I am grateful to Daniel Beck for kindly sharing a draft of his book with me prior to its publication.

https://doi.org/10.1515/9783110599688-001

childless: do they all belong to the same redactional layer?, and, more importantly, even if one agrees that they all aim at the same idea, which is their *exact* theological intent? Lastly, is it possible to reread the Christology of the Qur'ān (i.e. the latter's treatment of God's Word and of Jesus's messiahship) against the background of the Near-Eastern Christological developments of the 7th century? And if so, how should they and how should they not be linked?; this is to say, what specific type of contextual *connection* between them should be acknowledged in order to pay justice to their apparently complex imbrication and what particular type of *subordination* should be avoided in turn?

Before answering to these and other related questions, however (that is, before moving beyond the poor *binary* typology formerly alluded to, which certainly needs to be substituted with a more *complex*, sophisticated one)[2] it will be helpful to ponder and discuss the most relevant arguments on the quranic Jesus put forward over the past decades (with no attempt at exhaustivity, therefore).

The Study of the Quranic Jesus between the 1830s and Now

From Carl Friedrich Gerock to Denise Masson's Ecumenical Reading of the Qur'ān

Several monographs on the quranic Jesus were published in German, French, and English between 1839 and 1929, including Carl Friedrich Gerock's *Versuch einer Darstellung der Christologie des Koran,*[3] J.-P. Maneval's *La Christologie du Coran,*[4] William Goldsack's *Christ in Islam,*[5] Samuel Zwemer's *The Moslem Christ,*[6] and Basharat Ahmad's *Birth of Jesus in the Light of the Quran and in*

---

2 Not that I view binary logic as being rudimentary per se (see my forthcoming essay "Social Theory, Conceptual Imagination, and The Study of Pre-State Societies: From Lévi-Strauss to Pierre Clastres," forthcoming in *Anarchist Studies*); it simply proves here inoperative at best.

3 C. F. Gerock, *Versuch einer Darstellung der Christologie des Koran* (Hamburg: Perthes, 1839).

4 J.-P. Maneval, *La Christologie du Coran* (PhD dissertation, Faculté de théologie protestante de Montauban; Toulouse, France: Chauvin, 1867).

5 William Goldsack, *Christ in Islam: The Testimony of the Quran to Christ* (London: Christian Literature Society, 1905).

6 Samuel M. Zwemer, *The Moslem Christ: An Essay on the Life, Character, and Teachings of Jesus Christ according to the Koran and Orthodox Tradition* (Edinburgh and London: Oliphant, Anderson, and Ferrier, 1912).

the Light of the Gospels.[7] Yet due to the obsolete style of these, the first if indirect studies worth mentioning here are Josef Henninger's *Spuren christlicher Glaubenswahrheiten im Koran*[8] and Denise Masson's *Le Coran et la Révélation judéo-chrétienne*,[9] which were both published in the 1950s. Henninger patiently scrutinises the Christian views and doctrines reflected in the quranic corpus,[10] whereas Masson basically aims at bridging the divide between the theology of the Qur'ān and that of the Catholic Church. The Christology resulting from the 4th Lateran Council according to which the divine essence is uncreated, Thomas Aquinas's distinction between differences *ad extra* and differences *ad intra*, and Hans Urs von Balthasar's non-triadic understanding of the trinity, Masson affirms, may all be said to come rather close to the formulation of God's unmatched unicity in the Qur'ān. Her legitimate ecumenical concerns notwithstanding, Masson's too harmonising and somewhat ahistorical views were opportunely criticised in the 1960s and the 1970s by French Orientalists and Catholic theologians alike,[11] yet they were influential on the Second Vatican Council (1962–5) and encouraged the renewed attitude towards Islam that the Catholic Church displayed thereinafter.[12]

---

7 Basharat Ahmad, *Birth of Jesus in the Light of the Quran and in the Light of the Gospels* (Lahore, India: Dar-ul-Kutib-i-Islam, ca. 1929). See further the bibliography in Jan A. B. Jongeneel, with the assistance of Robert T. Coote, *Jesus Christ in World History: His Presence and Representation in Cyclical and Linear Settings* (Frankfurt: Peter Lang, 2008) 429.

8 Josef Henninger, *Spuren christlicher Glaubenswahrheiten im Koran* (Schöneck: ANZM, 1951); originally published in *NZM/NRSM* 1 (1945): 135–40, 304–14; 2 (1946): 56–65, 109–22, 289–304; 3 (1947): 128–40, 290–301; 4 (1948): 129–41, 284–93; 5 (1949): 127–40, 290–300; 6 (1950): 207–17, 284–97.

9 Denise Masson, *Le Coran et la Révélation judéo-chrétienne. Études comparées* (2 vols.; Paris: Maisonneuve, 1958); reedited in 1976 as *Monothéisme coranique et monothéisme biblique. Doctrines comparées* (Paris: Desclée).

10 See now too Jane Dammen McAuliffe, *Qur'ānic Christians: An Analysis of Classical and Modern Exegesis* (Cambridge and New York: Cambridge University Press, 2007); Gabriel Said Reynolds, "On the Presentation of Christianity in the Qur'ān and the Many Aspects of Qur'anic Rhetoric," *BJQHS* 12 (2014): 42–54.

11 See Regis Blachère, "Compte rendu de Denise Masson, *Le Coran et la Révélation judéo-chrétienne, études comparées*, Paris (A. Maisonneuve) 1958," *Arabica* 7.1 (1960): 93–5; André Caquot, "Compte rendu de Denise Masson, *Le Coran et la Révélation judéo-chrétienne. Études comparées*, Paris, A. Maisonneuve, 1958," *RHR* 157.1 (1960): 107–8; Hervé Bleuchot, "Compte rendu de Denise Masson, *Monothéisme coranique et monothéisme biblique. Doctrines comparées*,[Paris,] Desclée de Brouwer, 1976," *ROMM* 24.1 (1977): 281–85.

12 See further James Pallathupurayidam, *The Second Vatican Council and Islam: Change in the Catholic Attitude* (Ph.D. dissertation, McGill University, 1981); Renée Champion, "Masson, Denise," in *Dictionnaire des orientalistes de la langue française*, ed. François Pouillon (Paris: IISMM–Karthala, 2012) 704. See also Giulio Basetti-Sani, *Il Corano nella luce di Cristo: saggio per una*

Robert Charles Zaehner and the "Nestorian" Matrix of the Qur'ān's Christology

The very same year in which Masson's book was released, Robert Charles Zaehner published a brief essay on "The Qur'ān and Christ"; Zaehner's essay was included as an appendix in a volume titled *At Sundry Times: An Essay in the Comparison of Religions* containing the transcript of his Sir D. Owen Evans Lectures at the University College of Wales in January of 1957, and it was also the first modern study to explicitly focus on the study of quranic Jesus.[13]

Zaehner was a historian of religions and a specialist in Iranian and Indian studies (on which he published uninterruptedly between 1938 and 1974) who combined his academic position as professor of Eastern Religions and Ethics at Oxford University with his job as British Intelligence officer at the UK Embassy in Tehran.[14] As an Orientalist, Zaehner worked on middle-east religions; as a (Catholic-)Christian apologist, he was deeply concerned with the relation between these and Christianity, and his views proved influential within certain Christian sectors;[15] an illustration of this is Peter Kreeft and Ronald Tacelli's *Handbook of Christian Apologetics*, which draws repeatedly on Zaehner's insights on "salvation and other religions."[16] Yet Zaehner's 1958 paper on the quranic Jesus cannot be simply grouped among his apologetic writings. As Carlo Cereti, following Geoffrey Parrinder,[17] writes,

> [e]ven in his more scholarly books, Zaehner was prone to be influenced by his personal beliefs when analyzing religious phenomena. [And t]his was all the more true for a group of books that may be aptly defined as apologetic and polemical, arguing as they do in favor of his own Christian and ethical beliefs–works such as *Christianity and Other Religions* (1964), *The Convergent Spirit* (1963), *Evolution in Religion* (1971), and *Dialectical Christianity and Christian Materialism* (1971). More complex and intellectually stimulating [however] are two other impassioned works, *At Sundry Times* (1958) . . . and *Concordant Discord* (1970).[18]

---

reinterpretazione cristiana del libro sacro de l'Islam (Bologna: Editrice Missionaria Italiana, 1972; English translation by W. Russell Carroll and Bede Dauphinee, *The Koran in the Light of Christ* [Chicago: Franciscan Herald Press, 1977]).

13 R. C. Zaehner, *At Sundry Times: An Essay in the Comparison of Religions* (London: Faber and Faber, 1958; 2nd ed., Westport, CT: Greenwood, 1977) 195–217.

14 For Zaehner's biography and publications, see Geoffrey Parrinder, "Robert Charles Zaehner (1913–1974)," *HR* 16 (1976): 66–74; Carlo Cereti, "Zaehner, Robert Charles," *EnIr*, online edition, 2015, available at http://www.iranicaonline.org/articles/zaehner-robert.

15 See e.g. R. C. Zaehner, *Mysticism Sacred and Profane* (Oxford and New York: Oxford University Press, 1961) and *Christianity and Other Religions* (New York: Hawthorn, 1964), respectively.

16 Peter Kreeft and Ronald K. Tacelli, *Handbook of Christian Apologetics: Hundred of Answers to Crucial Questions* (IVP Academic; Downers Grove, IL: InterVarsity Press, 2009) 399.

17 Cf. Parrinder, "Zaehner," 69–70.

18 Cereti, "Zaehner."

In his 1957 lectures at the University College of Wales and at the Newman Association Graduate Division of the University Catholic Federation of Great Britain that very year,[19] Zaehner attempted to build a bridge (thus wider than Masson's) between Christianity and the religions of the Middle East, Islam included; and for that purpose he criticised what he believed to be lately introduced points of conflict in the Islamic interpretation of the Qur'ān, which he understood to be in basic agreement with the premises of Christian doctrine.[20] Not all of Zaehner's insights can be ruled out on this basis, however. I therefore disagree with Oddbjørn Leirvik's claim that Zaehner "combines a thematic approach [to the quranic Jesus] with a sort of *interpretatio christiana*"[21] when, following Tor Andrae,[22] in his 1958 appendix he suggests, for instance, that the Christology of the Qur'ān is less anti-Christian than "Nestorian" (i.e. East-Syrian) oriented;[23] for in this case Zaehner's rather unconventional view is partly sound, as I shall try to prove later in this book.

To put it succinctly: Zaehner rightly makes the point that, although God's Word and Spirit can be said to dwell in him, Jesus is fully and only human in the Qur'ān; as to Mary, he argues, she is not the Mother of God, for God's Word and Spirit pre-exist her and are cast upon her: "The human Jesus is produced directly by God's creative Word or *Logos*," he writes: "he is not a son acquired by God but is brought into existence in the Virgin's womb by the direct action of the Divine

---

19 See R. C. Zaehner, "Islam and Christ," *DR* (1957): 271–88.

20 For an assessment of Zaehner's attitude towards Islam, see further David R. Blanks, "Western Views of Islam in the Premodern Period: A Brief History of Past Approaches," in *Western Views of Islam in Medieval and Early Modern Europe: Perception of Other*, ed. David R. Blanks and Michael Frassetto (New York: St. Martin's Press, 1999) 24–5; Kristin Skottki, "Medieval Western Perceptions of Islam and the Scholars: What Went Wrong?," in *Cultural Transfers in Dispute: Representations in Asia, Europe and the Arab World since the Middle Ages*, ed. Jörg Feuchter, Friedhelm Hoffmann, and Bee Yun (Frankfurt and New York: Campus Verlag, 2011) 107–34, pp. 120–1.

21 Oddbjørn Leirvik, *Images of Jesus Christ in Islam* (London and New York: Continuum, 1999; 2nd ed., 2010) 24.

22 Tor Andrae, *Der Ursprung des Islams und das Christentum* (Uppsala: Almqvist and Wiksells, 1926).

23 Zaehner, *At Sundry Times*, 206–9. I personally prefer expressions like "East Syrian" (or "Eastern Diphysite") to the term "Nestorian," which constitutes – as Sebastian Brock stresses – a "misnomer" (see Sebastian P. Brock, "The 'Nestorian' Church: A Lamentable Misnomer," *BJRL* 78.3 [1996]: 23–35); yet "Nestorian" is the term Zaehner himself uses to denote the Christology of the Church of the East, for which reason I opt to keep it here as such. For a criticism of Brock's "pro-orthodox" view, see however Chapter 4 *in fine*.

Word, 'Be!'"[24] In fact, the Qur'ān teaches nothing different from this;[25] and this unquestionably resembles, in turn, the "theology of the indwelling Logos" of the Church of the East, according to which Colossians 2:9 ("For it is in Christ that the Godhead in all its fullness dwells embodied" [REB]) was paraphrased to mean "in [Jesus] the Logos dwells perfectly."[26]

It may be objected that, compared to East-Syrian Christology, the Qur'ān operates on a different level, as it does not address the question of the relationship between Christ's divinity and his humanity – put differently: Jesus lacks in it divine status, so one may argue that there is no need for the quranic authors to reciprocally articulate his divinity *and* his humanity, which was, in contrast, a fundamental concern for the theologians of the Church of the East.[27] Yet the

---

24 Zaehner, *At Sundry Times*, 206.

25 Cf. Q 2:87, 253; 5:110 (concerning Jesus's divine assistance by the Holy Spirit); 3:45; 4:171 (concerning Jesus as God's Word); 3:47, 59; 19:21 (concerning God's creation of Jesus) 4:171; 21:91; 66:12 (concerning Jesus as the manifestation of God's Spirit). Cf. too 3:59; 15:29; 38:72; 21:91; 66:12 (apropos Adam and Jesus). I shall examine these passages in the next chapter.

26 Jaroslav Pelikan, *The Christian Tradition: A History of the Development of Doctrine* (2 vols.; Chicago and London: University of Chicago Press, 1971–4) 2:41. It is from Pelikan, too, that I take the expression "theology of the indwelling Logos." "The man whom the Logos had assumed as his temple and dwelling," he writes, "was the Second Adam, made sinless by the grace of God. It was this assumed man, and not the indwelling Logos, who had been crucified"; cf. the reference to Jesus's death in Q 4:153–9, which may be read in this way *contra* its traditional interpretation in (and outside) Islam (see Neal Robinson, "Jesus," in *Encycopledia of the Qur'ān*, ed. J. D. McAuliffe [6 vols.; Leiden and Boston: Brill, 2001–6] 3:17–20; Gabriel Said Reynolds, "The Muslim Jesus: Dead or Alive?" *BSOAS* 72.2 [2009]: 237–58). On the hitherto overlooked quranic (crypto-)representation of Jesus as the Second Adam, see my comments on Q 15:29; 38:72; 21:91; 66:12 in Chapter 3.

27 According to the latter, Christ is *one* "person" (Syr. ܦܪܨܘܦܐ *parsōpā;* Gk. πρόσοπον *prosōpon*) with *two* "natures" (Syr. ܟܝܢܐ *kyanē*, sing. ܟܝܢܐ *kyanā*; Gk. φύσεις *physeis*, sing. φύσις *physis*), one *divine* and the other one *human*, to which therefore correspond *two* "individual manifestations" (Syr. ܩܢܘܡܐ *qnōmē*, sing. ܩܢܘܡܐ *qnōmā*; the Gk. ὑποστασεις *hypostaseis*, sing. ὑποστασις *hypostasis*, has a slightly different and more complex meaning, as it denotes both the "substance," i.e. the "underlying reality" of something and "what actually exists"; see in this respect Christopher Stead, *Philosophy in Christian Antiquity* [Cambridge and New York: Cambridge University Press, 1994] 176). This approach clearly differs from the Chalcedonian (*one* person and *one* substance, but *two* natures), whose foundations were laid in the Council of Chalcedon in 451 and which represents a less-straightforward type of Diphysitism (the theological view that Christ has "two" natures), as much as it differs from the Miaphysite or West Syrian (*one* person, *one* single nature, and hence *one* single manifestation of such nature). Syriac Christians – be they Miaphysites or Diphysites – regarded Chalcedonian Christology, moreover, as being politically dangerous and theoretically untenable, for it represented the Christology of the foreign Greek-speaking Byzantine Church and proved ultimately inconsistent according to their own doctrinal principles (there cannot be two natures in Christ and one

Qur'ān reflects the East-Diphysite premise that the earthly Jesus is only a man, and therefore labels him "the Messiah, son of Mary," instead of Son of God – a title that intriguingly echoes too, in chiastic fashion, the East-Diphysite claim according to which Mary is the "Bearer/Mother of the Messiah" (Gk. Χριστοτόκος *Christotokos*) instead of the "Bearer/Mother of God" (Gk. Θεοτόκος *Theotokos*), as Chalcedonians and Miaphysites (alike in this case) conversely sustain(ed).[28] Furthermore, as I shall argue in Chapter 5, affirming that the Qur'ān leaves no room to the divinity of God's Word would amount to an oversimplification of its message. Emphasising as Zaehner does, therefore, the apparent connections existing between the Christology of the Qur'ān and the Christology of the East-Syrian Church, is in my opinion, *pace* Leirvik – and, again, in spite of Zaehner's own religious views – anything but improper. Additionally, the meaningfulness of Zaehner's comments cannot be limited to the comparative study of religion, for even if the Qur'ān would become in the late 7th-century the "sacred book," i.e. the textual marker of a new religious community, the documents collected in it (not to speak of the earliest redactional layers of such documents!) resist any clear-cut religious definition.[29]

Henri Michaud and the Hypothesis of a Jewish-Christian Influence on the Qur'ān

The next study after Masson's and Zaehner's was Henri Michaud's *Jésus selon le Coran* in 1960.[30] Michaud's purpose was to undertake a comprehensive survey of the quranic Jesus-texts and to foster a climate of mutual understanding and tolerance among Christians and Muslims. In addition, he ventured a rather bold hypothesis, namely that Muḥammad's views of Jesus were influenced by Jewish-Christianity. This contention had already been made *inter alios* by Adolf von Harnack and Hans-Joachim Schoeps[31] but presents several

sole manifestation for both, claimed the Diphysites of East Syria and present-day Iraq; and vice versa: there cannot be one only substance and two natures, the Miaphysites of West Syria, the Coptic-speaking Miaphysites of Egypt, and the Gəʿəz-speaking Miaphysites of Ethiopia, affirmed in turn).

28 For a more thorough cross-examination of the Christology of the Qur'ān and that of the Church of the East, see chapters 4 and 5.

29 In short, it would be anachronistic to view the Qur'ān as a deposit of Islamic doctrine or *theologoumena*; see the Conclusion to this book.

30 Henri Michaud, *Jésus salon le Coran* (CTh 46; Neuchatel: Delachaux et Niestlé, 1960).

31 See Guy G. Stroumsa, "Jewish Christianity and Islamic Origins," in *Islamic Cultures, Islamic Contexts: Essays in Honor of Professor Patricia Crone*, ed. Behnam Sadeghi, Asad Q. Ahmed, Adam Silverstein, and Robert G. Hoyland (Leiden and Boston: Brill, 2015) 72–96.

problems. First, as Guy Stroumsa aptly notes, "our documentation on Jewish Christian communities rarely goes beyond the fourth century."[32] Secondly, "the precise mechanisms through which ideas [were] transmitted [into the Qur'ān] are too little known"[33] to draw a clear-cut conclusion as to the direct influence of Jewish-Christian motifs upon formative Islam. Thirdly, as Matt Jackson-McCabe and Daniel Boyarin persuasively argue, the category "Jewish Christianity" is inherently problematic, inasmuch as it is too theological and too anachronistic.[34] It would make little sense, for instance, to distinguish between pagan- (i.e. Pauline) and Jewish (i.e. non-Pauline) Christians within the early Jesus's movement. We should rather talk of Christ-believing Jews as a subtype of Messianic- and/or Apocalyptic- and/or Enochic Jews,[35] and consequently distinguish between (*a*) the Christ-believing Jews that accepted Paul's

---

32 Stroumsa, "Jewish Christianity and Islamic Origins," 76. A fact that Mustafa Akyol's recent book *The Islamic Jesus: How the King of the Jews Became a Prophet of the Muslims* (New York: St. Martin's Press, 2017) and Dominique Bernard's likewise recent monograph *Les disciples juifs de Jésus du Ier siècle à Mahomet: Recherches sur le mouvement ébionite* (Paris: Cerf, 2017) – as well as paradoxically Stroumsa himself – seem to overlook.

33 Stroumsa, "Jewish Christianity and Islamic Origins," 90.

34 "Two critical if typically unspoken assumptions," writes Jackson-McCabe, "undergird this notion of a Jewish *Christianity*. The first is that, even if the name itself had not yet been coined, a religion that can usefully be distinguished from Judaism as Christianity was in fact in existence immediately in the wake of Jesus' death, if not already within his own lifetime. The second is that those ancient groups who seem from our perspective to sit on the borderline between Judaism and Christianity are nonetheless better understood as examples of the latter" (Matt Jackson-McCabe, "What's in a Name? The Problem of 'Jewish Christianity'," in *Jewish Christianity Reconsidered: Rethinking Ancient Groups and Texts*, ed. Matt Jackson-McCabe [Minneapolis: Fortress, 2007], 7–38, p. 29). In turn, Boyarin highlights that "everything that has traditionally been identified as Christianity in particular existed in some non-Jesus [Jewish] movements of the first century and later as well," and that "there is no nontheological or non anachronistic way way at all to distinguish Christianity from Judaism until institutions are in place that make and enforce this distinction, and even then we know precious little about what the nonelite and nonchatering classes were thinking or doing" (Daniel Boyarin, "Rethinking Jewish Christianity: An Argument for Dismantling a Dubious Category [to which is Appended a Correction of my Border Lines]," *JQR* 99.1 (2009): 7–37, p. 28). On the late partings of the ways between "Christianity" and "Judaism," see Daniel Boyarin, *Border Lines: The Partition of Judaeo-Christianity* (DRLAR; Philadelphia: University of Pennsylvania Press, 2004).

35 On the interconnectedness of these categories, see e.g. Gabriele Boccaccini, *Beyond the Essene Hypothesis: The Parting of the Ways between Qumran and Enochic Judaism* (Grand Rapids, MI, and Cambridge: Eerdmans, 1998); idem, *Roots of Rabbinic Judaism: An Intellectual History, from Ezekiel to Daniel* (Grand Rapids, MI, and Cambridge: Eerdmans, 2002); Gabriele Boccaccini, ed., *Enoch and the Messiah Son of Man: Revisiting the Book of Parables* (Grand Rapids, MI, and Cambridge: Eerdmans, 2007).

original message of integrating the gentiles *qua* gentiles alongside Israel into the people of God; (*b*) the Christ-believing Jews, be they originally born Jews or proselytes, that opposed Paul's message by claiming that the gentiles had to convert to Judaism; (*c*) the non-Jewish Christ-believers that sided with one or another of these options; and (*d*) the non-Jewish Christ-believers that refused to join Israel.[36] Labelling the Christ-believing Jews that opposed Paul's message as "Jewish Christians" implicitly deprives them of their Judaism/Jewishness and loses sight of the fact that Paul and those Jews who accepted his message were Christ-believing Jews as well. As for the period elapsing between the 1st and the 4th century, why should we uncritically assume the view of the Christian heresiologists that the non-Pauline Christ-believing Jews and the gentiles who joined them are to be considered as Christians instead of Jews? Should we not equate Christianity with the somewhat artificial and political achievement of the aforementioned *d*-group alone, and thus exclusively label as Christians the people belonging to it whatever its eventual subdivisions?[37]

Geoffrey Parrinder's Theological Approach to the Quranic Jesus

Like Zaehner's, Masson's, and Michaud's books, Martin Pörksen's *Jesus in der Bibel und im Koran* (1964) serves too an ecumenic purpose.[38] I shall next briefly comment instead of Pörksen's essay, therefore, Geoffrey Parrinder's widespread monograph *Jesus in the Qur'ān*, which was published in 1965.[39] As the author declares, he had his book "written primarily for readers in the Western world, the general public as well as students of theology and the comparative study of religions",[40] and his main purpose was to offer to such readers and to those Muslim readers who had asked for it "a modern and impartial study of the teaching of the Qur'ān about Jesus"[41] which was wanting at that time.

---

36 See further Gabriele Boccaccini and Carlos A. Segovia, eds., *Paul the Jew: Rethinking the Apostle as a Figure of Second Temple Judaism* (Minneapolis: Fortress, 2016).
37 On the making of Christianity see once more Boyarin, *Border Lines*. On the subdivisions of "Jewish Christianity," Simon Claude Mimouni, *Le judéo-christianisme ancien. Essays historiques*, Préface par André Caquot (Patrimoines; Paris: Cerf, 1998).
38 Martin Pörksen, *Jesus in der Bibel und im Koran* (Bad Salzuflen, Germany: MBK, 1964).
39 Geoffrey Parrinder, *Jesus in the Qur'ān* (London: Faber and Faber, 1965; 2nd ed., Oxford: Oneworld, 1995).
40 Parrinder, *Jesus in the Qur'ān*, 9.
41 Parrinder, *Jesus in the Qur'ān*, 9.

Ultimately, however, Parrinder's approach is strongly and unambiguously theological:

> This is a study of religion – he writes – and it presupposes sympathy with religious faith. The old idea that only an agnostic could write impartially is less popular now than in the last century, for it is realized that one who regards religion as superstition may well be biased and cannot hope to discover the inner spirit of religion or command the attention of believers. It is noteworthy that some of the most eminent modern writers on Islam in English, French and German are Christians who approach Islam as a kindred religion. But many academic scholars are interested chiefly in linguistic or historical matters, and questions of theology tend to get left aside for lack of interest or competence. When the theologian enters this field he [sic!] must try to follow academic discipline, apply its standards in the examination of texts and teachings, yet bring out the meaning and importance of religion. . . .
>
> The interest of this book is chiefly theological, and so questions of textual criticism, a subject particularly delicate for Muslims, have largely been left aside.[42]

Questions of textual criticism should be paid special attention and sympathy with religious faith be entirely left aside, nevertheless, when writing from a historical perspective, which is absolutely necessary, in turn, to understand what the Qur'ān says about Jesus regardless of the way(s) in which Muslim and/or Christian believers may interpret it – on which we now have Roger Arnaldez's,[43] Neal Robinson's,[44] Maurice Borrmans,[45] Tarif Khalidi's,[46] Mark Beaumont's,[47] Paul-Gordon Chandler's,[48] Oddbjørn Leirvik's,[49] and Mona Siddiqui's[50] excellent essays.[51]

---

42 Parrinder, *Jesus in the Qur'ān*, 9–10.

43 Roger Arnaldez, *Jésus, fils de Marie, prophète de l'Islam* (Paris: Desclée, 1980).

44 Neal Robinson, *Christ in Islam and Christianity* (Albany, NY: State University of New York Press, 1991).

45 Maurice Borrmans, Jésus et les Musulmans d*'aujourd'hui* (Paris: Desclée, 1996).

46 Tarif Khalidi, *The Muslim Jesus: Sayings and Stories in Islamic Literature* (Cambridge, MA, and London: Harvard University Press, 2001).

47 I. Mark Beaumont, *Christology in Dialogue with Muslims: A Critical Analysis of Christian Presentations of Christ for Muslims from the Ninth and Twentieth Centuries* (Foreword by David Thomas; Carlisle, UK: Paternoster, 2005).

48 Paul-Gordon Chandler, *Pilgrims of Christ on the Muslim Road: Exploring a New Path between Two Faiths* (Lanham, MD, and Plymouth, UK: Rowman and Littlefield, 2007).

49 Leirvik, *Images of Jesus Christ in Islam.*

50 Mona Siddiqui, *Christians, Muslims, and Jesus* (New Haven, CT, and London: Yale University Press, 2013).

51 See also Donald Wismer, *The Islamic Jesus: An Annotated Bibliography of Sources in English and French* (New York: Garland, 1977; reprinted in London and New York: Routledge, 2016), and Akyol's aforementioned book on the Islamic Jesus, whose historical reconstruction of the quranic milieu remains, however, too conventional.

Put differently: commitment to the principles of secularism and the methods of historical-critical research needs to be unconditionally demanded from the historian of religious ideas *qua* historian, whose task is to unravel the eventual connections existing between a number of religious notions, texts, and practices, and to bring out their meaning and importance in the making of specific religious identities within specific social-political networks. Thus, Parrinder's efforts to compare the quranic and Christian views of Jesus, as well as to approach them as much as possible without overlooking (unlike Masson) the difficulties inherent in such a task,[52] present the inconvenience of privileging the religious beliefs of Muslims and Christians, and hence of two social collectives and their theologies, over the textual, discursive, and contextual analysis of the Qur'ān itself. Still, Parrinder's book remains a very useful introduction to the study of the quranic Jesus.

From Ali Merad to Heikki Räisänen's Historical Interpretation

Overall, Masson's, Zaehner's, Michaud, Pörksen and, to a lesser extent, Parrinder's approaches may be labelled as "dialogical" in the sense that they mean to overcome the "polemical" and "missionary" nature of all previous inquiries into the quranic Jesus-figure and replace it with a less apologetic and thus more nuanced reading of the Qur'ān in dialogue with Christian theological representation(s) of Jesus-Christ.[53] Similarly, Ali Merad's "Le Christ selon le Coran" (1968)[54] analyses the Qur'ān's teaching on Jesus, which Merad takes to be authoritative and theologically coherent[55] while at the same time epistemologically unclosed, in order to show that the sacred book of Islam encourages reflection on the part of Muslims and Christians alike concerning Jesus's nature, mission, example, and death.[56]

---

52 See in this respect chapters 13 and 14 of Parrinder's book, pp. 126–41.
53 Cf. Heikki Räisänen, "The Portrait of Jesus in the Qur'ān: Reflections from a Biblical Scholar," *MW* 70 (1980): 122–33; Leirvik, *Images of Jesus Christ in Islam*, 28.
54 Ali Merad, "Le Christ selon le Coran," *ROMM* 5 (1968): 79–94; English translation: "Christ According to the Qur'ān," *Encounters* 69 (1980): 2–17.
55 See the comments made below apropos Räisänen's assumptions and method.
56 "Certes, le Coran pose des vérités de foi, au sujet du Christ," he writes. "Mais sa visée fondamentale, à cet égard, semble être de provoquer la réflexion humaine, plutôt que de fournir les ultimes réponses. . . . Dès lors," he adds, "comment ne pas souhaiter, qu'à l'ère du Concile [Vatican II (on which see above the comments on Masson's book)], et à la faveur du thème essentiel du Christ, une volonté du dialogue puisse animer de plus en plus Chrétiens et Musulmans, dans une souci de compréhension réciproque, et de mutuel apaisement" (Merad, "Le Christ selon le

Conversely, Heikki Räisänen's *Das Koranische Jesusbild* (1971)[57] represents a remarkably original attempt – indeed the first one ever carried out – to evaluate the precise scope of the quranic Jesus passages in light of their own differential context, which, the author claims, must be taken into account as the only possible horizon in any scholarly exploration of the quranic Jesus:

> "Every detail in the Qur'ān, whatever its origin may be, must be interpreted in the light of the new qur'ānic context. The Qur'ān must be explained by the Qur'ān and not by anything else.... No matter what the Christians meant, for instance, when they spoke of Jesus as the 'Word' of God, for the point of view of the Qur'ān the only relevant question is: 'What could Muḥammad possibly mean by that expression in the context of *his* total view?' Seen against the background of Muḥammad's theology as a whole, the Qur'anic portrait of Jesus stands out as coherent and clear."[58]

For "the dangers inherent in the dialogical approach are those of superficiality and anachronism," writes Räisänen.[59] Therefore, he adds, "[a]gainst all dialogical claims it should be emphasized that a knowledge of the NT is not at all necessary for an understanding of the Qur'ān in its historical setting."[60]

Yet Räisänen's "historical" method[61] presents its own problems, as well. First, the quranic context is anything but clear. As I have written elsewhere,

> it is . . . difficult to know what precisely the Qur'ān is and when it acquired its present form. Testimonies about its different versions/recensions are well documented in the Islamic sources themselves; so too are reports about its textual additions and suppressions and the date of its alleged "Uthmanic" collection. Likewise, its origins are far from

Coran," 93). On human hope and fulfilment as "[le] thème essentiel du Christ," see Merad, "Le Christ selon le Coran," 92.

57 Heikki Räisänen, *Das Koranische Jesusbild: Ein Beitrag zur Theologie des Korans* (SFGMO 20; Helsinki: Finnischen Gesellschaft für Missiologie und Ökumenik, 1971). See also idem, "The Portrait of Jesus in the Qur'ān," which summarises the arguments put forward in *Das Koranische Jesusbild*.

58 Räisänen, "The Portrait of Jesus in the Qur'ān," 124.

59 Räisänen, "The Portrait of Jesus in the Qur'ān," 123.

60 Räisänen, "The Portrait of Jesus in the Qur'ān," 123. E.g. Räisänen underlines that even if undoubtedly the title "Word" in Q 4:171 "goes back to the Christian use of *Logos* as a Christological title . . . it is just as clear that Muḥammad did *not* take over the specific Christian meaning of that term. In the context mentioned," he explains, "the title seems to refer to the manner of Jesus' birth by the power of God's creative word of command. Jesus is God's 'Word,' but certainly not in the sense of the Christian Logos. It is futile to engage in a dialogue on this point in an attempt to Christianize the language of the Qur'ān," he therefore concludes (Räisänen, "The Portrait of Jesus in the Qur'ān," 127).

61 Räisänen, "The Portrait of Jesus in the Qur'ān," 123.

> clear. Recent scholarship on the Qur'ān shows that its alleged unity, background, and chronology posit many problems if approached from a historical-critical perspective, thus highlighting questions long overlooked in the interpretation of the Muslim scripture, such as: "What layers does it contain and how should they be studied?" "Which was their original character and function?" "What complex redactional process did they undergo?" "Which specific historical/cultural settings must one have in mind when addressing these issues?"[62]

Secondly, projecting onto it the "data" provided in the 9th and 10th centuries by the Islamic tradition would be not only anachronistic, but also immensely naïve, as many of such "data" – beginning with those "collected" in Ibn Hišām's biography (*sīra*) of Muḥammad – served the purpose of establishing a new *Heilsgeschichte* or "salvation history," rather than a history in the proper (modern) sense.[63] Thus, for instance, the connection between Muḥammad and the Qur'ān proves ultimately problematic, as I have elsewhere highlighted too:

> the quranic prophetical *logia* go back to a prophet, and it is very likely that such a prophet was no other than Muḥammad himself. But it is nonetheless important to acknowledge that he is only named in the Qur'ān four/five times (Q 3:144; 33:40; 47:2; 48:29; and 61:6 as Aḥmad). Now, these verses may well be later interpolations, as David Powers has recently suggested *apropos* Q 33:40;[64] but even if they are not, they cannot be read as providing an absolute clue to the character who is anonymously addressed in the quranic corpus as (merely) "you," unless one assumes that the Qur'ān is a uniform text containing only Muḥammad's *ipssima verba*[65] . . . To put it differently, from a purely literary standpoint . . . the Qur'ān mostly remains . . . an anonymous document. Moreover, how can we be sure that there is only one prophet behind the prophetical *logia* contained in the quranic corpus? The fact is that we cannot, even if we pretend otherwise; for again, such a reduction would imply reading the Qur'ān in light of the Muslim tradition, which [is] for the historian of late-antique religion as problematic as reading the texts gathered in the New Testament in light of the Christian theological tradition [would be]. And yet there are hints in the quranic corpus itself that [suggest that there is a single prophet behind it] . . .

---

62 Carlos A. Segovia, *The Quranic Noah and the Making of the Islamic Prophet: A Study of Intertextuality and Religious Identity Formation in Late Antiquity* (JCIT 4; Berlin and Boston: De Gruyter, 2015) 28. "To neglect these and other related issues," I further added, "would be like explaining the emergence of the earliest Christ-believing groups by exclusively relying on the author of Luke-Acts . . . or like accepting the Mishnaic and Talmudic legends about Yavneh as the actual birthplace of rabbinic Judaism" (XV).

63 See Gordon D. Newby, *The Making of the Last Prophet: A Reconstruction of the Earliest Biography of Muhammad* (Columbia: University of South Carolina Press, 1989).

64 David Powers, *Muḥammad Is Not the Father of Any of Your Men: The Making of the Last Prophet (*DRLAR; Philadelphia: University of Pennsylvania Press, 2011).

65 On which see Herbert Berg, "Context: Muḥammad," in *The Blackwell Companion to the Qur'ān*, ed. Andrew Rippin (Oxford: Blackwell, 2006) 187–204.

> So I am not claiming here that there actually are several quranic prophets instead of just one. However, for coherence's sake, I think it is necessary to . . . distinguish between the quranic prophet and Muḥammad as two literary figures and to understand that the prophetical *logia* of the Qur'ān are a puzzle that we still need to work out in some very crucial aspects. [Therefore] I [shall] denominate the prophet repeatedly alluded to in the Qur'ān as "the quranic prophet," without further qualification, and Ibn Hišām's literary hero as "Muḥammad."[66]

That is to say, theoretically speaking Räisänen's approach is perfectly valid,[67] but it fails to achieve its goal in the practice, in so far as it takes too much for granted concerning what we (wrongly) presume to know about the Qur'ān and its prophet.[68]

This notwithstanding, Räisänen makes an unquestionably interesting point. Comparing the Qur'ān with the New Testament,[69] he observes that the clearest parallels to the former's subordinationist Christology are to be found in Luke 9:20 and Acts 3:18 (where Jesus is described as "God's messiah");[70] Acts 2:22 (where he is portrayed as a "man" fully dependent on God); and Acts 3:13, 18 (where he is, in turn, depicted as "God's servant"):

> "Luke gives us a Christology characterized by the emphatic subordination of Jesus to God. Whereas the rest of the NT uses the title 'Christ' absolutely, Luke speaks of Jesus as *God's* Christ (Acts 3:18, Lk 9:20, etc.). Jesus is *God's* servant (Acts 3:13, 4:27) and Chosen One (Lk 9:35, Acts 3:20). His mighty acts were in fact worked by God through him (Acts 2:22), for God was with him (Acts 10:38)."[71]

I shall return in due time to these considerations. In the meantime, suffice it to say that – as Leirvik correctly notes – John 20:17, with its reference to "my Father and your Father, my God and your God" placed on Jesus's own lips, ought to be incorporated to the list too (cf. the analogous expression "my Lord and your Lord" in Q 3:51; 19:36; 43:64).[72]

---

66 Segovia, *The Quranic Noah and the Making of the Islamic Prophet*, 16–17.
67 In fact, chapters 3, 4, and 5 in this book aim at providing it a new conceptual framework.
68 "The Qur'ān," states for instance Räisänen, "is a single book . . . [in which] we can study the religious experience of a single individual within a relatively short period of time" (Räisänen, "The Portrait of Jesus in the Qur'ān," 132). See for discussion the Conclusion to the present study.
69 Räisänen, "The Portrait of Jesus in the Qur'ān," 127–9.
70 See further Chapter 3 below.
71 Räisänen, "The Portrait of Jesus in the Qur'ān," 127–8.
72 Leirvik, *Images of Jesus Christ in Islam*, 28.

Giuseppe Rizzardi, Claus Schedl, and Günther Risse

I should now like to refer to Giuseppe Rizzardi's, Claus Schedl's, and Günther Risse's studies, which came out in the 1970s and 1980s. Rizzardi[73] offers a detailed survey of the approaches to the Christology of the Qur'ān essayed by Catholic theologians, from Peter the Venerable, Guglielmo of Tripoli and John of Wales (12th and 13th centuries) to modern times. In turn, in his monograph *Muhammad und Jesus*[74] Claus Schedl undertakes an exhaustive analysis of the quranic Jesus-texts while simultaneously exploring what he believes to be the arithmetic pattern underlying several quranic *sūra*-s, which needs to be connected, he claims, with the numerical value of the word Λόγος *Logos* now applied to the Qur'ān itself instead of Christ;[75] additionally, he contends that the denial that "God is the messiah" in Q 5:17 is reminiscent of a "Nestorian" text of the mid-6th century[76] and that, far from discussing Jesus's divine sonship as such, the earliest quranic layers question the more general notion of divine begetting alone[77] – I shall return in due course to these arguments, as well.[78] Besides, Schedl published in 1987 an article comparing the number of chapters in the quranic corpus and the number of Jesus's *logia* in the Gospel of Thomas, which amount in both cases to 114;[79] as Neal Robinson aptly observes,

> Schedl's claim that the suras are constructed in accordance with arithmetical models is more problematic. He resorts to too many different models for his analyses to be entirely convincing. . . . Nevertheless the fact that the number of suras in the Qur'an is the same as the number of logia in the Gospel of Thomas suggests that arithmetic symbolism may have played some part in the final editing of the revelations if not in their initial composition.[80]

---

73 Giuseppe Rizzardi, *Il problema della cristologia coranica: storia dell'ermeneutica cristiana* (Milan: Istituto Propaganda Libraria, 1982).

74 Claus Schedl, *Muhammad und Jesus:Die christologisch relevanten Texte des Korans, neu übersetz und erlärkt* (Vienna, Freiburg, and Basel: Herder, 1978).

75 I shall go back to this argument in Chapter 5. See for discussion Neal Robinson, *Christ in Islam and Christianity*, 38–40.

76 Schedl, *Muhammad und Jesus*, 531.

77 Schedl, *Muhammad und Jesus*, 329.

78 See Chapter 5.

79 Claus Schedl, "Die 114 Suren des Koran und die 114 Logien Jesu im Thomas-Evangelium," *Der Islam* 64.2 (1987): 261–4.

80 Robinson, *Christ in Islam and Christianity*, 40.

Lastly, Günther Risse's 1989 study on the figure of Jesus in the Qur'ān and its historical religious background[81] makes the case that the Qur'ān's theology is specifically addressed against an extreme variant form of "Monophysite" Christianity.[82] I shall come back to Risse's argument later on too.[83]

Neal Robinson's Comparative Study on Christ in Islam and Christianity

Less audacious but not less ambitious than Risse's and Schedl's is Neal Robinson's widely acclaimed book *Christ in Islam and Christianity*,[84] whose first chapter outlines the major traits of the quranic Jesus and whose subsequent pages examine the classical Muslim commentaries and the traditional Christian responses to the quranic representation of Jesus, with special emphasis on the topic of Jesus's crucifixion, which furthermore has attracted considerable attention in the past two decades, with important studies by Todd Lawson,[85] Gabriel Said Reynolds,[86] and Suleiman Mourad.[87] Also, in 2003 Robinson contributed to Jane Dammen McAuliffe's *Encyclopaedia of the Qur'ān* with a lengthy entry on the quranic Jesus.[88]

Mention must be also made, to end with, of Roberto Tottoli's *I profeti biblici nella tradizione islamica* (1999),[89] which dedicates a few pages to the examination of the quranic Jesus; Édouard-Marie Gallez's *Le messie et son prophète*

81 Günther Risse, *"Gott ist Christus, der Sohn der Maria": Eine Studie zum Christusbild im Koran* (Bonn: Borengässer, 1989).

82 Risse, *"Gott ist Christus, der Sohn der Maria,"* 217.

83 See once more Chapter 5.

84 See n.43 above. See also idem, "Christian and Muslim Perspectives on Jesus in the Qur'ān," in *Fundamentalism and Tolerance: An Agenda for Theology and Society*, ed. Andrew Linzey and Peter J. Wexler (London: Bellew, 1991) 92–105, 171–172.

85 Todd Lawson, "The Crucifixion of Jesus in the Qur'ān and Quranic Commentary: A Historical Survey, Part I," *BHMIIS* 10.2 (1991): 34–62; idem, "The Crucifixion of Jesus in the Qur'ān and Quranic Commentary: A Historical Survey, Part II," *BHMIIS* 10.3 (1991): 6–40; idem, *The Crucifixion and the Qur'an: A Study in the History of Muslim Thought* (Oxford: Oneworld, 2009).

86 Gabriel Said Reynolds, "The Muslim Jesus: Dead or Alive?," *BSOAS* 72.2 (2009): 237–58.

87 Suleiman A. Mourad, "The Qur'ān and Jesus' Crucifixion and Death," in *New Perspectives on the Qur'ān: The Qur'ān in Its Historical Context 2*, ed. Gabriel Said Reynolds (RSQ; London and New York: Routledge, 2011) 349–57.

88 Neal Robinson, "Jesus," in *Encyclopaedia of the Qur'ān*, ed. Jane Dammen McAuliffe (6 vols.; Leiden and Boston: Brill, 2001–6) 3:7–21.

89 Roberto Tottoli, *I profeti biblici nella tradizione islamica* (Brescia: Paideia, 1999); English translation by Michael Robertson, *Biblical Prophets in the Qur'ān and Muslim Literature* (RSQ; London and New York: Routledge, 2002).

(2005),[90] which following partly Michaud and intensely relying, moreover, on Patricia Crone and Michael Cook's *Hagarism*[91] labels the Qur'ān's Christology as Jewish-Christian;[92] and, finally, Oddbjørn Leirvik's aforementioned volume *Images of Jesus Christ in Islam*, which includes a brief section on the quranic Jesus and its ongoing study in the second half of the 20th century; yet Leirvik suitably highlights some of the grammatical problems susceptible of being taken into consideration in the analysis of the Qur'ān's Jesus passages and their literary character.

Addendum. Investigations on the Emergence of Islam and 7th-Century Near-East Christianity

Without specifically focussing on the study of the quranic Jesus, other authors have explored – be it explicitly or implicitly – the links that can be traced between emergent Islam, on the one hand, and, on the other hand, 7th-century Christians and Christianity. I am thinking here for instance – to mention but the main titles thereof – of Louis Cheikho's *Le christianisme et la littérature chrétienne en Arabie avant l'islam* (1912–23),[93] Tor Andrae's *Der Ursprung des Islams und das Christentum* (1926),[94] Richard Bell's *The Origin of Islam in Its Christian Environment* (1926),[95] François Nau's *Les arabes chrétiens de Mésopotamie et de Syrie du VIe au VIIe siècle* (1933),[96] Henri Charles's *Le christianisme des arabes nomades sur le limes et dans le désert syro-mésopotamien aux alentours de l'hégire* (1936),[97] Josef Henninger's "Christentum im vorislamischen Arabien" (1948),[98] Günter Lüling's

---

90 Édouard-Marie Gallez, *Le messie et son prophète. Aux origines de l'islam* (2 vols.; Versailles: Éditions de Paris, 2005).

91 Patricia Crone and Michael Cook, *Hagarism: The Making of the Islamic Word* (Cambridge: Cambridge University Press, 1977).

92 See above my discussion of Michaud's monograph, as well as the Conclusion to the present study concerning the interpretation(s) of emergent Islam as a Jewish-Christian movement.

93 Louis Cheikho's *Le christianisme et la littérature chrétienne en Arabie avant l'islam* (3 vols.; Beirut: Imprimerie Catholique, 1912–23; 2nd ed., Beirut: Dar el-Machreq, 1989).

94 See n.20 above.

95 Richard Bell, *The Origin of Islam in Its Christian Environment* (London: Macmillan, 1926; reprinted in London and New York: Routledge, 2012).

96 François Nau, *Les arabes chrétiens de Mésopotamie et de Syrie du VIe au VIIe siècle* (CSA; Paris: Imprimerie National, 1933).

97 Henri Charles, *Le christianisme des arabes nomads sur le limes et dans le désert syro-mésopotamien aux alentours de l'hégire* (BEHE; Paris: Leroux, 1936).

98 Josef Henninger, "Christentum im vorislamischen Arabien," *NZM* 4 (1948): 222–4.

Über den Ur-Koran (1974),[99] J. Spencer Trimingham's *Christianity among the Arabs in pre-Islamic Times* (1979),[100] Alfred Havenith's *Les arabes chrétiens nomads au temps de Mohammed* (1988),[101] Robert Schick's *The Christian Communities of Palestine from Byzantine to Islamic Rule* (1995),[102] Irfan Shahîd's *Byzantium and the Arabs in the Sixth Century* (1995–2002),[103] Meir Jacob Kister's *Concepts and Ideas at the Dawn of Islam* (1997),[104] Christoph Luxenberg's *Die syro-aramäische Lesart des Koran: Ein Beitrag zur Entschlüsselung der Koransprache* (2000),[105] Sidney H. Griffith's "Christians and Christianity [in the Qur'ān]" (2001),[106] David Marshall's "Christianity in the Qur'ān" (2001),[107] Stephen Shoemaker's "Christmas in the Qur'ān" (2003),[108] Theresia Heinthaler's *Christliche Araber vor dem Islam* (2007),[109] Jane Dammen McAuliffe's *Qur'ānic Christians* (2007),[110] Guillaume Dye's "Lieux saints communs, partagés ou confisqués" (2012),[111] Haggai Mazuz's

99 Günter Lüling, Über den Ur-Qur'ān: Ansätze zur Rekonstruktion vorislamischer christlicher Strophenlieder im Qur'ān (Erlangen: Lüling, 1974; 2nd ed., 1993); English translation, *A Challenge to Islam for Reformation: The Rediscovery and Reliable Reconstruction of a Comprehensive pre-Islamic Christian Hymnal Hidden in the Koran under Earliest Islamic Reinterpretations* (Delhi: Banarsidass, 2003).

100 J. Spencer Trimingham *Christianity among the Arabs in pre-Islamic Times* (London: Longman; Beirut: Librairie du Liban, 1979).

101 Alfred Havenith, *Les arabes chrétiens nomads au temps de Mohammed*, Préface de Julien Ries (CCL; Louvain-la-Neuve: Centre d'Histoire des Religions, 1988).

102 Robert Schick, *The Christian Communities of Palestine from Byzantine to Islamic Rule: A Historical and Archaeological Study* (SLAEI; Princeton, NJ: Darwin, 1995).

103 Irfan Shahîd, *Byzantium and the Arabs in the Sixth Century* (2 vols.; DORLC; Washington DC: Dumbarton Oaks, 1995–2002).

104 Meir Jacob Kister, *Concepts and Ideas at the Dawn of Islam* (VCS; Aldershot, IK: Ashgate/Variorum, 1997).

105 Christoph Luxenberg, *Die syro-aramäische Lesart des Koran: Ein Beitrag zur Entschlüsselung der Koransprache The Syro-Aramaic Reading of the Koran* (Berlin: Schiler, 2000; 3rd ed., 2003); English translation, *The Syro-Aramaic Reading of the Koran: A Contribution to the Decoding of the Language of the Koran* (Berlin: Schiler, 2007).

106 Sidney H. Griffith, "Christians and Christianity [in the Qur'ān]," in *Encyclopaedia of the Qur'ān*, ed. Jane Dammen McAuliffe, 1:307–16.

107 David Marshall, "Christianity in the Qur'ān," in *Islamic Interpretations of Christianity*, ed. Lloyd Ridgeon (London and New York: Routledge, 2001) 3–29.

108 Stephen J. Shoemaker, "Christmas in the Qur'ān: The Qur'ānic Account of Jesus' Nativity and Palestinian Local Tradition," *JSAI* 28 (2003): 11–39.

109 Theresia Heinthaler, *Christliche Araber vor dem Islam: Verbreitung und konfessionelle Zugehörigkeit: eine Hinführung* (ECS 7; Leuven: Peeters, 2007).

110 See n.8 above.

111 Guillaume Dye, "Lieux saints communs, partagés ou confisqués : aux sources de quelques péricopes coraniques (Q 19 : 16–33)", in *Partage du sacré: transferts, dévotions mixtes, rivalités*

"Christians in the Qur'ān" (2012),[112] Jan Van Reeth's "Melchisédech le Prophète éternel selon Jean d'Apamée et le monarchianisme musulman" (2012),[113] Muriel Debié's "Les controverses miaphysites en Arabie et le Coran" (2015),[114] and Greg Fisher and Philip Wood's "Arabs and Christianity" (2015).[115]

Works dealing with the connections existing between formative Islam and 7th-century Near-Eastern Christianity differ on their scope and purpose as much as they do on their method. Yet two contrasting approaches, and a relative progression from one to another – which precludes neither exceptions nor the reversibility of what remains only a general tendency – can be easily discerned over the past decades: thus, while some early studies aim at deciphering the hypothetical influence of various "heterodox" Christian *groups* on Muḥammad's religious views,[116] more recent studies often attempt to unravel the ways in which Christian *ideas* may have made their way into the quranic corpus in the first decades of the Arab take-over of the Fertile Crescent.[117] Thereby the scholarly emphasis, too, has gradually shifted from a more or less speculative inquiry into the Arabian prophet's religious milieu to a historical-critical exploration of the Qur'ān's latest redactional layers and their plausible setting.[118] Arguably, reluctance to positively

interconfessionnelles, ed. Isabelle Depret and Guillaume Dye (Brussels-Fernelmont: EME, 2012) 55–121.

112 Haggai Mazuz, "Christians in the Qur'ān: Some Insights Derived from the Classical Exegetical Approach," *SO* 112 (2012): 41–53.

113 Jan M. F. Van Reeth, "Melchisédech le Prophète éternel selon Jean d'Apamée et le monarchianisme musulman," *OC* 96 (2012): 8–46.

114 Muriel Debié, "Les controverses miaphysites en Arabie et le Coran," in *Les controverses religieuses en syriaque*, ed. Flavia Ruani (ES 13; Paris: Geuthner, 2015) 137–56.

115 Greg Fisher and Philip Wood (with contributions from George Bevan, Geoffrey Greatrex, Basema Hamarneh, Peter Schadler, and Walter Ward), "Arabs and Christianity," in *Arabs and Empires before Islam*, ed. Greg Fisher (Oxford and New York: Oxford University Press, 2015) 276–372.

116 Therefore echoing John of Damascus's early description of Islam as a Christian "heresy," on which see Gilles Courtieu, "La *threskeia* des Ismaélites Etude de la première définition synthétique de l'islam par Jean de Damas," in *Hérésies: une construction d'identités religieuses*, ed. Christian Brouwer, Guillaume Dye, and Anja van Rompaey (Brussels: Éditions de l'Université de Bruxelles, 2015) 105–260.

117 See e.g. Shoemaker and Dye aforementioned essays.

118 See e.g. Guillaume Dye, "The Qur'ān and its Hypertextuality in Light of Redaction Criticism," forthcoming in *Early Islam: The Religious Milieu of Late Antiquity*, ed. Guillaume Dye (LAMINE; Chicago: Chicago Oriental Institute). Van Reeth, "Melchisédech le Prophète éternel selon Jean d'Apamée et le monarchianisme musulman," represents a remarkable exception: "Selon la théologie biblique," he writes, "Dieu parle par la bouche des prophètes. Le prophète est « le héraut de Yahweh, qui proclame les paroles que Dieu lui suggère ». À cette fin, Dieu établit une relation toute particulière, directe et personnelle, avec son prophète élu, lui mettant

delimit the former given the lack of reliable information that we have about it has played a determinant role in this gradual shift.[119]

Purpose and Argument of this Book, with a Note on the Notion of "Symptomatic Reading"

Three Preliminary Notions: Polyphony, Periphery, Hypertextuality

Whatever the date of the Jesus passages contained in the Qur'ān – an issue that I will examine at some length in Chapter 4 – limiting the Christian, if peripheral, trimmings of formative (i.e. pre-Marwanid) Islam[120] to, roughly, the second half of the 7th century, is however, as I hope to show in this book, unnecessary – and *a*

littéralement et pour ainsi dire physiquement ses paroles dans la bouche, tout en pénétrant son âme, en prenant possession de l'esprit de son serviteur. Cependant, la vocation prophétique garde toujours un caractère éphémère et non-substantiel; elle ne semble en rien changer la nature du prophète, qui reste celle d'un simple être humain, mortel et faillible.Diamétralement opposée à cette prophétologie juive est la révélation personnifiée telle qu'elle est professée par le christianisme orthodoxe, qui voit en Jésus Christ l'incarnation du Logos, de la Parole divine créatrice. Or, il existe une forme épiphanique de la révélation qui se situe entre ces deux extrêmes. . . . la prophétologie musulmane originelle, telle qu'elle se dégage de plus en plus des recherches récentes concernant la formation du Coran et les origines de l'Islam, semble bien représenter une troisième voie, à mi-chemin entre la tradition prophétique vétérotestamentaire et la christologie officielle des Églises. C'est cette prophétologie et la tradition exégétique qui l'accompagne que nous voulons analyser. Elle repose sur un principe prophétique éternel et divin, qui en chaque génération s'incarne dans la personne des prophètes successifs. Nous voulons . . . essayer de retrouver les racines de cette prophétologie dans le Coran et d'en retracer les sources, ce qui devrait nous permettre . . . de déterminer de façon plus précise la religion monothéiste, chrétienne ›hétérodoxe‹, dont Muḥammad a pu être un adepte et qui semble avoir été présente sur le sol du Hedjaz depuis déjà quelques générations" (8–9). I shall return to Van Reth's interpretation in Chapter 5.

119 Undeniably influential in this respect has been John Wansbrough's *The Sectarian Milieu: Contents and Composition of Islamic Salvation History* (Oxford and New York: Oxford University Press, 1978; reprinted with a foreword, translation, and expanded notes by Gerald R. Hawting in Amherst, NY: Prometheus Books, 2006). See further Herbert Berg, "The Needle in the Haystack: Islamic Origins and the Nature of the Early Sources," in *The Coming of the Comforter: When, Where, and to Whom? Studies on the Rise of Islam and Various Other Topics in Memory of John Wansbrough*, ed. Carlos A. Segovia and Basil Lourié (OJC 3; Piscataway, NJ: Gorgias Press, 2012) 271–302; Françoise Micheau, *Les débuts de l'islam. Jalons pour one nouvelle histoire* (Paris: Téraèdre, 2012), ch. 3.

120 On the Marwanid beginnings of Islam see Micheau, *Les débuts de l'islam*, ch. 7; Carlos A. Segovia, "Identity Politics and Scholarship in the Study of Islamic Origins: The Inscriptions of the Dome of the Rock as a Test Case," forthcoming in *Identity, Politics and the Study of Islam:*

fortiori misguiding. For Christian ideas can be detected in the very earliest layers of the quranic corpus as well, and actually throughout all its redactional strata – these ideas are sometimes encrypted and sometimes visible, but I fear it is only our tendency to reduce Christianity to a few basic (often Jesus-centred) notions, together with our habit of taking Islam as a defined religious entity right from the start, that prevents us from recognising them.

More precisely: the Qur'ān resembles an intricate polyphonic composition in which divergent theologies interact but whose *basso continuo*, at least till a certain point in the chronology of the document, is somewhat Christian whether we like it or not – which needless to say does not mean that Islam started as an intra-Christian phenomenon, let alone as a Christian "heresy." It is rather the notion of *periphery* that I will advocate in the pages that follow.[121]

Intertextuality – or maybe it would be more accurate to speak of *hypertextuality*[122] – shall also be given a prominent role in this study, as the Qur'ān's peculiar Christology does not only draw on a number of pre-existent, circulating ideas, but also sub-texts and inter-texts.[123] And special attention needs to be paid too to the Qur'ān's own intra-textuality, by which I mean the ways in which its successive textual layers witness to the elaboration and revision of particular ideas and their eventual substitution by new ones.

I have earlier dealt with a number of overlapping intertextual trajectories present in the quranic corpus, including one relative to the quranic Jesus, against the background of religious identity formation in late antiquity. I have

---

Current Dilemmas in the Study of Religions, ed. Matt Sheddy (CESIF; Sheffield, UK, and Bristol, CT: Equinox).

121 I have already used the terms "periphery" and "peripheral" in my essay "A Messianic Controversy behind the Making of Muḥammad as the Last Prophet?," forthcoming in *Early Islam: The Religious Milieu of Late Antiquity*, ed. Guillaume Dye (LAMINE; Chicago: Chicago Oriental Institute) but originally presented to the 1st Nangeroni Meeting of the Early Islamic Studies Seminar in Milan in June of 2015, and where I put forward a hypothesis on the Christian background of emergent Islam that stresses the latter's East-Diphysite components. See further chapters 4 and 5.

122 In the sense that the intertextual web in which the Qur'ān ought to be inscribed consists of so many threads pointing in so many directions that it forms a multilayered network. On the notion of "hypertextuality," see Daniel Dubuisson, *The Western Construction of Religion: Myths, Knowledge, and Ideology*, translated by William Sayers (Baltimore, MD, and London: John Hopkins University Press, 2003) 32.

123 Cf. my brief analysis of the Adam narratives in Q 15:28–31 and 38:71–4 in "The Jews and Christians of Pre-Islamic Yemen (Ḥimyar) and the Elusive Matrix of the Qur'ān's Christology," in *Jewish Christianity and Islamic Origins: Papers presented at the Eighth Annual ASMEA Conference (Washington DC, October 29–31, 2015)*, ed. Francisco del Río Sánchez (JAOC; Turnhout, BE: Brepols, 2018) 91–104, p. 94 n.14.

tried to prove, for instance, that the quranic portrayal of Jesus's birth in Q 3:46 and 19:29–30 echoes the Arabic Gospel of the Infancy 1:2, which must in turn be read as an adaptation of a previous Noahic motif that goes back to the Second Temple Period and was later applied to Jesus in both the New Testament and the New Testament apocrypha.[124] Originally set out in the Enochic corpus and other related writings as a kind of messianic symbol, this motif made its way well into late antique times and was reused in different contexts to describe Melchizedek, Jesus, and Moses alongside other related motifs that were likewise used to describe these and other figures. In short, the quranic portrayal of Jesus's birth in Q 3:46 and 19:29–30 must be placed in an ongoing tradition of variant textual reinterpretations of a single motif whose ideological background is, however, much more complex. In turn, in my contribution to the volume in memory of John Wansbrough that I edited with Basil Lourié[125] I explored the parabolic use of natural order as opposed to human disobedience in the prologue to the Book of the Watchers and its fragmentary quranic parallels, more specifically the quranic reuse of 1Enoch 1–5 for paraenetic purposes in Q 7:36; 10:6; 16:81; 24:41, 44, 46. Therefore, my intent was to place these seemingly unrelated quranic passages within a well-known and continuing intellectual tradition that goes back, once more, to the Second Temple Period, and of which one may find numerous textual examples in the prophetic, apocalyptic, and wisdom literature of that period; yet this required outlining the more probable source of its quranic instantiation, which in my view should be searched for in 1Enoch 1–5 (especially 2:1–5:4). I have devoted a third and somewhat more complex article to the symptomatic rereading of Q 56:1–56 in light of Apocalypse of Abraham.[126] My purpose in it was not only to show that Q 56:1–56 draws almost verbatim on ApAb 21–2 (especially 21:7; 22:1, 3–5), but also that Paul's Abrahamic argument as reinterpreted in an overtly supersessionary fashion by the Church is subliminally reused against the Jews in the quranic passage in order to lay the foundations of a new founding (and again supersessionary) myth – a new myth that is fully indebted, however, to the post-Pauline Jewish discussion of Paul's Abrahamic argument in

124 Carlos A. Segovia, "Noah as Eschatological Mediator Transposed: From 2 Enoch 71–72 to the Christological Echoes of 1 Enoch 106:3 in the Qur'ān," *Henoch* 33.1 (2011): 130–45; see also idem, *The Quranic Noah and the Making of the Islamic Prophet*, 21–7.

125 Carlos A. Segovia, "Thematic and Structural Affinities between 1 Enoch and the Qur'ān: A Contribution to the Study of the Judaeo-Christian Apocalyptic Setting of the Early Islamic Faith," in *The Coming of the Comforter: When, Where, and to Whom? Studies on the Rise of Islam and Various Other Topics in Memory of John Wansbrough*, ed. Carlos A. Segovia and Basil Lourié, 231–67.

126 Carlos A. Segovia, "'Those on the Right' and 'Those on the Left': Rereading Qur'ān 56:1–56 (and the Founding Myth of Islam) in Light of Apocalypse of Abraham 21–2," *OC* (2017): 197–211.

the Apocalypse of Abraham.[127] Lastly, in my recent monograph on the quranic Noah narratives[128] I have attempted to show that the quranic Noah narratives helped, first, to strengthen the eschatological credentials of the quranic prophet by means of a creative re-reading of several previous texts, including Ephraem's and Narsai's writings, and then facilitated the consensual model for Muḥammad's *sīra*. My aim, in short, was to (re)place the Qur'ān at the crossroads of the conversations and controversies of old to which its Noah narratives witness and to symptomatically (re)read them in light of some of the events that they mirror or to which they provide a literary and conceptual framework, be they episodes in the life of an anonymous prophet, portions on the shaping of a new charismatic figure that not unexpectedly (albeit only provisionally) takes a number of messianic traits – from whence the title of its Afterword: "Re-imagining Muḥammad as a New Messiah" – or phases in the development of a new religious identity.

Introducing the Argument of the Book and Its Parts

In this book I look at the Qur'ān from an altogether different angle but with a similar lens. My overall purpose is to reread its Jesus passages in light of the Christological developments contemporary with the composition of the quranic corpus. Thus In Chapter 2 ("Jesus in the Quranic Corpus: Texts and Contexts") I *survey* the quranic passages that mention Jesus, providing the reader with their text and translation, a summary of their content and context within the corpus, and a number of cross-references. In turn, in Chapter 3 ("Reassessing the Typology, and Date, and Ideology of the Jesus Passages – and Their Setting") I try to move beyond the limits imposed by their conventional classification and dating. Thus I undertake a *symptomatic reading* of the quranic Jesus passages that attempts at disclosing their "buried problematic" through a careful examination of their rhetoric and imagery;[129] a new, typological classification is the main

127 Carlos A. Segovia, "Discussing/subverting Paul: Polemical Re-readings and Competitive Supersessionist Misreadings of Pauline Inclusivism in Late Antiquity: A Case Study on the Apocalypse of Abraham, Justin Martyr, and the Qur'ān," in *Paul the Jew: A Conversation between Pauline and Second Temple Scholars*, ed. Gabriele Boccaccini and Carlos A. Segovia (Minneapolis: Fortress, 2016) 341–61.

128 Segovia, *The Quranic Noah and the Making of the Islamic Prophet*.

129 The notion of "symptomatic reading" was coined in the mid-1960s by Louis Althusser in *Lire le Capital*, written in collaboration with Étienne Balibar, Roger Establet, Pierre Macherey, and Jacques Rancière (TQ; Paris: Maspero, 1965; English translation by Ben Brewster, *Reading Capital* [London: New Left Books, 1970]). As John Thurston (from whom I take the expression "buried problematic") writes, "[a]ccording to Althusser, Marx's symptomatic reading of the

outcome of such reading, plus a tentative hypothesis concerning their underlying ideology, which turns from anti-Jewish to anti-Christian, and their plausible twofold setting in mid- to late-7th-century Palestine. Chapter 4 ("Moving Backwards: A Peripheral Form of Christianity?") opens up a different venue by offering a new *interpretation* of the Qur'ān's initial rejection of mainstream Christology in light of 6th-to-7th-century Yemenite- and East Syriac Christianity; additionally, I *examine* too the Qur'ān's criticism of imperial ecclesiology. Next, in Chapter 5 ("From the Qur'ān's Early Christology to the Elaboration of the Muhamadan *Kerygma*") I *analyse* the transformation of the early Qur'ān's Christology into a prophetical *kerygma* and a monotheistic creed. Like Daniel Beck, I understand the Qur'ān's earliest Christology as the view that God's Word is revealed to mankind by a heavenly messenger without substantive intermediation of any human prophet; like Jan Van Reeth,[130] I take such heavenly messenger to be, moreover, both God's own "epiphanic form" – as understood in the pre-Islamic esoteric traditions studied by Henry Corbin[131] – and his Messiah. Also, I maintain that it is at a later stage in the composition of the quranic corpus that the figure of an initially anonymous prophet – whose name was afterwards deduced from his qualified title – is introduced as the exclusive recipient of God's Word, and hence as God's apostle at the expense of the heavenly messenger, who is conveniently transformed into something like the prophet's occasional inspirer. Finally, the latter's identification with the Paraclete announced by Jesus in John's Gospel

classical economists found that they were answering unposed questions dictated to them by the ideology within which they worked. In *Capital* Marx posed the questions behind the work of the classical political economists Adam Smith and David Ricardo, and thus broke with its ideological problematic. Since any new problematic must be formulated in terms carried over from the discarded problematic, Althusser reads *Capital* symptomatically in order to clarify in terms adequate to them the principles of its new problematic" (John Thurston, "Symptomatic Reading," in *Encyclopedia of Contemporary Literary Theory: Approaches, Scholars, Terms*, ed. Irena R. Makaryk [Toronto, Buffalo, and London: University of Toronto Press, 1993] 638). Shortly afterwards, Macherey applied Althusser's technique to the study of literary texts in order to unpack their unconscious ideology (see Pierre Macherey, *Pour une théorie de la production littéraire* [Paris: Maspero, 1966]; English translation by Geoffrey Wall, *A Theory of Literary Production* [London: Routledge and Kegan Paul, 1978]). Likewise, my purpose here is to uncover the *unsaid* behind the said within each particular *text*, although the former should be instead depicted, in this case, as the latter's implicit thought world and tacit meaning. Therefore too, this book can be read both as a historical study and a philosophical essay on a number of (meta)religious ideas whose theoretical setting(s) must be deciphered as much as their historical background needs to be unearthed.

130 Van Reeth, "Melchisédech le Prophète éternel selon Jean d'Apamée et le monarchianisme musulman."

131 See especially Henry Corbin, *Le paradoxe du monthéisme* (Paris: L'Herne, 1981) 133–61.

is construed as foretold by Jesus himself in a gesture that redistributes their respective roles. Recalling at this point the symbolic subordination of John the Baptist to Jesus in the New Testament and other later Christian writings is surely unnecessary. Pointing out that all this allowed for a complete *subversion* of the Qur'ān's early Christology may not seem so obvious; yet apparently its memory was preserved within the proto-Shiite tradition[132] and is fundamental to understand the very beginnings of the Qur'ān (or, better, of its earliest, possibly pre-Muhamadan, *Grundschriften*). Lastly, in the Afterword I attempt at evaluating the results thus obtained in dialogue with Anders Petersen's renewed definition of the term "apologetics."[133]

Overall, my point is that, whether present or absent from its pages, the quranic Jesus, paradoxically, is the key to unravelling not only the intriguing beginnings, but also the fascinating development of the Qur'ān's complex, multi-phased theology, which in my view amounts to much more than a simple call to monotheism – and hence perhaps too the key to deciphering what the Qur'ān, despite its many gripping themes and labyrinthine byways, is ultimately about.

132 Mohammad Ali Amir-Moezzi, "Muḥammad le Paraclete et 'Alī le Messie. Nouvelles remarques sur les origines de l'islam et de l'imamologie shi'ite," in *L'Ésotérisme Shi'ite. Ses racines et ses prolongements/Shi'i Esotericism: Its Roots and Developments*, ed. Mohammad Ali Amir-Moezzi, with Maria De Cillis, Daniel De Smet, and Orkhan Mir-Kasimov (BEHESR 177; Turnhout, BE: Brepols and The Institute of Ismaili Studies, 2016) 19–54.
133 See Anders Klostergaard Petersen, "The Diversity of Apologetics: From Genre to a Mode of Thinking," in *Critique and Apologetics: Jews, Christians and Pagans in Antiquity*, ed. Jörg Ulrich, David Brakke, and Anders-Christian Jacobsen (ECCA; Frankfurt am Main: Peter Lang, 2009) 15–41; idem, "Apologetics," in *Vocabulary for the Study of Religion*, ed. Robert Segal and Kocku von Stuckrad (3 vols.; Leiden and Boston: Brill, 2015) 1:110–14.

2 Jesus in the Quranic Corpus: Texts and Contexts

Distribution of the Relevant Passages

Jesus is mentioned in thirty nine verses of the quranic corpus as (*a*) "Jesus" (ʿĪsā),[1] (*b*) "Jesus son of Mary" (ʿĪsā b. Maryam),[2] (*c*) "the son of Mary" (ibn Maryam),[3] (*d*) "the Messiah" (*al-masīḥ*),[4] (*e*) "the Messiah son of Mary" (*al-masīḥ* b. Maryam),[5] (*f*) "the Messiah, Jesus son of Mary" (*al-masīḥ* ʿĪsā b. Maryam),[6] (*g*) "God's servant (*ʿabd*),"[7] (*h*) "God's messenger (*rasūl*),"[8] (*i*) "a Word (*kalimat*^{un}) from God,"[9] (*j*) "the Word of Truth" (*qawl al-ḥaqq*),[10] (*k*) "God's Word (*kalima*)" and "a Spirit (*rūḥ*) from him,"[11] (*l*) a "prophet" (*nabī*),[12] (*m*) one among the "righteous" (*ṣaliḥūn*)[13] and (*n*) among "those brought near" to God (*muqarrabūn*)[14] – or else indirectly.[15]

Below is a table with the relevant passages grouped by *sūra*, followed by their text, translation, a summary of their content, and a brief preliminary analysis[16]:

---

1 Q 2:136; 3:52, 55, 59, 84; 4:163; 6:85; 42:13; 43:59, 63; 61:14. On the name ʿĪsā and its plausible East-Syrian background, see Dye, Guillaume and Manfred Kropp, "Le nom de Jésus (ʿĪsā) dans le Coran, et quelques autres noms bibliques: remarques sur l'onomastique coranique," in *Figures bibliques en islam*, ed. Guillaume Dye and Fabien Nobilio (Brussels-Fernelmont: EME, 2011) 171–98. In contrast, Christoph Luxenberg, *The Syro-Aramaic Reading of the Koran: A Contribution to the Decoding of the Language of the Koran* (Berlin: Schiler, 2007) 41–3, argues for an adaptation of the Hebrew ʾĪšay.

2 Q 2:87, 253; 5:46, 78, 110, 112, 114, 116; 19:34; 33:7; 57:27; 61:6.

3 Q 23:50; 43:57.

4 Q 4:172; 5:72; 9:30.

5 Q 5:17, 72, 75; 9:31.

6 Q 3:45; 4:157, 171.

7 Q 19:30.

8 Q 4:157, 171; 57:27; 61:6.

9 Q 3:39, 45.

10 Q 19:34.

11 Q 4:171.

12 Q 2:136; 3:84; 19:30; 33:7.

13 Q 6:85.

14 Q 3:45.

15 See the comments on Q 21:91; 66:12.

16 Basic cross-references and minor matters – so to speak – are discussed in the footnotes, while those relevant for the argument of the book are addressed in the commentary on each passage.

https://doi.org/10.1515/9783110599688-002

Q2	Q3	Q4	Q5	Q6	Q9	Q19
v. 87	vv. 33–63	vv. 155–9	v. 17	vv. 84–7	v. 30–1	vv. 2–36
v. 136	v. 84	v. 163	v. 46			
v. 253		v. 171–2	v. 72–5			
			v. 78			
			vv. 110–18			

Q21	Q23	Q33	Q42	Q43	Q57	Q61
v. 91	v. 50	vv. 7–8	v. 13	vv. 57–64	vv. 25–7	v. 6
						v. 14

Q66
v. 12

The Texts, with a Brief Commentary

Sūrat al-Baqara (Q 2, "The Cow")

No. 1: **Q 2:87**

A defence of Jesus, whom God has assisted with the Holy Spirit and who bears witness to God and the Torah of Moses, against the Jews.

وَلَقَدْ آتَيْنَا مُوسَى الْكِتَابَ وَقَفَّيْنَا مِنْ بَعْدِهِ بِالرُّسُلِ ۖ وَآتَيْنَا عِيسَى ابْنَ مَرْيَمَ الْبَيِّنَاتِ وَأَيَّدْنَاهُ بِرُوحِ
الْقُدُسِ ۗ أَفَكُلَّمَا جَاءَكُمْ رَسُولٌ بِمَا لَا تَهْوَىٰ أَنْفُسُكُمُ اسْتَكْبَرْتُمْ فَفَرِيقًا كَذَّبْتُمْ وَفَرِيقًا تَقْتُلُونَ 2:87

2:87 Indeed we gave Moses the book, and we followed up after him with messengers. And we gave Jesus, son of Mary, clear signs, and supported him with the Holy Spirit.[17] But is it not so that whenever a messenger brought to you what you yourselves did not desire you acted arrogantly – so that some you called liars, and some you killed?

This passage is placed within a larger, anti-Jewish, text (namely, vv. 83–103, which follow two former anti-Jewish pericopes: 2:40–74, 75–82). Cf. 2:136 (where Jesus is mentioned too alongside Moses); 3:50 (where Jesus is said to both confirm and update the Torah); 5:46 (which endorses a similar idea without the reference to Moses and additionally mentions the Gospel); and 5:78 (which mentions

17 Cf. 2:253; 5:110.

David instead of Moses alongside Jesus and likewise displays an even stronger anti-Jewish rhetoric), as well as the references to Jesus's mission to Israel in 3:49; 43:59; 61:6. Cf. too 2:253 (which lacks the reference to Moses and the anti-Jewish rhetoric but presents a similar wording as regards the connection between Jesus, God, and the Holy Spirit, albeit Jesus is conferred special status in it); and 5:110 (which likewise includes a reference to Jesus being divinely assisted by the Holy Spirit). Cf. also 3:49–55; 4:157–9; 5:46, 78, 110 (with display, too, a more-or-less-overt anti-Jewish rhetoric in defence of Jesus); 4:171–2 (where Jesus is said to be a spirit from God) and 21:91 + 66:12 (where he is somewhat obliquely, but intimately, connected to God's own spirit).

No. 2: **Q 2:136**

Jesus is mentioned, together with Moses, within a list of previous prophets including Abraham, Ishmael, Isaac, and Jacob.

قُولُوا آمَنَّا بِاللَّهِ وَمَا أُنْزِلَ إِلَيْنَا وَمَا أُنْزِلَ إِلَىٰ إِبْرَاهِيمَ وَإِسْمَاعِيلَ وَإِسْحَاقَ وَيَعْقُوبَ وَالْأَسْبَاطِ وَمَا أُوتِيَ
مُوسَىٰ وَعِيسَىٰ وَمَا أُوتِيَ النَّبِيُّونَ مِنْ رَبِّهِمْ لَا نُفَرِّقُ بَيْنَ أَحَدٍ مِنْهُمْ وَنَحْنُ لَهُ مُسْلِمُونَ 2:136

2:136 Say, "We believe in God and what has been sent to us,[18] and what was sent to Abraham,[19] and Ishmael, and Isaac, and Jacob, and the tribes, and what was given to Moses and Jesus, and what was given to the prophets by their Lord. We make no distinction between them – and to him we are submissive."

Lists similar to this one (which is reproduced verbatim in 3:84) are relatively frequent in the quranic corpus; cf. 4:163; 6:85; 33:7–8; 42:13; as well as 57:26–7). Since the preceding verse (2:135) points to Abraham as an authoritative figure against the claim made by the Christians (and the Jews) that it is they who walk in the straight path, the statement that no difference is to be made among the prophets is generally interpreted as a dismissal of Jesus's prevalence over these. Cf. however 2:253 (where the opposite claim is made) and 3:84 (which is identical to 2:136 but is not preceded there by an anti-Christian formula). I shall go back to this issue in the next chapter. Cf. too the references to Jesus's mission to Israel in 3:43; 43:59;61:6, his vindication in 4:157–9, and very especially the accusation against the Jews in 4:150.

18 Cf. 3:53.
19 إبرهيم *'brhym* in the "Uthmanic" codex = Ibrāhīm,as the standard (i.e. canonical) reading has it, or Abrāhām after the Syro-Aramaic אברהם/ܐܒܪܗܡ, with the ي *y* functioning as *mater lectionis* for *ā*?; see further Luxenberg,*The Syro-Aramaic Reading of the Koran*, 54, 93, 100.

No. 3: **Q 2:253**

Jesus bears witness to God and is divinely assisted by the Holy Spirit. Yet this time he is distinguished over other prophets.

تِلْكَ الرُّسُلُ فَضَّلْنَا بَعْضَهُمْ عَلَىٰ بَعْضٍ ۘ مِنْهُمْ مَنْ كَلَّمَ اللَّهُ ۖ وَرَفَعَ بَعْضَهُمْ دَرَجَاتٍ ۚ وَآتَيْنَا
عِيسَى ابْنَ مَرْيَمَ الْبَيِّنَاتِ وَأَيَّدْنَاهُ بِرُوحِ الْقُدُسِ ۗ وَلَوْ شَاءَ اللَّهُ مَا اقْتَتَلَ الَّذِينَ مِنْ بَعْدِهِمْ مِنْ بَعْدِ مَا
جَاءَتْهُمُ الْبَيِّنَاتُ وَلَٰكِنِ اخْتَلَفُوا فَمِنْهُمْ مَنْ آمَنَ وَمِنْهُمْ مَنْ كَفَرَ ۚ وَلَوْ شَاءَ اللَّهُ مَا اقْتَتَلُوا وَلَٰكِنَّ اللَّهَ
يَفْعَلُ مَا يُرِيدُ 2:253

2:253 These are the messengers – we have favoured some of them over others, among them those with whom God spoke; and some of them he raised in rank. We gave Jesus, son of Mary, clear signs, and supported him with the Holy Spirit.[20] If God had so willed, those who came after them would not have struggled among themselves after the clear signs had come to them. But they differed from each other: some believed, some of them did not. If God had so willed, they would not have struggled among themselves, but God does whatever he wills.

Cf. 2:87 (which presents a similar wording as regards the connection between Jesus, God, and the Holy Spirit); and 5:110 (which likewise include a reference to Jesus being divinely assisted by the Holy Spirit). Cf. also 4:171–2 (where Jesus is said to be a spirit from God); and 21:91 + 66:12 (where he is more intimately, if implicitly, connected to God's spirit).

Sūrat Āl ʿImrān **(Q 3, "The House of ʿImrān")**

No. 4: **Q 3:33–63**

An account of Jesus's birth and infancy, divine instruction, mission to Israel, miracles, and teachings – and of Israel's rejection of his mission. The narrative includes a brief speech by Jesus and is preceded by the story of the miraculous births of Mary and John the Baptist.

إِنَّ اللَّهَ اصْطَفَىٰ آدَمَ وَنُوحًا وَآلَ إِبْرَاهِيمَ وَآلَ عِمْرَانَ عَلَى الْعَالَمِينَ 3:33
ذُرِّيَّةً بَعْضُهَا مِنْ بَعْضٍ ۗ وَاللَّهُ سَمِيعٌ عَلِيمٌ 34
إِذْ قَالَتِ امْرَأَتُ عِمْرَانَ رَبِّ إِنِّي نَذَرْتُ لَكَ مَا فِي بَطْنِي مُحَرَّرًا فَتَقَبَّلْ مِنِّي ۖ إِنَّكَ أَنْتَ السَّمِيعُ الْعَلِيمُ 35

20 Cf. 2:87; 5:110.

فَلَمَّا وَضَعَتْهَا قَالَتْ رَبِّ إِنِّي وَضَعْتُهَا أُنْثَىٰ وَاللَّهُ أَعْلَمُ بِمَا وَضَعَتْ وَلَيْسَ الذَّكَرُ كَالْأُنْثَىٰ ۖ وَإِنِّي سَمَّيْتُهَا
مَرْيَمَ وَإِنِّي أُعِيذُهَا بِكَ وَذُرِّيَّتَهَا مِنَ الشَّيْطَانِ الرَّجِيمِ 36
فَتَقَبَّلَهَا رَبُّهَا بِقَبُولٍ حَسَنٍ وَأَنْبَتَهَا نَبَاتًا حَسَنًا وَكَفَّلَهَا زَكَرِيَّا ۖ كُلَّمَا دَخَلَ عَلَيْهَا زَكَرِيَّا الْمِحْرَابَ وَجَدَ
عِنْدَهَا رِزْقًا ۖ قَالَ يَا مَرْيَمُ أَنَّىٰ لَكِ هَٰذَا ۖ قَالَتْ هُوَ مِنْ عِنْدِ اللَّهِ ۖ إِنَّ اللَّهَ يَرْزُقُ مَنْ يَشَاءُ بِغَيْرِ حِسَابٍ 37
هُنَالِكَ دَعَا زَكَرِيَّا رَبَّهُ ۖ قَالَ رَبِّ هَبْ لِي مِنْ لَدُنْكَ ذُرِّيَّةً طَيِّبَةً ۖ إِنَّكَ سَمِيعُ الدُّعَاءِ 38
فَنَادَتْهُ الْمَلَائِكَةُ وَهُوَ قَائِمٌ يُصَلِّي فِي الْمِحْرَابِ أَنَّ اللَّهَ يُبَشِّرُكَ بِيَحْيَىٰ مُصَدِّقًا بِكَلِمَةٍ مِنَ اللَّهِ وَسَيِّدًا
وَحَصُورًا وَنَبِيًّا مِنَ الصَّالِحِينَ 39
قَالَ رَبِّ أَنَّىٰ يَكُونُ لِي غُلَامٌ وَقَدْ بَلَغَنِيَ الْكِبَرُ وَامْرَأَتِي عَاقِرٌ ۖ قَالَ كَذَٰلِكَ اللَّهُ يَفْعَلُ مَا يَشَاءُ 40
قَالَ رَبِّ اجْعَلْ لِي آيَةً ۖ قَالَ آيَتُكَ أَلَّا تُكَلِّمَ النَّاسَ ثَلَاثَةَ أَيَّامٍ إِلَّا رَمْزًا ۗ وَاذْكُرْ رَبَّكَ كَثِيرًا وَسَبِّحْ بِالْعَشِيِّ
وَالْإِبْكَارِ 41
وَإِذْ قَالَتِ الْمَلَائِكَةُ يَا مَرْيَمُ إِنَّ اللَّهَ اصْطَفَاكِ وَطَهَّرَكِ وَاصْطَفَاكِ عَلَىٰ نِسَاءِ الْعَالَمِينَ 42
يَا مَرْيَمُ اقْنُتِي لِرَبِّكِ وَاسْجُدِي وَارْكَعِي مَعَ الرَّاكِعِينَ 43
ذَٰلِكَ مِنْ أَنْبَاءِ الْغَيْبِ نُوحِيهِ إِلَيْكَ ۚ وَمَا كُنْتَ لَدَيْهِمْ إِذْ يُلْقُونَ أَقْلَامَهُمْ أَيُّهُمْ يَكْفُلُ مَرْيَمَ وَمَا كُنْتَ لَدَيْهِمْ إِذْ
يَخْتَصِمُونَ 44
إِذْ قَالَتِ الْمَلَائِكَةُ يَا مَرْيَمُ إِنَّ اللَّهَ يُبَشِّرُكِ بِكَلِمَةٍ مِنْهُ اسْمُهُ الْمَسِيحُ عِيسَى ابْنُ مَرْيَمَ وَجِيهًا فِي الدُّنْيَا
وَالْآخِرَةِ وَمِنَ الْمُقَرَّبِينَ 45
وَيُكَلِّمُ النَّاسَ فِي الْمَهْدِ وَكَهْلًا وَمِنَ الصَّالِحِينَ 46
قَالَتْ رَبِّ أَنَّىٰ يَكُونُ لِي وَلَدٌ وَلَمْ يَمْسَسْنِي بَشَرٌ ۖ قَالَ كَذَٰلِكِ اللَّهُ يَخْلُقُ مَا يَشَاءُ ۚ إِذَا قَضَىٰ أَمْرًا فَإِنَّمَا
يَقُولُ لَهُ كُنْ فَيَكُونُ 47
وَيُعَلِّمُهُ الْكِتَابَ وَالْحِكْمَةَ وَالتَّوْرَاةَ وَالْإِنْجِيلَ 48
وَرَسُولًا إِلَىٰ بَنِي إِسْرَائِيلَ أَنِّي قَدْ جِئْتُكُمْ بِآيَةٍ مِنْ رَبِّكُمْ ۖ أَنِّي أَخْلُقُ لَكُمْ مِنَ الطِّينِ كَهَيْئَةِ الطَّيْرِ فَأَنْفُخُ
فِيهِ فَيَكُونُ طَيْرًا بِإِذْنِ اللَّهِ ۖ وَأُبْرِئُ الْأَكْمَهَ وَالْأَبْرَصَ وَأُحْيِي الْمَوْتَىٰ بِإِذْنِ اللَّهِ ۖ وَأُنَبِّئُكُمْ بِمَا تَأْكُلُونَ وَمَا
تَدَّخِرُونَ فِي بُيُوتِكُمْ ۚ إِنَّ فِي ذَٰلِكَ لَآيَةً لَكُمْ إِنْ كُنْتُمْ مُؤْمِنِينَ 49
وَمُصَدِّقًا لِمَا بَيْنَ يَدَيَّ مِنَ التَّوْرَاةِ وَلِأُحِلَّ لَكُمْ بَعْضَ الَّذِي حُرِّمَ عَلَيْكُمْ ۚ وَجِئْتُكُمْ بِآيَةٍ مِنْ رَبِّكُمْ فَاتَّقُوا اللَّهَ
وَأَطِيعُونِ 50
إِنَّ اللَّهَ رَبِّي وَرَبُّكُمْ فَاعْبُدُوهُ ۗ هَٰذَا صِرَاطٌ مُسْتَقِيمٌ 51
فَلَمَّا أَحَسَّ عِيسَىٰ مِنْهُمُ الْكُفْرَ قَالَ مَنْ أَنْصَارِي إِلَى اللَّهِ ۖ قَالَ الْحَوَارِيُّونَ نَحْنُ أَنْصَارُ اللَّهِ آمَنَّا بِاللَّهِ
وَاشْهَدْ بِأَنَّا مُسْلِمُونَ 52
رَبَّنَا آمَنَّا بِمَا أَنْزَلْتَ وَاتَّبَعْنَا الرَّسُولَ فَاكْتُبْنَا مَعَ الشَّاهِدِينَ 53
وَمَكَرُوا وَمَكَرَ اللَّهُ ۖ وَاللَّهُ خَيْرُ الْمَاكِرِينَ 54
إِذْ قَالَ اللَّهُ يَا عِيسَىٰ إِنِّي مُتَوَفِّيكَ وَرَافِعُكَ إِلَيَّ وَمُطَهِّرُكَ مِنَ الَّذِينَ كَفَرُوا وَجَاعِلُ الَّذِينَ اتَّبَعُوكَ فَوْقَ
الَّذِينَ كَفَرُوا إِلَىٰ يَوْمِ الْقِيَامَةِ ۖ ثُمَّ إِلَيَّ مَرْجِعُكُمْ فَأَحْكُمُ بَيْنَكُمْ فِيمَا كُنْتُمْ فِيهِ تَخْتَلِفُونَ 55
فَأَمَّا الَّذِينَ كَفَرُوا فَأُعَذِّبُهُمْ عَذَابًا شَدِيدًا فِي الدُّنْيَا وَالْآخِرَةِ وَمَا لَهُمْ مِنْ نَاصِرِينَ 56
وَأَمَّا الَّذِينَ آمَنُوا وَعَمِلُوا الصَّالِحَاتِ فَيُوَفِّيهِمْ أُجُورَهُمْ ۗ وَاللَّهُ لَا يُحِبُّ الظَّالِمِينَ 57

ذَٰلِكَ نَتْلُوهُ عَلَيْكَ مِنَ الْآيَاتِ وَالذِّكْرِ الْحَكِيمِ 58
إِنَّ مَثَلَ عِيسَىٰ عِنْدَ اللَّهِ كَمَثَلِ آدَمَ ۖ خَلَقَهُ مِنْ تُرَابٍ ثُمَّ قَالَ لَهُ كُنْ فَيَكُونُ 59
الْحَقُّ مِنْ رَبِّكَ فَلَا تَكُنْ مِنَ الْمُمْتَرِينَ 60
فَمَنْ حَاجَّكَ فِيهِ مِنْ بَعْدِ مَا جَاءَكَ مِنَ الْعِلْمِ فَقُلْ تَعَالَوْا نَدْعُ أَبْنَاءَنَا وَأَبْنَاءَكُمْ وَنِسَاءَنَا وَنِسَاءَكُمْ وَأَنْفُسَنَا
وَأَنْفُسَكُمْ ثُمَّ نَبْتَهِلْ فَنَجْعَلْ لَعْنَتَ اللَّهِ عَلَى الْكَاذِبِينَ 61
إِنَّ هَٰذَا لَهُوَ الْقَصَصُ الْحَقُّ ۚ وَمَا مِنْ إِلَٰهٍ إِلَّا اللَّهُ ۚ وَإِنَّ اللَّهَ لَهُوَ الْعَزِيزُ الْحَكِيمُ 62
فَإِنْ تَوَلَّوْا فَإِنَّ اللَّهَ عَلِيمٌ بِالْمُفْسِدِينَ 63

3:33 God chose Adam and Noah, the family of Abraham and the family of ʻImrān, over all men[21]

34 – they were descendants one from another. God is hearing, knowing.

35 The wife of ʻImrān said, "My Lord, I do vow to you what is in my womb, as an offering. So accept it from me – you are the Hearing, the Knowing."

36 Then, when she delivered her [= Mary], she said, "My Lord, I have delivered a female" – God knew well what she had delivered, and that the male is not like the female – "and I have named her Mary, and I seek for her refuge in you, and for her offspring, from the accursed Satan."[22]

---

21 The plural العلمين occurs seventy-three times in the Qurʾān: forty-one times in genitive form following the noun ربّ *rabb* ("Lord") which denotes God (ربّ العلمين: so 1:2; 2:131; 5:28; 6:45,71,162; 7:54,61,67,104,121; 10:10,37; 26:16,23,47,77,98,109,127,145,164,180; 27:8,44; 28:30; 32:2; 37:87,182; 39:75; 40:64–6; 41:9; 43:46; 45:36; 56:80; 59:16; 69:43; 81:29; 83:6) and thirty-two times in several phrases following the prepositions ل *li-* ("for," fourteen times: 3:96,108; 6:90; 12:104; 21:71,91,107; 25:1; 29:10,15; 30:22; 38:87; 68:52; 81:27), على *ʻalà* ("over," "above," nine times: 2:47,122,251; 3:33,42; 6:86; 7:140; 44:32; 45:16), من *min* ("from," "among," five times: 5:20,115; 7:80; 26:165; 29:28), عن *ʻan* ("with respect to," "in front of," three times: 3:97; 15:70; 29:6), and only once following the preposition فى *fī* ("in," "among?": 37:79). It is to be translated as "all men/women," instead of "the worlds." Cf. 3:33 and Israel's election in 2:47,122; 44:32; 45:16; Mary's in 3:42; and Ishmael's, Elijah's, Jonas's and Lot's in 6:86. Likewise, in 3:97 and 29:6 God is declared to be rich "with respect to all men," i.e. in contrast to these; whereas in 29:10 God knows what "all men" conceal in their hearts. See also Alfred-Louis de Prémare, *Les fondations de l'islam. Entre écriture et histoire* (Paris: Seuil, 2002) 437–8, n.156; Arthur J. Droge, *The Qur'ān: A New Annotated Translation* (Sheffield, UK, and Bristol, CT: Equinox, 2013) 1 n.3.

22 الشّيطان الرّجيم *al-šayṭān al-raǧīm*, often misunderstood to mean "stoned." See Manfred Kropp, "Der äthiopische Satan = *šayṭān* und seine koranischen Ausläufer; mit einer Bemerkung über verbales Steinigen," *OC* 89 (1995): 93–102; idem, "Beyond Single Words: Māʼida – Shayṭān – jibt and ṭāghūt. Mechanisms of transmission into the Ethiopic (Gəʻəz) Bible and the Qurʾānic text," in *The Qurʾān in Its Historical Context*, ed. Gabriel Said Reynolds (RSQ; London and New York: Routledge, 2008) 204–16.

37 Her Lord accepted her [= Mary] gladly and made her grow up well, and Zachariah took care of her. Whenever Zachariah entered the sanctuary[23] to [visit] her, he found [some] provision [of food] with her. He said, "Mary!, where does this come to you from?" She replied, "From God – God provides to whomever he wills without reckoning."
38 There Zachariah prayed to his Lord saying, "My lord, grant me a good offspring from yourself – surely you are the hearer of prayer"[24];
39 and the angels called him while he was standing, praying in the sanctuary: "God gives you good tidings of John, confirming a word from God.[25] [He will be] honourable, and chaste, and a prophet among the righteous."[26]
40 He said, "My Lord, how shall I have a boy? I am already old and my wife is barren." He said, "Thus! God does whatever he wills."[27]
41 He said, "My Lord, give me a sign." He said: "Your sign is that you will not speak to anyone for three days, save by gestures. Remember your Lord often and glorify [him] in the evening and the morning."[28]
42 And [remember] when the angels said, "Mary, God has chosen you and purified you – he has chosen you among all other women.
43 Mary, be obedient to your Lord, prostrate yourself and bow down with those who bow down."[29]
44 This is from the stories of the unseen. We have inspired you with it, for you were not with them when they cast their pens as to which of them would take care of Mary; nor were you with them when they disputed.
45 [Remember] when the angels said, "God gives you good tidings of a word from him.[30] His name is the Messiah,[31] Jesus son of Mary, honoured in this world and the hereafter, and one of those brought near [to God].
46 He will speak to the people from the cradle[32] and will be among the righteous."[33]
47 She said, "My Lord, how shall I have a child, when no man has touched me?" He said, "Thus! God creates whatever he wills. When he decrees something, he simply says, 'Be!,' and it becomes.[34]

23 Cf. Protevangelium of James 6–8; Pseudo-Matthew 4–8; Story of Joseph the Carpenter 3–4. In all these sources, it is clear that Mary is upraised inside the Jerusalem temple.
24 (Cf. Psalm 65:2.)
25 Cf. v. 45 below, as well as 4:171.
26 Cf. 6:85.
27 Cf. v. 47. Cf. too 19:8–9, 20–1.
28 Cf. vv. 38–41 and 19:2–11.
29 Cf. the Adam narratives analysed in the next chapter.
30 Cf. v. 39 and 4:171.
31 (Cf. Luke 9:20; Acts 3:18.)
32 Cf. 5:110; 19:29–30.
33 Cf. again 6:85.
34 Cf. vv. 40, 59. Cf. too 19:8–9, 20–1, 35.

48 He [= God] will teach him the Writing,[35] and Wisdom, and the Torah, and the Gospel,[36]
49 and [will make him] a messenger to the sons of Israel."
50 [He said to them,] "I have brought you a sign from your Lord: I shall create for you the form of a bird out of clay; then I will breath into it and it shall become a bird, with God's permission.[37] I shall heal the blind and the leper and bring the dead back to life, with God's permission.[38] And I will tell you what you [are allowed to] eat and what you may store up in your houses. This, indeed, is a sign for you, if you are believers.
51 [I come to you] confirming the Torah [given to you] before me,[39] and to allow you some things that were previously forbidden to you. I have brought you a sign from your Lord,

35 الكتاب *al-kitāb*. Like Muslim exegetes, modern scholars usually interpret *kitāb* to mean "book" and tend to identify it with the "Qur'ān" itself, which they portray, therefore, as displaying here and elsewhere some kind of more or less straightforward self-referentiality (see Stefan Wild, ed., *Self-referentiality in the Qur'ān* [DA 11; Wiesbaden: Harrassowitz, 2007]; Anne-Sylvie Boisliveau, *Le Coran par lui-même. Vocabulaire et argumentation du discours coranique autoréférentiel* [Leiden and Boston: Brill, 2014] 25). Yet such identification proves problematic. First, because *kitāb* has other meanings as well (Droge, *The Qur'ān*, 2, n.2), including "writing" (arguably its, albeit more vague, original meaning) and "decree" (see further John Wansbrough, *Quranic Studies: Sources and Methods of Scriptural Interpretation* [LOS; Oxford: Oxford University Press, 1977; reprinted with a Foreword, Translations, and Expanded Notes by Andrew Rippin in Amherst, NY: Prometheus Books, 2004] 75;Daniel A. Madigan, The *Qur'ān's Self-image* [Princeton, NJ: Princeton University Press, 2001] 177–9; Jan Retsö, *The Arabs in Antiquity: Their History from the Assyrians to the Umayyads* [London and New York: RoutledgeCurzon, 2003] 42; idem, "Arabs and Arabic in the Age of the Prophet," in *The Qur'ān in Context: Historical and Literary Investigations into the Qur'ānic Milieu*, ed. Angelika Neuwirth, Nicolai Sinai, and Michael Marx [TSQ 6; Leiden and Boston: Brill, 2010, 281–92, p. 284]). Secondly, because, despite their relatedness, *kitāb* and *qur'ān* (which should in turn be translated as "reading" or "recitation") are anything but clear-cut synonyms; cf. 10:37; 41:3; 42:7, 14–15, 17; 43:3–4; 56:77–8; 85:21–2, where their difference is quite patent, as well as the allusion to "that *kitāb*" instead of "this *kitāb*" in 2:2 (on the difference between *kitāb* and *qur'ān* see Wansbrough, *Quranic Studies*, 75; Retsö, *The Arabs in Antiquity*, 41–7; "Arabs and Arabic in the Age of the Prophet," 284–5, 288–9; Daniel A. Madigan, "The Limits of Self-referentiality in the Qur'ān," in *Self-referentiality in the Qur'ān*, ed. Wild, 59–69). And, lastly, because we have no reasons to presume that the Qur'ān formed a single unitary text (i.e. something like a "book") prior to its collection and subsequent canonisation (see further Wansbrough, *Quranic Studies*, 20–52;Alfred-Louis de Prémare, *Aux origines du Coran: questions d'hier, approaches d'aujourd'hui* [Paris: Téraèdre, 2004] 29–46). Cf. too 4:159, where *kitāb* can be translated as "Scripture."

36 الإنجيل *al-inǧīl* (sing.); cf. 5:46, 110; 57:27. For an interpretation of this term as meaning the Diatessaron, i.e. the standard Gospel text (or more precisely, harmony) in Syrian Christianity until about 400 CE, see Jan M. F. Van Reeth, "L'Évangile du prophète," in *al-Kitāb: La sacralité du texte dans le monde de l'Islam. Actes du Symposium international tenu à Leuven et Louvain-la-Neuve du 29 mai au 1 juin 2002*, ed. Daniel De Smet, Godefroy Callatay, and Jan M. F. van Reeth (Brussels: SBEO, 2004) 155–74.

37 Cf. 5:110.

38 Cf. 5:110.

39 Cf. 5:46; 61:6.

so fear God and obey me.[40] God is my Lord and your Lord, so worship him[41] – this is a straight path."[42]

52 When Jesus saw their disbelief, he said, "Who are my helpers for God?" The disciples said, "We are God's helpers! We believe in God. Bear witness that we submit [to him].

53 Our Lord, we believe in what you have sent down[43] and we follow the messenger – so count us among [your] witnesses!"[44]

54 They [= the sons of Israel, i.e. the Jews] schemed [against Jesus], but God too schemed [against them] – God is the best of schemers.

55 [Remember] when God said, "Jesus!, I am going to take you and raise you to myself[45] and purify you from those who disbelieve; and I will place those who follow you above the disbelievers until the Day of Resurrection; then to me you shall [all] return, and I shall judge between you concerning your differences;

56 the disbelievers, I shall punish them with a harsh punishment in [both] this world and the hereafter, and no one will be able to help them!"[46]

57 As for the believers and righteous – he will grant them a full reward, for God does not love the evildoers.

58 This – we recite it to you from [God's] verses[47] and [God's] wise reminder.

59 Indeed, the appearance of Jesus before God is like the appearance of Adam, whom he created from the dust. He said to him, "Be!," and he became.[48]

60 The truth is from your God, so do not be among the doubters.

61 Then whoever argues with you about it after this knowledge has come to you – tell him, "Come! Let us call our sons and your sons, our women and your women, ourselves and yourselves! Let us pray humbly [together] and invoke the curse of God among the liars [among us]!"

62 This verily is a true narration – indeed it is. There is no God but God, and he surely is the Mighty, the Wise.

63 But if they turn away – well, God knows [who are] the corrupters.

Cf. 2:87; 4:157–9; 5:46, 78, 110 (which likewise display a more or less overt anti-Jewish rhetoric in defence of Jesus), and especially 2:87; 5:46; 61:6 (which present Jesus's mission to Israel as a confirmation of the Torah). Cf. too the reference to Jesus's mission to Israel in 43:59.

---

40 Cf. 43:63.

41 Cf. 5:72, 117; 19:36; 43:64.

42 Cf. 5:117; 6:87; 19:36; 43:61, 64.

43 Cf. 2:136

44 Cf. 5:111–12; 61:14.

45 Cf. 4:158; 5:117.

46 Cf. 5:72.

47 See the comments on *kitāb* and *qur'ān* apropos v. 48.

48 Cf. v. 47. Cf. too 19:35.

The identification Joachim = ‘Imrān has often been attributed to scribal confusion[49]. Most scholars are aware that the name chosen by the quranic author(s) to name Mary’s father (‘Imrān) is reminiscent of the biblical Amram, who is introduced as the father of Aaron, Moses, and Miriam in Exodus 6:20; Numbers 26:59; and 1 Chronicles 23:13. They do also know that Jesus’s mother (Mary) is referred to as Aaron’s sister, and hence implicitly as Amran’s daughter, in Q 19:28 (see below). In their view, confusing Mary (which is spelled מרים *mrym* = Miryam in Hebrew) with Aaron’s sister (i.e. confusing her with another Miriam) made it possible for the quranic author(s) to additionally confuse Mary (Miriam) with the daughter of Amram. Yet this at-first-sight-odd identification may not be as casual as it is normally taken to be. For it may serve to reflect and expand the traditional Christian typological re-placement of the Mosaic revelation by Christ by (*a*) explicitly substituting Amran (i.e. Moses’s father) by Joachim/‘Imrān and Miriam (i.e. Moses’s sister) by Mary, and therefore by (*b*) implicitly substituting Aaron (i.e. Moses’s brother) by John the Baptist (cf. too the intriguing reference in Luke 1:5 to John’s mother, Elisabeth, as being herself a descendant of Aaron). Be that as it may, the quranic authors operate both here and in Q 19 a fourfold replacement: Amram → ‘Imrān; Aaron → John (Yaḥyā); Moses → Jesus (‘Īsā); Miriam → Mary (Maryam). Cf. Jesus’s and Mary’s distinction in 2:87, 253; 5:110; 19:21, 30–3; 23:50; 43:57, 59.

The account of Mary’s miraculous birth (vv. 34–7) follows Mary’s infancy narratives in Protevangelium of James 1–10; Pseudo-Matthew 1–8; and The Story of Joseph the Carpenter 2–4, while that of John the Baptist (vv. 37–41) draws on Luke 1:5–25, 57–80.

In turn, the story of Jesus speaking from the cradle in v. 46 is reminiscent of Arabic Infancy Gospel 1:2 (or the latter’s Syriac *Grundschrift*); cf. too 1 Enoch 106:2–3, where the newborn Noah similarly speaks from the midwife’s arms – the apocalyptic Noah being a model for Jesus in the New Testament and the New Testament Apocrypha.[50] On Jesus’s turning clay birds into living birds, cf. Infancy Gospel of Thomas 2–3; Pseudo-Matthew 26–8; and Arabic Gospel of the Infancy

---

49 See Roberto Tottoli, “‘Imrān,” in *Encyclopaedia of the Qur’ān*, ed. Jane Dammen McAuliffe (6 vols.; Leiden and Boston: Brill, 2001–6) 2:509; Pierre Lory, “‘Imrân et sa famille,” in *Dictionnaire du Coran*, ed. Mohammad Ali Amir-Moezzi (Paris: Laffont, 2007) 417–9; Angelika Neuwirth, “The House of Abraham and the House of Amram: Genealogy, Patriarchal Authority, and Exegetical Professionalism,” in *The Qur’ān in Context: Historical and Literary Investigations into the Qur’ānic Milieu*, ed. Angelika Neuwirth, Nicolai Sinai, and Michael Marx (Leiden and Boston: Brill, 2010) 499–531, pp. 503–28.

50 See Carlos A. Segovia, *The Quranic Noah and the Making of the Islamic Prophet: A Study of Intertextuality and Religious Identity Formation in Late Antiquity* (JCIT 4; Berlin and Boston: de Gruyter, 2015) 21–5.

36 (where, curiously, such miracle is presented as a confirmation of Jesus's divine sonship). On the formula "with God's permission," cf. 5:110.

I shall come back to vv. 47 and 59 in the next chapter and to the portrayal of Jesus as "a word from God" in vv. 39, 45 in Chapter 5.

See also Jesus's speeches in 5:112, 114, 116–18; 19:24–6, 30–3; 43:63–4; 61:6, 14.

Lastly, it is evident that this five-part pericope – (1) vv. 33; (2) vv. 34–41; (3) vv. 42–8; (4) 49–57; (5) vv. 58–63 – must be connected to 19:2–36 (see below). Cf. too the close similarities (as Guillaume Dye pointed to me in a personal communication of March 15, 2017) with Acts 2:22–5.

No. 5: **Q 3:84**

This verse reproduces verbatim 2:136 (see above).

Sūrat al-Nisā' **(Q 4, "Women")**

No. 6: **Q 4:155–9**

An anti-Jewish passage denying Jesus's crucifixion and announcing that, in due time, he will be acknowledged to be the Messiah by the Jews.

فَبِمَا نَقْضِهِمْ مِيثَاقَهُمْ وَكُفْرِهِمْ بِآيَاتِ اللَّهِ وَقَتْلِهِمُ الْأَنْبِيَاءَ بِغَيْرِ حَقٍّ وَقَوْلِهِمْ قُلُوبُنَا غُلْفٌ ۚ بَلْ طَبَعَ اللَّهُ عَلَيْهَا
بِكُفْرِهِمْ فَلَا يُؤْمِنُونَ إِلَّا قَلِيلًا 155
وَبِكُفْرِهِمْ وَقَوْلِهِمْ عَلَىٰ مَرْيَمَ بُهْتَانًا عَظِيمًا 156
وَقَوْلِهِمْ إِنَّا قَتَلْنَا الْمَسِيحَ عِيسَى ابْنَ مَرْيَمَ رَسُولَ اللَّهِ وَمَا قَتَلُوهُ وَمَا صَلَبُوهُ وَلَٰكِنْ شُبِّهَ لَهُمْ ۚ وَإِنَّ الَّذِينَ
اخْتَلَفُوا فِيهِ لَفِي شَكٍّ مِنْهُ ۚ مَا لَهُمْ بِهِ مِنْ عِلْمٍ إِلَّا اتِّبَاعَ الظَّنِّ ۚ وَمَا قَتَلُوهُ يَقِينًا 157
بَلْ رَفَعَهُ اللَّهُ إِلَيْهِ ۚ وَكَانَ اللَّهُ عَزِيزًا حَكِيمًا 158
وَإِنْ مِنْ أَهْلِ الْكِتَابِ إِلَّا لَيُؤْمِنَنَّ بِهِ قَبْلَ مَوْتِهِ ۖ وَيَوْمَ الْقِيَامَةِ يَكُونُ عَلَيْهِمْ شَهِيدًا 159

4:155 Because of their breaking of the covenant, and their disbelief in God's signs, and their killing of the prophets without any right, and their saying, "Our hearts are wrapped" – God has rather sealed them on account of their disbelief, so they cannot believe, save a few [among them] –

156 on account of their disbelief and their saying against Mary a great slander,

157 and because of their saying, "We have killed the Messiah, Jesus son of Mary [and] God's messenger" – but they did not kill him, they did not crucify him, it [only] seemed like that to them... Those who differ about it are in doubt about it, they have no knowledge about it – they only follow an assumption. For they did not kill him.

158 No! God raised him to himself.[51] God is mighty, wise.
159 [There is] not [even] one among the People of the Scripture[52] who shall not believe in him [= Jesus] before his [own] death. Moreover, in the Day of Resurrection he [= Jesus himself] will bear witness against them [= the disbelievers among the Jews, i.e. those who do not acknowledge Jesus to be the Messiah raised by God].

The wording in v. 157 is ambiguous, as ولكن شبه لهم *wa-lākin šubbiha lahum* can mean three different things: (*a*) "someone was made to resemble him to them," i.e. someone else was crucified instead of Jesus (which is the habitual understanding of this phrase)[53]; (*b*) "it seemed like that to them," or "it was made to appear so to them," i.e. the Jews believed that they had killed Jesus, yet they did not kill him, because God took him and had someone else killed in his instead; and (*c*) although "it seemed like that to them" the Jews did not truly kill Jesus, for he was resurrected by God and will return in the end of times. Besides, in "his death" in v. 159 is rendered in Ubayy's recension as "their death," in allusion to the death of each individual Jew – shortly before dying they, too, will have to admit the truth about Jesus, which they now (pretend to) ignore (v. 157). Cf. too the reference to Jesus's death in 5:117, as well as the statement about the living martyrs in 3:169. I will return to these issues in Chapter 5.

No. 7: **Q 4:163**

Jesus is included within a list of prophets including Noah, Abraham, Ishmael, Isaac, Jacob,Job, Jonah, Aaron, Solomon, and David.

إِنَّا أَوْحَيْنَا إِلَيْكَ كَمَا أَوْحَيْنَا إِلَىٰ نُوحٍ وَالنَّبِيِّينَ مِنْ بَعْدِهِ ۚ وَأَوْحَيْنَا إِلَىٰ إِبْرَاهِيمَ وَإِسْمَاعِيلَ وَإِسْحَاقَ
وَيَعْقُوبَ وَالْأَسْبَاطِ وَعِيسَىٰ وَأَيُّوبَ وَيُونُسَ وَهَارُونَ وَسُلَيْمَانَ ۚ وَآتَيْنَا دَاوُودَ زَبُورًا 4:163

4:163 We have inspired you as we [earlier] inspired Noah and the prophets after him, and as we inspired Abraham, and Ishmael, and Isaac, and Jacob, and the tribes, and Jesus, and Job, and Jonah, and Aaron, and Salomon, and we gave David [the] Psalms.

Cf. the shorter list provided in 2:136 and 3:84. Cf. too the prophetical lists in 6:85; 33:7–8; 42:13.

---

51 Cf. 3:55; 5:117.

52 أهل الكتاب *ahl al-kitāb*. This expression is polysemic; cf. 3:65 (where it designates the Jews and the Christians alike) 4:171 (where it is applied to the Christians alone), and this verse (where it rather means the Jews).

53 At least since Ibn Isḥāq; see Gordon D. Newby, *The Making of the Last Prophet: A Reconstruction of the Earliest Biography of Muhammad* (Columbia: University of South Carolina Press, 1989) 209–10.

No. 8: **Q 4:171–2**

An anti-trinitarian passage describing Jesus as a messenger and servant of God – though he is simultaneously referred to as God's Word and a spirit from him.

يَا أَهْلَ الْكِتَابِ لَا تَغْلُوا فِي دِينِكُمْ وَلَا تَقُولُوا عَلَى اللَّهِ إِلَّا الْحَقَّ ۚ إِنَّمَا الْمَسِيحُ عِيسَى ابْنُ مَرْيَمَ رَسُولُ
اللَّهِ وَكَلِمَتُهُ أَلْقَاهَا إِلَىٰ مَرْيَمَ وَرُوحٌ مِنْهُ ۖ فَآمِنُوا بِاللَّهِ وَرُسُلِهِ ۖ وَلَا تَقُولُوا ثَلَاثَةٌ ۚ انْتَهُوا خَيْرًا لَكُمْ إِنَّمَا
ۚ اللَّهُ إِلَٰهٌ وَاحِدٌ ۖ سُبْحَانَهُ أَنْ يَكُونَ لَهُ وَلَدٌ ۘ لَهُ مَا فِي السَّمَاوَاتِ وَمَا فِي الْأَرْضِ ۗ وَكَفَىٰ بِاللَّهِ
وَكِيلًا 4:171
لَنْ يَسْتَنْكِفَ الْمَسِيحُ أَنْ يَكُونَ عَبْدًا لِلَّهِ وَلَا الْمَلَائِكَةُ الْمُقَرَّبُونَ ۚ وَمَنْ يَسْتَنْكِفْ عَنْ عِبَادَتِهِ وَيَسْتَكْبِرْ
فَسَيَحْشُرُهُمْ إِلَيْهِ جَمِيعًا 172

4:171 O people of the Scripture, do not exaggerate/err[54] in your religion/judgement[55] and do not say about God save the truth. The Messiah, Jesus son of Mary, is but the messenger of God[56] and his Word, which he conveyed to Mary, and a spirit from him. So believe in God and his messengers and do not say "Three!"[57]; cease [doing that], it is better for you.[58] God is but one God[59] – may he be praised! How could he have a child? To him belongs all there is in the heavens and on the earth. God is sufficient as a helper [to mankind].

172 The Messiah does not disdain to be a servant of God,[60] nor do the angels, who are near [to God]. Whoever disdains his service and becomes arrogant – he [= God] will gather them towards him, all of them.

On Jesus as "God's Word"/"a word from God," cf. 3:39, 45. Cf. also 5:17 and 9:30 (which deny Jesus's divinity); 5:72–5 (which contain the same denial plus that of the Trinity); and 5:116–17 (which claim that neither Jesus nor his mother are divine). Cf. too 3:79–80; 9:31; 18:102 (which hold that neither God's angels, prophets, and servants, nor the Messiah, can be taken as lords); and the strict monotheist formulas in 2:116; 6:101; 10:68; 17:111; 18:4; 19:35, 88–94; 23:91; 39:4; 43:81; 72:3; 112. On the connection between Jesus and the Spirit, see 2:87; 2:253;

54 The *rasm* or consonantal skeleton (ٮعلوا) is ambiguous, i.e. it may be interpreted both ways (تغلوا *taġlū* / تعلوا *ta'lū*) ; see Christoph Luxenberg, "A New Interpretation of the Arabic Inscription in Jerusalem's Dome of the Rock," in *The Hidden Origins of Islam: New research into Its Early History*, ed. Karl-Heinz Ohlig and Gerd-R. Puin (Amherst, NY: Prometheus Books, 2010) 125–51, p. 137.

55 دين *dīn*.

56 Cf. 5:75.

57 Cf. 5:73.

58 Cf. 5:73.

59 Cf. 5:73; 9:31. (See also Isaiah 45:7.)

60 Cf. 19:30. (See also Acts 3:13, 4:27.)

5:110; 21:91; 66:12. Clearly, the identity of Word and Spirit overturns the trinity. See further the Afterword.

Sūrat al-Māʾida (Q 5, "The Table")

No. 9: **Q 5:17**

Another passage denying Jesus's identification with God – i.e. Jesus's divine nature.

لَقَدْ كَفَرَ الَّذِينَ قَالُوا إِنَّ اللَّهَ هُوَ الْمَسِيحُ ابْنُ مَرْيَمَ ۚ قُلْ فَمَنْ يَمْلِكُ مِنَ اللَّهِ شَيْئًا إِنْ أَرَادَ أَنْ يُهْلِكَ الْمَسِيحَ
ابْنَ مَرْيَمَ وَأُمَّهُ وَمَنْ فِي الْأَرْضِ جَمِيعًا ۗ وَلِلَّهِ مُلْكُ السَّمَاوَاتِ وَالْأَرْضِ وَمَا بَيْنَهُمَا ۚ يَخْلُقُ مَا يَشَاءُ ۚ
وَاللَّهُ عَلَىٰ كُلِّ شَيْءٍ قَدِيرٌ 5:17

5:17 Certainly they disbelieve – those who say "God is the Messiah, son of Mary."[61] Say, "Who would be able to do anything against God if he wished to destroy the Messiah, son of Mary, and his mother,[62] and whoever is on earth – or all [of them] together? To God belongs the kingdom of the heavens and the earth and whatever is between them. He creates whatever he wills. God is powerful over everything.

Cf. 4:171–2 above and 5:72–5, 116–17 below.

No. 10: **Q 5:46**

A brief allusion to Jesus and the Gospel, which is described as a divine guide in confirmation of the Torah.

وَقَفَّيْنَا عَلَىٰ آثَارِهِمْ بِعِيسَى ابْنِ مَرْيَمَ مُصَدِّقًا لِمَا بَيْنَ يَدَيْهِ مِنَ التَّوْرَاةِ ۖ وَآتَيْنَاهُ الْإِنْجِيلَ فِيهِ هُدًى وَنُورٌ
وَمُصَدِّقًا لِمَا بَيْنَ يَدَيْهِ مِنَ التَّوْرَاةِ وَهُدًى وَمَوْعِظَةً لِلْمُتَّقِينَ 5:46

5:46 And we sent on their footsteps Jesus, son of Mary, confirming that which was before him in the Torah,[63] and we gave him the Gospel,[64] containing guidance and light and confirming that which was before it in the Torah, as guidance and admonition to the fearful.

Cf. 3:50 (where Jesus is said both to confirm and update the Torah). See also the references to Jesus's mission to Israel in 3:49–55; 5:78, 110; 43:59; 61:6.

---

61 Cf. 5:72.

62 Cf. 23:50.

63 Cf. 3:51; 61:6.

64 Cf. 3:48; 5:110; 57:27. See n.36 above.

No. 11: **Q 5:72–5**

Another passage denying Jesus's identification with God, and the trinity.

لَقَدْ كَفَرَ الَّذِينَ قَالُوا إِنَّ اللَّهَ هُوَ الْمَسِيحُ ابْنُ مَرْيَمَ ۖ وَقَالَ الْمَسِيحُ يَا بَنِي إِسْرَائِيلَ اعْبُدُوا اللَّهَ رَبِّي وَرَبَّكُمْ ۖ
إِنَّهُ مَنْ يُشْرِكْ بِاللَّهِ فَقَدْ حَرَّمَ اللَّهُ عَلَيْهِ الْجَنَّةَ وَمَأْوَاهُ النَّارُ ۖ وَمَا لِلظَّالِمِينَ مِنْ أَنْصَارٍ 5:72
لَقَدْ كَفَرَ الَّذِينَ قَالُوا إِنَّ اللَّهَ ثَالِثُ ثَلَاثَةٍ ۘ وَمَا مِنْ إِلَٰهٍ إِلَّا إِلَٰهٌ وَاحِدٌ ۚ وَإِنْ لَمْ يَنْتَهُوا عَمَّا يَقُولُونَ لَيَمَسَّنَّ الَّذِينَ
كَفَرُوا مِنْهُمْ عَذَابٌ أَلِيمٌ 73
أَفَلَا يَتُوبُونَ إِلَى اللَّهِ وَيَسْتَغْفِرُونَهُ ۚ وَاللَّهُ غَفُورٌ رَحِيمٌ 74
مَا الْمَسِيحُ ابْنُ مَرْيَمَ إِلَّا رَسُولٌ قَدْ خَلَتْ مِنْ قَبْلِهِ الرُّسُلُ وَأُمُّهُ صِدِّيقَةٌ ۖ كَانَا يَأْكُلَانِ الطَّعَامَ ۗ انْظُرْ كَيْفَ
نُبَيِّنُ لَهُمُ الْآيَاتِ ثُمَّ انْظُرْ أَنَّىٰ يُؤْفَكُونَ 75

5:72 Certainly they disbelieve – those who say "God is the Messiah, son of Mary."[65] The Messiah rather said, "Sons of Israel!, worship God, [who is] my Lord and your Lord.[66] He who associates [anything] with God[67] – God has forbidden him [from entering] the Garden, so his abode [will be] the Fire. The evildoers have no helpers.[68]

5:73 Certainly they disbelieve – those who say "God is the third of three,"[69] as there is no God but one God.[70] If they do not desist from what they are saying,[71] surely a painful punishment will strike the disbelievers among them.

5:74 Will they not turn to God in repentance and seek his forgiveness? God is forgiving, compassionate.

5:75 The Messiah son of Mary was only a messenger.[72] [Other] messengers have passed away before him. As for his mother, she was a truthful woman.[73] They both ate food [unlike God and the angels, for they were both human].[74] See how we make clear the signs to them, and see how deluded they are.

Cf. 4:171–2 (which likewise reject Jesus's divine sonship and the trinity); 5:17 (which opens in the same way) and 9:30 (which also deny Jesus's divine status); and 5:116–17 (which claim that neither Jesus nor his mother are divine). Cf. too 3:79–80; 9:31; 18:102 (which hold that neither God's angels, prophets, and servants, nor the Messiah, can be taken as lords); and the strict monotheist

65 Cf. 5:17.
66 Cf. 3:51; 5:117; 19:36; 43:61, 64.
67 Cf. 9:31.
68 Cf. 3:56.
69 Cf. 4:171.
70 Cf. 4:171.
71 Cf. 4:171.
72 Cf. 4:171.
73 Cf. 5:116.
74 Cf. 6:14; 11:70.

formulas in 2:116; 6:101; 10:68; 17:111; 18:4; 19:35, 88–94; 23:91; 39:4; 43:81; 72:3; 112. On the expression “my Lord and your Lord,” cf. 3:51; 19:36; 43:64.

No. 12: **Q 5:78**

A short text stating that Jesus and David have cursed the disbelieving Jews.

لُعِنَ الَّذِينَ كَفَرُوا مِنْ بَنِي إِسْرَائِيلَ عَلَىٰ لِسَانِ دَاوُودَ وَعِيسَى ابْنِ مَرْيَمَ ۚ ذَٰلِكَ بِمَا عَصَوْا وَكَانُوا
يَعْتَدُونَ 5:78

5:78 Those of the Sons of Israel who disbelieved were cursed by the tongue of David and Jesus, son of Mary – because they had disobeyed and transgressed.

This passage is placed within a larger anti-Jewish pericope (5:78–81). Cf. 2:87, as well as the reference to Jesus *and* Moses in 2:136. Cf. too the allusions to Jesus’s mission to Israel in 3:49–55; 5:46, 110; 43:59; 61:6.

No. 13: **Q 5:110–18**

A reminder of Jesus’s distinction, assistance by the Spirit, divine instruction, miracles, confrontation with the Jews, and disciples, followed by a polemical proclamation denying Jesus’s and Mary’s divine nature.

إِذْ قَالَ اللَّهُ يَا عِيسَى ابْنَ مَرْيَمَ اذْكُرْ نِعْمَتِي عَلَيْكَ وَعَلَىٰ وَالِدَتِكَ إِذْ أَيَّدْتُكَ بِرُوحِ الْقُدُسِ تُكَلِّمُ النَّاسَ فِي
الْمَهْدِ وَكَهْلًا ۖ وَإِذْ عَلَّمْتُكَ الْكِتَابَ وَالْحِكْمَةَ وَالتَّوْرَاةَ وَالْإِنْجِيلَ ۖ وَإِذْ تَخْلُقُ مِنَ الطِّينِ كَهَيْئَةِ الطَّيْرِ بِإِذْنِي
فَتَنْفُخُ فِيهَا فَتَكُونُ طَيْرًا بِإِذْنِي ۖ وَتُبْرِئُ الْأَكْمَهَ وَالْأَبْرَصَ بِإِذْنِي ۖ وَإِذْ تُخْرِجُ الْمَوْتَىٰ بِإِذْنِي ۖ وَإِذْ كَفَفْتُ
بَنِي إِسْرَائِيلَ عَنْكَ إِذْ جِئْتَهُمْ بِالْبَيِّنَاتِ فَقَالَ الَّذِينَ كَفَرُوا مِنْهُمْ إِنْ هَٰذَا إِلَّا سِحْرٌ مُبِينٌ 5:110
وَإِذْ أَوْحَيْتُ إِلَى الْحَوَارِيِّينَ أَنْ آمِنُوا بِي وَبِرَسُولِي قَالُوا آمَنَّا وَاشْهَدْ بِأَنَّنَا مُسْلِمُونَ 111
إِذْ قَالَ الْحَوَارِيُّونَ يَا عِيسَى ابْنَ مَرْيَمَ هَلْ يَسْتَطِيعُ رَبُّكَ أَنْ يُنَزِّلَ عَلَيْنَا مَائِدَةً مِنَ السَّمَاءِ ۖ قَالَ اتَّقُوا اللَّهَ
إِنْ كُنْتُمْ مُؤْمِنِينَ 112
قَالُوا نُرِيدُ أَنْ نَأْكُلَ مِنْهَا وَتَطْمَئِنَّ قُلُوبُنَا وَنَعْلَمَ أَنْ قَدْ صَدَقْتَنَا وَنَكُونَ عَلَيْهَا مِنَ الشَّاهِدِينَ 113
قَالَ عِيسَى ابْنُ مَرْيَمَ اللَّهُمَّ رَبَّنَا أَنْزِلْ عَلَيْنَا مَائِدَةً مِنَ السَّمَاءِ تَكُونُ لَنَا عِيدًا لِأَوَّلِنَا وَآخِرِنَا وَآيَةً مِنْكَ ۖ
وَارْزُقْنَا وَأَنْتَ خَيْرُ الرَّازِقِينَ 114
قَالَ اللَّهُ إِنِّي مُنَزِّلُهَا عَلَيْكُمْ ۖ فَمَنْ يَكْفُرْ بَعْدُ مِنْكُمْ فَإِنِّي أُعَذِّبُهُ عَذَابًا لَا أُعَذِّبُهُ أَحَدًا مِنَ الْعَالَمِينَ 115
وَإِذْ قَالَ اللَّهُ يَا عِيسَى ابْنَ مَرْيَمَ أَأَنْتَ قُلْتَ لِلنَّاسِ اتَّخِذُونِي وَأُمِّيَ إِلَٰهَيْنِ مِنْ دُونِ اللَّهِ ۖ قَالَ سُبْحَانَكَ مَا
يَكُونُ لِي أَنْ أَقُولَ مَا لَيْسَ لِي بِحَقٍّ ۚ إِنْ كُنْتُ قُلْتُهُ فَقَدْ عَلِمْتَهُ ۚ تَعْلَمُ مَا فِي نَفْسِي وَلَا أَعْلَمُ مَا فِي نَفْسِكَ ۚ
إِنَّكَ أَنْتَ عَلَّامُ الْغُيُوبِ 116

مَا قُلْتُ لَهُمْ إِلَّا مَا أَمَرْتَنِي بِهِ أَنِ اعْبُدُوا اللَّهَ رَبِّي وَرَبَّكُمْ ۚ وَكُنْتُ عَلَيْهِمْ شَهِيدًا مَا دُمْتُ فِيهِمْ ۖ فَلَمَّا
تَوَفَّيْتَنِي كُنْتَ أَنْتَ الرَّقِيبَ عَلَيْهِمْ ۚ وَأَنْتَ عَلَىٰ كُلِّ شَيْءٍ شَهِيدٌ 117
إِنْ تُعَذِّبْهُمْ فَإِنَّهُمْ عِبَادُكَ ۖ وَإِنْ تَغْفِرْ لَهُمْ فَإِنَّكَ أَنْتَ الْعَزِيزُ الْحَكِيمُ 118

5:110 [Remember] when God said, " Jesus, son of Mary!, remember my favour upon you and upon your mother, when I supported you with the Holy Spirit[75] [so that] you could speak to the people from the cradle, and in adulthood[76]; and when I taught you the Writing, and wisdom, and the Torah, and the Gospel[77]; and when you created the form of a bird out of clay with my permission, and you breathed into it and it became a [living] bird with my permission[78]; and [when] you healed the blind and the leper with my permission[79]; and when you brought forth the dead with my permission[80]; when I restrained the Sons of Israel from [violently attacking] you – when you brought them clear signs, the disbelievers among them said, 'This is nothing but magic!'[81];

111 and when I inspired the disciples [telling them], 'Believe in me and in my messenger!' – they said, 'We believe – bear witness that we are submissive'"[82].

112 And when the disciples said, 'Jesus, son of Mary, is your Lord able to send down for us a table[83] from heaven?'[84] He said, 'Fear God, if you believe [in him]!'

113 They said, 'We would like to eat from it to satisfy our hearts and know with certainty that you have spoken the truth to us, and [thus] be counted among its witnesses.'[85]

114 Jesus, son of Mary, said, 'Oh God! Our Lord! Send down for us a table from heaven, as a festival for [all of] us, from the first of us to the last of us and as a sign from you.'

115 God said, 'Yes, I will send it down for you. Whoever of you disbelieves after that – I shall punish him as I have never punished any other man.'

116 [Remember] when God said, "Jesus, son of Mary! Did you say to the people, 'Take me and my mother as Gods besides God'?"[86] He said, " Glory be to you! I did not say what I have no right to. Had I said it, you would have known it. [For] you know what it is in me, while I do not know what is in you – you are, certainly, the Knower of the unseen.

75 Cf. 2:87, 253.

76 Cf. 3:46; 19:29–30.

77 Cf. 3:48; 5:46; 57:27. See nn.35–6 above.

78 Cf. 3:50.

79 Cf. 3:50.

80 Cf. 3:50.

81 Cf. 61:6.

82 Cf. 3:52–3; 61:14.

83 المائدة *al-māʾida*. On the presumable Ethiopic origin of this non-Arabic word, see Kropp, "Beyond Single Words." On the meaning of this puzzling passage, see the commentary below.

84 (Cf. Acts 10:9–16.)

85 Cf. 3:53.

86 Cf. 5:75. Cf. too 9:31.

117 I only said to them what you commanded me to: 'Worship God, [as he is] my Lord and your Lord!'[87] I witnessed to their words[88] as long as I was among them, but when you raised me [to yourself],[89] you became their witness – for everything is under your sight.[90]
118 If you punish them – surely they are your servants. If you forgive them – surely you are the Mighty, the Wise."

Cf. the references to Jesus and the Spirit in 2:87, 253; 4:171–2; 21:91; 66:12; the allusion to Jesus's ability to speak from the cradle in 3:46;19:29–30; the speeches delivered by Jesus in 3:49–52; 19:24–6, 30–3; 43:63–4; 61:6, 14; the list of Jesus's miracles in 3:49; the references to his disciples in 3:52–3; 61:14; the denial of Jesus's divinity in 4:171–2; 5:17, 72–5; 9:30–1 (plus the monotheistic formulas mentioned in the commentary on those passages); and Mary's defence in both 4:156 and the Jesus-birth narratives in *sūra*-s 3 and 19. I will go back to the denial of Mary's divinity in Chapter 5.

As I have already suggested, the reference to Jesus speaking from the cradle draws presumably on the AIG 1 (and indirectly 1 En 106), whereas the miracle of the clay birds recalls IGT 2–3, PsM 26–8, and AIG 36. In turn, the "table" in vv. 112–15, whose interpretation is much disputed,[91] is likely a allusion to the eucharist, as Droge perspicaciously suggests[92] – without providing any further explanation, though. Notice in this respect the reference to the confirmation of Jesus's "truth" in v. 113 as well as the otherwise enigmatic (or else superfluous) "ranking" phrase in v. 114: تكون لنا عيدا لأوّلنا وآخرنا ("as a festival for [all of] us, from the first of us to the last of us") which may be taken to depict the disciples' "lining up" to receive the eucharist from Jesus himself. In any event, the widespread supposition that this passage alludes to the Lord's Supper is erroneous, as the reference to the confirmation of Jesus's truth would make no sense in a pre-resurrection context; nor would the divine authentication of such truth, which in my view explains the image of the sending down of the "table" as a metonym for the eucharist. Likewise, it cannot allude to Peter's vision in Acts 10:9–16, since therein the vision is only individual (i.e. it only concerns Peter). Even more lose are the cross-references to Psalms 23:5and 78:19, or the conjecture that a miracle is here at stake. As for John 6:22–40, it may well be the subtext which the quranic

87 Cf. 3:51; 5:72; 19:36; 43:61, 64.
88 Lit., "over them."
89 Cf. 3:55; 4:158.
90 Lit., "you are a witness over everything."
91 See Matthias Radscheit, "Table," in *Encyclopaedia of the Qur'ān*, ed. McAuliffe, 5:188–91.
92 Droge, *The Qur'ān*, 74 n.163,

author(s) wanted to expand, or comment on, but if it is, this, again, would take us back to Jesus being the "bread from heaven."

Sūrat al-An'ām (Q 6, "Livestock")

No. 14: **Q 6:84–7**

Jesus is included within a list of righteous men together with Isaac, Jacob, David, Solomon, Joseph, Moses, Aaron, Zechariah, John the Baptist, Elijah, Ishmael, Elisha, Jonah, and Lot.

وَوَهَبْنَا لَهُ إِسْحَاقَ وَيَعْقُوبَ ۚ كُلًّا هَدَيْنَا ۚ وَنُوحًا هَدَيْنَا مِنْ قَبْلُ ۖ وَمِنْ ذُرِّيَّتِهِ دَاوُودَ وَسُلَيْمَانَ وَأَيُّوبَ
وَيُوسُفَ وَمُوسَىٰ وَهَارُونَ ۚ وَكَذَٰلِكَ نَجْزِي الْمُحْسِنِينَ 6:84
وَزَكَرِيَّا وَيَحْيَىٰ وَعِيسَىٰ وَإِلْيَاسَ ۖ كُلٌّ مِنَ الصَّالِحِينَ 85
وَإِسْمَاعِيلَ وَالْيَسَعَ وَيُونُسَ وَلُوطًا ۚ وَكُلًّا فَضَّلْنَا عَلَى الْعَالَمِينَ 86
وَمِنْ آبَائِهِمْ وَذُرِّيَّاتِهِمْ وَإِخْوَانِهِمْ ۖ وَاجْتَبَيْنَاهُمْ وَهَدَيْنَاهُمْ إِلَىٰ صِرَاطٍ مُسْتَقِيمٍ 87

6:84 We gave him [= Abraham] Isaac and Jacob – each one we guided, and Noah we guided before [them]. And among his [= Abraham's] descendants were David, and Solomon, and Joseph, and Moses, and Aaron – [for] this is how we reward the good-doers –
85 and Zachariah, and John, and Jesus, and Elijah – they, all, were righteous –
86 and Ishmael, and Elisha, and Jonah, and Lot – we favoured them over all men –
87 and some of their fathers, and their offspring, and their brothers – we chose them and guided them to a straight path.[93]

Cf. the prophetic lists in 2:136; 3:84; 4:163; 33:7–8; 42:13, as well as the reference to Jesus as a righteous in 3:46. On Jesus and Elijah, see 3:55; 4:158; 5:117; 19:57. On John the Baptist, 3:38–41; 19:2–11, and the comments on 61:6.

Sūrat al-Tawba (Q 9, "Repentance")

No. 15: **Q 9:30–1**

The Jews are accused of believing that 'Uzayr (Ezra?) is the son of God; likewise, the Christians are accused of believing and Jesus is the son of God. Furthermore, the Jews are accused of taking their rabbis, and the Christians of taking their monks

93 Cf. 3:51; 5:117; 19:36; 43:61, 64.

(or more likely their bishops) and Jesus as lords besides God, whose uniqueness is subsequently stressed.

وَقَالَتِ الْيَهُودُ عُزَيْرٌ ابْنُ اللَّهِ وَقَالَتِ النَّصَارَى الْمَسِيحُ ابْنُ اللَّهِ ۖ ذَٰلِكَ قَوْلُهُم بِأَفْوَاهِهِمْ ۖ يُضَاهِئُونَ قَوْلَ
الَّذِينَ كَفَرُوا مِن قَبْلُ ۚ قَاتَلَهُمُ اللَّهُ ۚ أَنَّىٰ يُؤْفَكُونَ 9:30
اتَّخَذُوا أَحْبَارَهُمْ وَرُهْبَانَهُمْ أَرْبَابًا مِّن دُونِ اللَّهِ وَالْمَسِيحَ ابْنَ مَرْيَمَ وَمَا أُمِرُوا إِلَّا لِيَعْبُدُوا إِلَٰهًا وَاحِدًا ۖ
لَّا إِلَٰهَ إِلَّا هُوَ ۚ سُبْحَانَهُ عَمَّا يُشْرِكُونَ 31

9:30 The Jews say, "'Uzayr is the son of God,"[94] and the Christians say, "The Messiah is the Son of God." This is what they utter with their mouths. They reproduce the words of those who disbelieved before [them]. [May] God fight them. How is it that they are [so] deluded?

31 They have taken their chief-rabbis[95] and their bishops[96] as lords besides God, and [also] the Messiah, Jesus son of Mary, while they have been commanded to worship but one God – there is no God but him.[97] Glory be to him above all what they associate [to him]![98]

Cf. 4:171–2; 5:17, 72–5, 116–17 (which deny Jesus's divinity); 3:79–80; 9:31; 18:102 (which hold that neither God's angels, prophets, and servants, nor the Messiah, can be taken as lords); and the strict monotheist formulas in 2:116; 6:101; 10:68; 17:111; 18:4; 19:35, 88–94; 23:91; 39:4; 43:81; 72:3; 112. I shall return to this very problematic passage in Chapter 4.

Sūrat Maryam (Q 19, "Mary")

No. 16: **Q 19:2–36**

A detailed narrative of Jesus's birth that echoes that in Sūra *3, followed by a monotheistic proclamation.*

---

94 Possibly Ezra. A reference to 4 Ezra 14:9 ("You are about to be taken away from the world of men, and thereafter you will remain with my son and with those like you until the end of time" [REB]) is unlikely, as this text does not affirm that Ezra is the Son of God. Attempts to identify a particular Jewish group who may have worshiped Ezra (or Enoch, after 1 Enoch 71:14) have systematically failed to achieve any positive result. In my view, the accusation itself is rhetorical, though necessary after the *Vorlage* of 9:31 was edited and expanded. See further Chapter 4.

95 أخبار *aḥbār*. See further Chapter 4, where I provide the reason for this translation, which I prefer to "scholars" or "teachers".

96 رهبان *ruhbān*. See once more Chapter 4, where I likewise provide the reason for translating *ruhbān* as "bishops" instead of "monks."

97 Cf. 5:73; 4:171.

98 Cf. 5:72.

ذِكْرُ رَحْمَتِ رَبِّكَ عَبْدَهُ زَكَرِيَّا 19:2
إِذْ نَادَىٰ رَبَّهُ نِدَاءً خَفِيًّا 3
قَالَ رَبِّ إِنِّي وَهَنَ الْعَظْمُ مِنِّي وَاشْتَعَلَ الرَّأْسُ شَيْبًا وَلَمْ أَكُنْ بِدُعَائِكَ رَبِّ شَقِيًّا 4
وَإِنِّي خِفْتُ الْمَوَالِيَ مِنْ وَرَائِي وَكَانَتِ امْرَأَتِي عَاقِرًا فَهَبْ لِي مِنْ لَدُنْكَ وَلِيًّا 5
يَرِثُنِي وَيَرِثُ مِنْ آلِ يَعْقُوبَ ۖ وَاجْعَلْهُ رَبِّ رَضِيًّا 6
يَا زَكَرِيَّا إِنَّا نُبَشِّرُكَ بِغُلَامٍ اسْمُهُ يَحْيَىٰ لَمْ نَجْعَلْ لَهُ مِنْ قَبْلُ سَمِيًّا 7
قَالَ رَبِّ أَنَّىٰ يَكُونُ لِي غُلَامٌ وَكَانَتِ امْرَأَتِي عَاقِرًا وَقَدْ بَلَغْتُ مِنَ الْكِبَرِ عِتِيًّا 8
قَالَ كَذَٰلِكَ قَالَ رَبُّكَ هُوَ عَلَيَّ هَيِّنٌ وَقَدْ خَلَقْتُكَ مِنْ قَبْلُ وَلَمْ تَكُ شَيْئًا 9
الَ رَبِّ اجْعَلْ لِي آيَةً ۚ قَالَ آيَتُكَ أَلَّا تُكَلِّمَ النَّاسَ ثَلَاثَ لَيَالٍ سَوِيًّا 10
فَخَرَجَ عَلَىٰ قَوْمِهِ مِنَ الْمِحْرَابِ فَأَوْحَىٰ إِلَيْهِمْ أَنْ سَبِّحُوا بُكْرَةً وَعَشِيًّا 11
يَا يَحْيَىٰ خُذِ الْكِتَابَ بِقُوَّةٍ ۖ وَآتَيْنَاهُ الْحُكْمَ صَبِيًّا 12
وَحَنَانًا مِنْ لَدُنَّا وَزَكَاةً ۖ وَكَانَ تَقِيًّا 13
وَبَرًّا بِوَالِدَيْهِ وَلَمْ يَكُنْ جَبَّارًا عَصِيًّا 14
وَسَلَامٌ عَلَيْهِ يَوْمَ وُلِدَ وَيَوْمَ يَمُوتُ وَيَوْمَ يُبْعَثُ حَيًّا 15
وَاذْكُرْ فِي الْكِتَابِ مَرْيَمَ إِذِ انْتَبَذَتْ مِنْ أَهْلِهَا مَكَانًا شَرْقِيًّا 16
فَاتَّخَذَتْ مِنْ دُونِهِمْ حِجَابًا فَأَرْسَلْنَا إِلَيْهَا رُوحَنَا فَتَمَثَّلَ لَهَا بَشَرًا سَوِيًّا 17
قَالَتْ إِنِّي أَعُوذُ بِالرَّحْمَٰنِ مِنْكَ إِنْ كُنْتَ تَقِيًّا 18
قَالَ إِنَّمَا أَنَا رَسُولُ رَبِّكِ لِأَهَبَ لَكِ غُلَامًا زَكِيًّا 19
قَالَتْ أَنَّىٰ يَكُونُ لِي غُلَامٌ وَلَمْ يَمْسَسْنِي بَشَرٌ وَلَمْ أَكُ بَغِيًّا 20
قَالَ كَذَٰلِكِ قَالَ رَبُّكِ هُوَ عَلَيَّ هَيِّنٌ ۖ وَلِنَجْعَلَهُ آيَةً لِلنَّاسِ وَرَحْمَةً مِنَّا ۚ وَكَانَ أَمْرًا مَقْضِيًّا 21
فَحَمَلَتْهُ فَانْتَبَذَتْ بِهِ مَكَانًا قَصِيًّا 22
فَأَجَاءَهَا الْمَخَاضُ إِلَىٰ جِذْعِ النَّخْلَةِ قَالَتْ يَا لَيْتَنِي مِتُّ قَبْلَ هَٰذَا وَكُنْتُ نَسْيًا مَنْسِيًّا 23
فَنَادَاهَا مِنْ تَحْتِهَا أَلَّا تَحْزَنِي قَدْ جَعَلَ رَبُّكِ تَحْتَكِ سَرِيًّا 24
وَهُزِّي إِلَيْكِ بِجِذْعِ النَّخْلَةِ تُسَاقِطْ عَلَيْكِ رُطَبًا جَنِيًّا 25
فَكُلِي وَاشْرَبِي وَقَرِّي عَيْنًا ۖ فَإِمَّا تَرَيِنَّ مِنَ الْبَشَرِ أَحَدًا فَقُولِي إِنِّي نَذَرْتُ لِلرَّحْمَٰنِ صَوْمًا فَلَنْ أُكَلِّمَ الْيَوْمَ
إِنْسِيًّا 26
فَأَتَتْ بِهِ قَوْمَهَا تَحْمِلُهُ ۖ قَالُوا يَا مَرْيَمُ لَقَدْ جِئْتِ شَيْئًا فَرِيًّا 27
يَا أُخْتَ هَارُونَ مَا كَانَ أَبُوكِ امْرَأَ سَوْءٍ وَمَا كَانَتْ أُمُّكِ بَغِيًّا 28
فَأَشَارَتْ إِلَيْهِ ۖ قَالُوا كَيْفَ نُكَلِّمُ مَنْ كَانَ فِي الْمَهْدِ صَبِيًّا 29
قَالَ إِنِّي عَبْدُ اللَّهِ آتَانِيَ الْكِتَابَ وَجَعَلَنِي نَبِيًّا 30
وَجَعَلَنِي مُبَارَكًا أَيْنَ مَا كُنْتُ وَأَوْصَانِي بِالصَّلَاةِ وَالزَّكَاةِ مَا دُمْتُ حَيًّا 31
وَبَرًّا بِوَالِدَتِي وَلَمْ يَجْعَلْنِي جَبَّارًا شَقِيًّا 32
وَالسَّلَامُ عَلَيَّ يَوْمَ وُلِدْتُ وَيَوْمَ أَمُوتُ وَيَوْمَ أُبْعَثُ حَيًّا 33
ذَٰلِكَ عِيسَى ابْنُ مَرْيَمَ ۚ قَوْلَ الْحَقِّ الَّذِي فِيهِ يَمْتَرُونَ 34

مَا كَانَ لِلَّهِ أَنْ يَتَّخِذَ مِنْ وَلَدٍ ۖ سُبْحَانَهُ ۚ إِذَا قَضَىٰ أَمْرًا فَإِنَّمَا يَقُولُ لَهُ كُنْ فَيَكُونُ 35
وَإِنَّ اللَّهَ رَبِّي وَرَبُّكُمْ فَاعْبُدُوهُ ۚ هَٰذَا صِرَاطٌ مُسْتَقِيمٌ 36

19:2 A remembrance of the mercy of your Lord on his servant Zachariah:
3 When he called his Lord, in secret –
4 he said, "My bones, my Lord, are weak and my hair is white, but I have never been disappointed when I have, my Lord, called on you.
5 And alas!, I fear for my offspring, as my wife is barren. So give me an heir
6 who may inherit from me and from the house of Jacob, and make him, my Lord, pleasing [to you]."
7 [We said,] "Zachariah!, we give you good tidings of a boy whose name will be John – a name we have never given to anyone before."
8 He said, "My Lord, how shall I have a boy? I am old and my wife is barren."
9 "Thus! Your Lord has said: 'It is easy for me, since I created you when you were nothing.'"[99]
10 He said, "My Lord, give me a sign." He said: "Your sign is that you will not speak to anyone for three days."
11 So he came out to his people from the sanctuary[100] and told them to sanctify [God] morning and evening.[101]
12 "John, hold fast to the Scripture!" – And we gave him wisdom as a child,
13 and affection from us, and purity; he was righteous
14 and dutiful to his parents, he was neither despotic nor disobedient.
15 Peace be upon him the day he was born, and the day he dies, and the day he will be raised alive![102]
16 And remember Mary in the Writing[103]: when she withdrew from her family to an eastern place,
17 and she hided herself from them, we sent to her our Spirit, which took for her human form.
18 She said, "I take shelter with the Merciful from you, if you are fearful [of God]."
19 He said, "I am only a messenger of your Lord, sent to grant you a pure boy."
20 She said, "How shall I have a boy, when no man has touched me and I am not a prostitute."
21 He said, "Thus! Your Lord has said, 'It is easy for me. He will be a sign to the people an a mercy from us. It is a thing decreed.'"[104]

99 Cf. vv. 20–1.

100 Cf. 3:37.

101 Cf. vv. 2–11 with 3:38–41.

102 Cf. v. 33.

103 Droge is aware of the ambiguity inherent in the wording: "The formula may be intended to 'remind' the audience of a particular story 'in the Book' (i.e. in the 'Torah' or 'Gospel'), or it may indicate that the Prophet had (or was thought to have) been instructed to undertake the production of a 'Book' (i.e. the Qur'ān in written form)" (*The Qur'ān*, 194 n.20). I think the second option is, at least here (cf. n.35 above), far more plausible.

104 Cf. vv. 8–9.

22 So she conceived him and withdrew with him to a distant place.
23 The pains of childbirth drove there to the trunk of the palm-tree. She said, "I wish I were dead by now and forgotten!"
24 But from beneath her he [= Jesus] called out to her: "Do not sorrow! Your Lord has given you a deliverer.[105]
25 Now, shake the trunk of the palm-tree towards you, and it shall drop fresh dates for you.
26 Eat, drink, and refresh your eyes. If you happen to see anyone, say, 'I have viewed a fast to the Merciful, so I will not speak to anyone today.'"
27 Then she brought him to her people, carrying him. They said, "Mary! This is something really strange!
28 Sister of Aaron![106] Your father was not a bad man, nor was your mother a prostitute!"
29 But she pointed him [thus inviting them to address him]. They said, "How are we to speak to one who is [still] in the cradle, a [mere] child?"
30 He said, "I am God's servant. He has given me the Scripture and made me a prophet,
31 and blessed me wherever I am, and commended to me prayer and charity as long as I live,
32 as well as to respect my mother – he has not made me a tyrant or a miserable.
33 Peace be upon me the day I was born, and the day I die, and the day I will be raised alive."[107]
34 This is Jesus, son of Mary – a statement of the truth about which they are in doubt.
35 It does not correspond to God to adopt a child. Glory to him! When he decrees something, he simply says 'Be!,' and it becomes.[108]
36 "God is my Lord and your Lord, so worship him – this is a straight path!"[109]

Four parts are discernible in this narrative: (1) vv. 2–11; (2) vv. 12–15; (3) vv. 16–33; (4) vv. 34–6 – maybe an addition to the text originally contained in vv. 2–33, about which it is difficult to tell whether it echoes, or else provides the model to, 3:33–63 (see above). Be that as it may, these verses convey a defence of Mary against accusations, likely on the part of Jews, questioning the legitimacy of her pregnancy (cf. 4:156). I shall return to this issue in Chapter 3.

***Sūrat al-Anbiyya'* (Q 21, "The Prophets")**

No. 17: **Q 21:91**

An encrypted Adamic Christological fragment?

105 I partly follow Luxenberg's emended translation (*The Syro-Aramaic Reading of the Koran*, 127–42).
106 See the comments on 3:33–63.
107 Cf. vv. 16–33 with 3:42–8. Cf. too vv. 30–3 with 12–15.
108 Cf. 3:40, 59.
109 Cf. vv. 34–6 with 3:58–63. Cf. too v. 36 with 3:51; 5:72, 117; 6:87; 43:61, 64.

وَالَّتِي أَحْصَنَتْ فَرْجَهَا فَنَفَخْنَا فِيهَا مِنْ رُوحِنَا وَجَعَلْنَاهَا وَابْنَهَا آيَةً لِلْعَالَمِينَ 21:91

21:91 And she [= Mary] who guarded her private chastity – we breathed into her of our spirit, and made her and her son a sign for all men.

Cf. 66:12. These two verses do not mention Jesus but Mary. Yet he seems to be implicitly alluded to in 66:12 (notice the 3rd person-singular masculine pronoun *hi* suffixed to the preposition *fī*, "in"; cf. the 3rd person-singular feminine pronoun *hā* suffixed to the same preposition in 21:91) as he into whom God breathed his own spirit – like Adam in 15:29 and 38:72. Moreover, 21:91 follows a reminder about John the Baptist (in vv. 89–90 of *sūra* 21) that echoes in an abridged manner 3:38–41 and 19:7–15. Cf. too 2:87, 253; 5:110 (which include a reference to Jesus being divinely assisted by the Holy Spirit); and 4:171–2 (where Jesus is said to be a spirit from God). Anyway, I shall return to this remarkably intriguing verse (and 66:12) in the next chapter.

Sūrat al-Mu'minūn (Q 23, "The Believers")

No. 18: **Q 23:50**

Jesus and his mother are presented as a sign – and placed in a high place.

وَجَعَلْنَا ابْنَ مَرْيَمَ وَأُمَّهُ آيَةً وَآوَيْنَاهُمَا إِلَىٰ رَبْوَةٍ ذَاتِ قَرَارٍ وَمَعِينٍ 23:50

23:50 We made the son of Mary and his mother[110] a sign and sheltered them on a high place with water springs.

The reference to Jesus and Mary (lit., "the son of Mary and his mother") brings an end to a threefold narrative about Noah (23:23–30), an anonymous prophet (23:31–44), and Moses (23:45–9). Mary and her son are said to have been made a sign and placed by God in a high place supplied with water (like e.g. the Kathisma Church, on which see the next chapter). Cf. too their divine distinction in 2:87, 253; 3:33, 42, 45–6; 5:110; 19:21, 30–3; 43:57, 59, and the prophetic lists in 2:136; 3:84; 4:163; 6:85; 33:7–8; 42:13.

110 Cf. 5:17.

Sūrat al-Aḥzāb (Q 33, "The Factions")

No. 19: **Q 33:7–8**

Jesus is mentioned within a list of prophets with whom God has established his covenant, including Noah, Abraham, and Moses – an eschatological warning follows the prophetical sequence.

وَإِذْ أَخَذْنَا مِنَ النَّبِيِّينَ مِيثَاقَهُمْ وَمِنْكَ وَمِنْ نُوحٍ وَإِبْرَاهِيمَ وَمُوسَىٰ وَعِيسَى ابْنِ مَرْيَمَ ۖ وَأَخَذْنَا مِنْهُمْ مِيثَاقًا غَلِيظًا 33:7
لِيَسْأَلَ الصَّادِقِينَ عَنْ صِدْقِهِمْ ۚ وَأَعَدَّ لِلْكَافِرِينَ عَذَابًا أَلِيمًا 8

33:7 [Remember] when we made a covenant with the prophets, and with you, and with Noah, Abraham, Moses, and Jesus son of Mary. We made a firm covenant with them
8 so that he may ask the truthful about their truth. He has prepared a painful punishment for the disbelievers.

Cf. the prophetical lists in 2:136; 3:84; 4:163; 6:85; 42:13.

Sūrat al-Šūrā (Q 42, "Consultation")

No. 20: **Q 42:13**

Jesus is mentioned this time within a list of men instructed by God, including Noah, Abraham, and Moses, who thus bear witness to the unity of God's religion – a proclamation of God's freedom to choose whomever he wishes follows such list.

شَرَعَ لَكُمْ مِنَ الدِّينِ مَا وَصَّىٰ بِهِ نُوحًا وَالَّذِي أَوْحَيْنَا إِلَيْكَ وَمَا وَصَّيْنَا بِهِ إِبْرَاهِيمَ وَمُوسَىٰ وَعِيسَىٰ ۖ
42:13 أَنْ أَقِيمُوا الدِّينَ وَلَا تَتَفَرَّقُوا فِيهِ ۚ كَبُرَ عَلَى الْمُشْرِكِينَ مَا تَدْعُوهُمْ إِلَيْهِ ۚ اللَّهُ يَجْتَبِي إِلَيْهِ مَنْ يَشَاءُ
وَيَهْدِي إِلَيْهِ مَنْ يُنِيبُ

42:13 He has ordained for you, from the religion, what he had [previously] charged Noah with, and what we have inspired you with, and what we charged Abraham, Moses, and Jesus with. Therefore, you shall observe the religion and not to be divided about it. What you call them to is hard for the idolaters. God chooses for himself whom he wills and guides to himself whom he turns [to himself in repentance].

Cf. the prophetical lists in 2:136; 3:84; 4:163; 6:85; 33:7–8

Sūrat al-Zuḫruf (Q 43, "Ornaments")

No. 21: **Q 43:57–64**

A defence of Jesus, seemingly against the polytheists, which further highlights Jesus's divine distinction and his mission to Israel – followed by an eschatological warning voiced by Jesus himself.

وَلَمَّا ضُرِبَ ابْنُ مَرْيَمَ مَثَلًا إِذَا قَوْمُكَ مِنْهُ يَصِدُّونَ 43:57
وَقَالُوا أَآلِهَتُنَا خَيْرٌ أَمْ هُوَ ۚ مَا ضَرَبُوهُ لَكَ إِلَّا جَدَلًا ۚ بَلْ هُمْ قَوْمٌ خَصِمُونَ 58
إِنْ هُوَ إِلَّا عَبْدٌ أَنْعَمْنَا عَلَيْهِ وَجَعَلْنَاهُ مَثَلًا لِبَنِي إِسْرَائِيلَ 59
وَلَوْ نَشَاءُ لَجَعَلْنَا مِنْكُمْ مَلَائِكَةً فِي الْأَرْضِ يَخْلُفُونَ 60
وَإِنَّهُ لَعِلْمٌ لِلسَّاعَةِ فَلَا تَمْتَرُنَّ بِهَا وَاتَّبِعُونِ ۚ هَٰذَا صِرَاطٌ مُسْتَقِيمٌ 61
وَلَا يَصُدَّنَّكُمُ الشَّيْطَانُ ۖ إِنَّهُ لَكُمْ عَدُوٌّ مُبِينٌ 62
وَلَمَّا جَاءَ عِيسَىٰ بِالْبَيِّنَاتِ قَالَ قَدْ جِئْتُكُمْ بِالْحِكْمَةِ وَلِأُبَيِّنَ لَكُمْ بَعْضَ الَّذِي تَخْتَلِفُونَ فِيهِ ۖ فَاتَّقُوا اللَّهَ
وَأَطِيعُونِ 63
إِنَّ اللَّهَ هُوَ رَبِّي وَرَبُّكُمْ فَاعْبُدُوهُ ۚ هَٰذَا صِرَاطٌ مُسْتَقِيمٌ 64

43:57 When the son of Mary is presented as an example, behold!, your people turn away
58 and say, "Are our gods better, or is he?" They only mention him to you to argue [with you] – nay!, they are prone to dispute, this people.
59 He was only a servant whom we blessed, and we made him an example for the Sons of Israel. If we wished so, surely we could have made angels out of you as [our/your?] successors on earth.
60 Certainly [you have] knowledge about the Hour,
61 so do not be doubtful about it and follow me – this is a straight path.[111]
62 Do not let Satan avert you, for clearly he is your enemy!
63 When Jesus brought clear signs, he said,[112] "I have brought you wisdom to enlighten you on your differences, so be fearful of God and obey me.[113]
64 God is my Lord and your Lord, so worship him – this is a straight path!"[114]

Cf. Jesus's speeches in 3:49–52; 5:112, 114, 116–18; 19:24–6, 30–3; 43:63–4;61:6, 14. Cf. too the divine distinction bestowed on Jesus and his mother in 2:87, 253; 3:33, 42, 45–6; 5:110; 19:21, 30–3; 23:50. On the expression "my Lord and your Lord," cf. 3:51; 5:72; 19:36. Cf. too the eschatological coda in 33:8.

111 Cf. v. 64 and 3:51; 5:117; 6:87; 19:36.
112 Cf. 5:110; 61:6.
113 Cf. 3:51.
114 Cf. v. 61 and 3:51; 5:72, 117; 6:87; 19:36.

Sūrat al-Ḥadīd (Q 57, "Iron")

No. 22: **Q 57:25–7**

Jesus is mentioned together with other prophets who bear witness to God, namely Noah and Abraham. Positive references are then made to the Gospel, the mercifulness of Jesus's followers, and the Church leaders (i.e. the bishops), although their authority is described as an innovation which, moreover, not everyone has assumed in the proper manner.

لَقَدْ أَرْسَلْنَا رُسُلَنَا بِالْبَيِّنَاتِ وَأَنْزَلْنَا مَعَهُمُ الْكِتَابَ وَالْمِيزَانَ لِيَقُومَ النَّاسُ بِالْقِسْطِ ۖ وَأَنْزَلْنَا الْحَدِيدَ فِيهِ بَأْسٌ
شَدِيدٌ وَمَنَافِعُ لِلنَّاسِ وَلِيَعْلَمَ اللَّهُ مَنْ يَنْصُرُهُ وَرُسُلَهُ بِالْغَيْبِ ۚ إِنَّ اللَّهَ قَوِيٌّ عَزِيزٌ 57:25
وَلَقَدْ أَرْسَلْنَا نُوحًا وَإِبْرَاهِيمَ وَجَعَلْنَا فِي ذُرِّيَّتِهِمَا النُّبُوَّةَ وَالْكِتَابَ ۖ فَمِنْهُمْ مُهْتَدٍ ۖ وَكَثِيرٌ مِنْهُمْ فَاسِقُونَ 26
ثُمَّ قَفَّيْنَا عَلَىٰ آثَارِهِمْ بِرُسُلِنَا وَقَفَّيْنَا بِعِيسَى ابْنِ مَرْيَمَ وَآتَيْنَاهُ الْإِنْجِيلَ وَجَعَلْنَا فِي قُلُوبِ الَّذِينَ اتَّبَعُوهُ
رَأْفَةً وَرَحْمَةً وَرَهْبَانِيَّةً ابْتَدَعُوهَا مَا كَتَبْنَاهَا عَلَيْهِمْ إِلَّا ابْتِغَاءَ رِضْوَانِ اللَّهِ فَمَا رَعَوْهَا حَقَّ رِعَايَتِهَا ۖ
فَآتَيْنَا الَّذِينَ آمَنُوا مِنْهُمْ أَجْرَهُمْ ۖ وَكَثِيرٌ مِنْهُمْ فَاسِقُونَ 27

57:25 We sent our messengers with clear signs, and with them we sent the Scripture and the balance, so that people may do justice. And we sent down iron, in which there is harsh violence but also benefit for the people. And [all this] for God to know who will help him and his messengers in the future. Surely God is strong, mighty.

26 We sent Noah and Abraham, and bestowed prophethood on their offspring, and [gave them] the Scripture. Yet among them there is [often] one rightly guided, while most of them are wicked.[115]

27 Then we sent our messengers on their footsteps, we sent Jesus, son of Mary, we gave him the Gospel,[116] and placed in the hearts of his followers kindness and mercy. But episcopacy[117] – they invented it, [as] we did not prescribe it for them; they [only instituted it] seeking God's approval, but have not observed it properly. We gave the believers among them their reward, but most of them are wicked.[118]

The subsequent verses (28–9), which recommend to follow God's messenger, may or may not be connected to this brief three-verse passage, depending on whether Jesus is identified with such messenger or not. Cf. the allusions to the Gospel in 2:87; 5:46, 110. On the bishops (rather than monks), see further Chapter 4. They are positively mentioned too in 5:82, and less favourably in 9:31, 34.

---

115 Cf. the following verse, *in fine*.
116 Cf. 3:48; 5:46, 110.
117 رهبانيّة *ruhbāniyya*. See Chapter 4, where I provide the reason for translating *ruhbān* as "bishops" instead of "monks," and thereby *ruhbāniyya* as "episcopacy". Cf. too 9:31.
118 Cf. the preceding verse, *in fine*.

Sūrat al-Ṣaff (Q 61, "The Lines")

No. 23: **Q 61:6**

A defence of Jesus's mission to Israel, followed by Jesus's foretelling of a future prophet named Aḥmad.

وَإِذْ قَالَ عِيسَى ابْنُ مَرْيَمَ يَا بَنِي إِسْرَائِيلَ إِنِّي رَسُولُ اللَّهِ إِلَيْكُمْ مُصَدِّقًا لِمَا بَيْنَ يَدَيَّ مِنَ التَّوْرَاةِ
وَمُبَشِّرًا بِرَسُولٍ يَأْتِي مِنْ بَعْدِي اسْمُهُ أَحْمَدُ ۖ فَلَمَّا جَاءَهُمْ بِالْبَيِّنَاتِ قَالُوا هَٰذَا سِحْرٌ مُبِينٌ 61:6

61:6 [Remember] when Jesus, son of Mary, said, "Sons of Israel! I am God's messenger to you, confirming the Torah [given to you] before me[119] and giving you good tidings of a messenger to come after me, whose name[120] will be Aḥmad." But when he brought them clear signs, they said "This is nothing but magic!"[121]

أحمد *aḥmad* (lit., "most praised") is likely a misreading of παράκλητος *paráklētos*, possibly due to the inherently ambiguous Syriac transliteration ܦܪܩܠܝܛܐ *prqlyṭ'* (= [*a*] παράκλητος *paraklētos* [Paraclete, "comforter"] or [*b*] περίκλυτος *peryklytos* ["most praised"], indistinctly) of the original Greek term ΠΑΡΑΚΛΗΤΟΣ *PARAKLĒTOS* mentioned in John 14:16, 26; 15:26; 16:7; 1 John 2:1. It is commonly identified with Muḥammad, which shares the same verbal root (*ḥ.m.d.*) and therefore has a similar, though less emphatic, meaning (the "praised one"). See the comments on 17:79–80 in Chapter 5. Yet Ubayy b. Ka'b's recension omits this specific reference and substitutes it with an allusion to a new community.[122] Cf. Jesus's speeches in 3:49–52; 5:112, 114, 116–18; 19:24–6, 30–3; 43:63–4; 61:14.

No. 24: **Q 61:14**

Jesus's disciples are presented as a model for the believers – the passage also includes a brief speech by Jesus.

---

119 Cf. 3:51; 5:46.
120 Or "title"; see the comments on this term below.
121 Cf. 5:110.
122 "... announcing a prophet to you, whose community will be the last one among [God's] communities (*ummatuhu aḫīr al-umam*), and by means of whom God will put the seal on the prophets and the messengers (*yaḫtum allāhu bidi al-anbiyā' wall rasūl*)" (Arthur Jeffery, *Materials for the History of the Text of the Qur'ān: The Old Codices* [Leiden and Boston: Brill, 1970] 170, my translation).

يَا أَيُّهَا الَّذِينَ آمَنُوا كُونُوا أَنْصَارَ اللَّهِ كَمَا قَالَ عِيسَى ابْنُ مَرْيَمَ لِلْحَوَارِيِّينَ مَنْ أَنْصَارِي إِلَى اللَّهِ ۖ قَالَ الْحَوَارِيُّونَ نَحْنُ أَنْصَارُ اللَّهِ ۖ فَآمَنَتْ طَائِفَةٌ مِنْ بَنِي إِسْرَائِيلَ وَكَفَرَتْ طَائِفَةٌ ۖ فَأَيَّدْنَا الَّذِينَ آمَنُوا عَلَىٰ عَدُوِّهِمْ فَأَصْبَحُوا ظَاهِرِينَ 61:14

61:14 O you who believe, be God's helpers – as when Jesus, the son of Mary, said to the disciples, "Who are my helpers for God?" The disciples said, "We are God's helpers!" A group among the Sons of Israel believed, while a[nother] group disbelieved, so we supported those who believed agains their opponents, and [thus] they prevailed.

The wording is similar to that in 3:52, with contains too a short dialogue between Jesus and his disciples. Cf. too the reference to Jesus's disciples and the Jews there and in 3:52–4; 5:110–11, as well as the speeches delivered by Jesus in 3:49–51; 5:112, 114, 116–18; 19:24–6, 30–3; 43:63–4; 61:6.

Sūrat al-Taḥrīm (Q 66, "The Forbidding")

No. 25: **Q 66:12**

Another encrypted Adamic Christological fragment?

وَمَرْيَمَ ابْنَتَ عِمْرَانَ الَّتِي أَحْصَنَتْ فَرْجَهَا فَنَفَخْنَا فِيهِ مِنْ رُوحِنَا وَصَدَّقَتْ بِكَلِمَاتِ رَبِّهَا وَكُتُبِهِ وَكَانَتْ مِنَ الْقَانِتِينَ 66:12

66:12 And Mary, daughter of ʻImrān, who guarded her chastity – we breathed into him of our spirit, and she accepted the words of her Lord and his writings, and became one of the obedient. (66:12)

See the comments on 21:91. On the name ʻImrān, see 3:33.

3 Reassessing the Typology, Date, and Ideology of the Jesus Passages – and Their Setting

Towards a New Classification, Formal and Thematic

Formal Division

Formal differences between the aforementioned passages allusive to Jesus, those displaying narratives of his birth, those that have him performing speeches, those which reflect credal formulas, and those serving polemical purposes are obvious despite their occasional overlapping. Formally speaking, then, it is possible to venture the following division:

(*A*) Brief mentions of Jesus (2:87, 136, 253; 3:84; 4:163; 5:78; 6:85; 23:50; 33:7; 42:13; 57:27)

(B_1) Narratives about his life and death (3:45–60; 19:16–33)

(B_2) Prologues to such narratives (3:33–43/4; 19:2–15)

(*C*) Speeches by Jesus himself (3:49–52; 19:24–6, 30–3, 36; 43:63–4; 61:6, 14)

(*D*) Confessional formulas including a reference to Jesus (2:136; 3:84; 4:171; 5:72–5)

(*E*) Polemical texts likewise including a reference to Jesus (2:136?; 3:33–59?, 60–3; 4:155–9, 171–2; 5:17; 9:30–1; 19:34–5; 43:57–8)

(*F*) Unclear passages (21:91; 66:12)

This *formal* approach may be said to provide, moreover, a first basic classification of the relevant passages – or, better, of those that seem to be relevant at first sight.[1]

Thematic Division

Thematically, instead, it is helpful to differentiate, if only roughly and preliminarily, between those passages that I have labeled "descriptive" and "theological," respectively – for, as I have suggested, this rudimentary, twofold division presents its own problems.[2]

1 I shall refer to the passages missing in this list in Chapter 5.

2 See Chapter 1.

https://doi.org/10.1515/9783110599688-003

Now, concerning the "descriptive" passages one must not only distinguish, as it is customary,[3] between:

(α) Passages mentioning Jesus as a messenger, a prophet, or righteous among others (2:136, 253, 3:84; 4:163; 6:85; 33:7; 42:13; 57:27)
(β) Passages about Jesus's birth (3:45–7;19:16–33)
(γ) Passages about Jesus's sayings and miracles (3:49–52; 5:110, 112–15; 19: 24–6, 30–3, 36; 43:63–4; 61:6, 14)
(δ) Passages about Jesus's mission to Israel (3:38–55; 5:46; 5:110; 43:57–9; 61:6)
(ε) Passages about Jesus's death (3:54–5; 4:155–9)
(ζ) Passages mentioning Mary (3:36–7, 42–7; 4:156; 5:73, 110, 116–17; 19:16–33; 21:91; 23:50; 66:12)
(η) Passages connecting Jesus and the Spirit (2:87, 253; 4:171; 5:110)
(θ) Passages mentioning the Gospel (3:48; 5:46, 110; 57:27)
(ι) Passages mentioning John the Baptist's (3:38–41; 19:7–15)
(κ) Passages mentioning Jesus's followers (2:253; 3:61–3; 4:171–2; 5:17, 72–5, 116–17; 9:30–1; 19:34; 42:13?; 57:27)

but also, not less importantly, between:

(λ) Passages stressing Jesus's distinction (2:87, 253; 4:171; 43:59)
(μ) Passages defending Jesus against the Jews (2:87, 136?; 3:45–55?; 5:78; 5:110)
(ν) Passages stressing Jesus's and Mary's distinction (5:110; 23:50)
(ξ) Passages defending Jesus and Mary against the Jews (3:45–55?; 4:155–9; 19:16–33?)
(ο) Passages stressing Mary's distinction (3:42; 21:91)
(π) Passages defending Mary against the Jews (3:33/42–8?; 4:156; 19:16–33?)
(ρ) Passages mentioning Jesus's disciples (3:52–3; 5:111–15; 61:14)
(σ) Passages mentioning Adam (3:59)

Notice too that some texts (e.g. 2:87, 253; 3:45–55; 4:155–9, 171–2; 5:17, 72–5, 73, 110, 116–17; 9:30–1; 19:16–33; 21:91; 42:13; 57:27; 61:6) fall simultaneously under various rubrics, while at a closer look others are susceptible of a counter-intuitive classification (see e.g. the comments on 2:136 below).

As for the "theological" passages, those stressing God's uniqueness and questioning Jesus's divine sonship (which are rightly taken to reflect the overall

3 See e.g. Geoffrey Parrinder, *Jesus in the Qur'ān* (London: Faber and Faber, 1965; 2nd ed., Oxford: Oneworld, 1995).

theology of the Qur'ān but do present their own nuances) ought to be subdivided into:

(τ) Passages that affirm that God is childless (4:171; 19:35)
(υ) Passages that deny Jesus's divinity (4:171–2; 5:17, 72, 75; 9:30–1)
(φ) Passages that deny Jesus's and Mary's divinity (5:75, 116–17)
(χ) Passages that deny the trinity (4:171, 5:73)

Thus there is no reason to confuse, as is sometimes done, the latter two text types[4]; nor is there any reason to suppose that all τ-texts (of which there are a good many more in the corpus than those listed above)[5] serve the purpose of downplaying Jesus's divinity, as their scope is actually broader – while the reverse argument is instead true: denying Jesus's divine sonship amounts to affirming that God is childless.[6]

In addition, there are two supplementary text types which are worth mentioning as well, namely:

(ψ) Passages (or, rather, a passage) connecting Jesus with the quranic prophet (61:6)
(ω) Passages hinting at an Adamic Christology (21:91; 66:12)

The latter category is quite puzzling, to say the least – but not much more problematic than the former one, as we shall see.

Lastly, the use of specific names/titles for Jesus ("Jesus," "Jesus son of Mary," "the Messiah," "the Messiah, Jesus son of Mary," etc.) apparently lacks significance in this respect. Put differently: depending on the passage in question, themes α to ω are linked to different names, but there seems to be no underlying pattern behind their distribution – in short, Jesus's names appear to be employed in a random fashion.[7]

---

4 See the discussion in Gabriel Said Reynolds, "On the Presentation of Christianity in the Qur'ān and the Many Aspects of Qur'anic Rhetoric," *BJQHS* 12 (2014): 52–4. Reynolds, however, does not provide a satisfactory answer to the question of what is the purpose, and hence the meaning, of 5:73; 5:116–17; instead, he merely asks: "In the case of *al-Mā'ida* (5) 116, for example, could it be that the Qur'ān is taunting Christians by intentionally exaggerating their devotion to Mary? Could this verse be more about the Qur'ān's creative rhetoric and less about the Collyridians?" (53–4), a "heretical" Christian group mentioned by Epiphanius (d. 403) in his *Panarion* (7.1.6), whose followers (mostly Arab women) Epiphanius accuses of worshiping Mary. See further Chapter 5.

5 See the comments on 4:171–2 in Chapter 2.

6 See further Chapter 5.

7 Random, too, is the fact that choosing Greek letters for the aforementioned entries, which amount to 24, therefore gives α and ω as the first and the last of them.

I shall now analyse a few passages in order to put forward a tentative hypothesis about the two historical periods in which the Jesus passages may have entered the quranic corpus.

Deciphering the Date of the Jesus Passages

Overlooked Texts in Defence of Jesus (and Mary) against the Jews

Despite them having being systematically overlooked, the μ-texts are key to understanding the Christology of the Qur'ān. The defence of Jesus (μ), Mary (π), or both of them (ξ) against the Jews is, in fact, salient and recurrent in the corpus. Yet it is also extensive beyond its recognisable boundaries – hence not limited to 2:87; 4:155–9; 5:78; 5:110 (and perhaps too, more broadly, 3:33/42–55 and 19:16–33). The text mirrored in Q 2:136 and 3:84:

> Say, "We believe in God and what has been sent to us,[8] and what was sent to Abraham, and Ishmael, and Isaac, and Jacob, and the tribes, and what was given to Moses and Jesus, and what was given to the prophets by their Lord. We make no distinction between them – and to him we are submissive"

may well serve as a test case hereof. I shall examine the two passages separately, as although the wording coincides in both, the context visibly differs from one to another.

The Vindication of the Quranic Prophet in Q 3:84

V. 84 in *Sūrat Āl 'Imrān* (Q 3, "The House of 'Imrān) follows a three-verse section (vv. 81–3) whose purpose is to *vindicate* the quranic prophet by presenting him as one among the prophets with whom God has made a covenant (v. 81), and thus as someone who ought to be helped (v. 81). Furthermore, those who deny him are accused of, and warned against, breaking God's covenant (vv. 82–3). In turn, vv. 85–92 and 100–20 expand on the differences existing between the believers and the disbelievers, i.e. between the followers of the quranic prophet and those who deny him and thereby "deny the truth" (v. 86). Therefore, "We make no distinction between them" in v. 84 should be read as meaning that those who *reject* the quranic prophet make an unacceptable *distinction* between God's prophets.

8 Cf. 3:53.

But who are those accused of denying the quranic prophet's mission? Judging from the inclusion of Jesus in the list reproduced in v. 84, one might think of them as Christians. Yet vv. 93–9 address them as the Sons of Israel – that is to say, as Jews. But then, the reference to Jesus (together with Moses) in v. 84 needs to be explained otherwise. Q 2:136 may well provide the clue to this, as I shall examine later on.

In sum, the purpose of the author of 3:84 is not to affirm that the quranic prophet is only one among God's prophets *but* – like vv. 81–3 and 86 – to authenticate his mission against those who reject it. It should suffice to quote vv. 81–6 to make it clear (my emphasis):

وَإِذْ أَخَذَ اللَّهُ مِيثَاقَ النَّبِيِّينَ لَمَا آتَيْتُكُمْ مِنْ كِتَابٍ وَحِكْمَةٍ ثُمَّ جَاءَكُمْ رَسُولٌ مُصَدِّقٌ لِمَا مَعَكُمْ لَتُؤْمِنُنَّ بِهِ
وَلَتَنْصُرُنَّهُ ۚ قَالَ أَأَقْرَرْتُمْ وَأَخَذْتُمْ عَلَىٰ ذَٰلِكُمْ إِصْرِي ۖ قَالُوا أَقْرَرْنَا ۚ قَالَ فَاشْهَدُوا وَأَنَا مَعَكُمْ مِنَ
الشَّاهِدِينَ 3:81
فَمَنْ تَوَلَّىٰ بَعْدَ ذَٰلِكَ فَأُولَٰئِكَ هُمُ الْفَاسِقُونَ 82
أَفَغَيْرَ دِينِ اللَّهِ يَبْغُونَ وَلَهُ أَسْلَمَ مَنْ فِي السَّمَاوَاتِ وَالْأَرْضِ طَوْعًا وَكَرْهًا وَإِلَيْهِ يُرْجَعُونَ 83
قُلْ آمَنَّا بِاللَّهِ وَمَا أُنْزِلَ عَلَيْنَا وَمَا أُنْزِلَ عَلَىٰ إِبْرَاهِيمَ وَإِسْمَاعِيلَ وَإِسْحَاقَ وَيَعْقُوبَ وَالْأَسْبَاطِ وَمَا أُوتِيَ
مُوسَىٰ وَعِيسَىٰ وَالنَّبِيُّونَ مِنْ رَبِّهِمْ لَا نُفَرِّقُ بَيْنَ أَحَدٍ مِنْهُمْ وَنَحْنُ لَهُ مُسْلِمُونَ 84
وَمَنْ يَبْتَغِ غَيْرَ الْإِسْلَامِ دِينًا فَلَنْ يُقْبَلَ مِنْهُ وَهُوَ فِي الْآخِرَةِ مِنَ الْخَاسِرِينَ 85
كَيْفَ يَهْدِي اللَّهُ قَوْمًا كَفَرُوا بَعْدَ إِيمَانِهِمْ وَشَهِدُوا أَنَّ الرَّسُولَ حَقٌّ وَجَاءَهُمُ الْبَيِّنَاتُ ۚ وَاللَّهُ لَا يَهْدِي الْقَوْمَ
الظَّالِمِينَ 86

3:81 [Remember] when God made [his] covenant with the prophets. He said, "Whatever I have given you of the Scripture and wisdom, *if a messenger comes to you confirming what you have with you, you must believe in him and help him*. Do you agree and accept my covenant on this condition?" They said, "We agree." He said, "Then bear witness and I will bear witness too."

82 Those who turn away after this – they are the wicked.

83 Do they seek something different from God's religion, when all [creatures] in the heavens and the earth have submitted to him willingly or unwillingly, and to him they shall return?

84 *Say, "We believe in God and what has been sent to us,*[9] *and what was sent to Abraham, and Ishmael, and Isaac, and Jacob, and the tribes, and what was given to Moses and Jesus, and what was given to the prophets by their Lord. We make no distinction between them – and to him we are submissive."*

85 Whoever desires a religion other than [complete] submission [to God] – this will not be accepted from him, and he will be among the losers in the hereafter.

9 Cf. 3:53.

86 *How is God to guide a people who have disbelieved after having believed,* [after having] *borne witness that the messenger is truthful and* [after having] *received clear signs?* God does not guide the evildoers.

The Parallel Vindication of the Jesus in Q 2:136

In turn, v. 136 in *Sūrat al-Baqara* (Q 2, "The Cow") is found within a long nineteen-verse anti-Jewish pericope (2:122–41)[10] containing two anti-Christian interpolations (in vv. 135 and 140). One wonders, then, if this verse does not serve an anti-Jewish purpose too; the rhetoric points indeed into that direction, and 4:150 brings additional confirmation to it, yet some further clarification is necessary for this argument to be consistent.

Abraham is the focus of two pericopes in *Sūrat al-Baqara* (Q 2), the first of which comprises vv. 122–41. In its opening lines, the author reworks Paul's Abrahamic argument in Galatians 3 and Romans 4, according to which God's promise to Abraham is broader than his covenant, in a way that recalls its supersessionary reworking in Matthew 3:9–10, the Epistle of Barnabas, Aristides's *Apology*, and Justin Martyr's *Dialogue with Trypho*.[11] Thus in v. 124 God says to Abraham: "I will make you a leader (*imām*) for the people"; Abraham then asks: "And of my offspring?"; to which God abruptly responds: "My covenant does not include the wrongdoers." This statement is commonly understood to refer to the unfaithful *among* the Sons of Israel – hence not to all Jews. But Arthur Droge insightfully observes[12] that "religion, not genealogy, determines who are the 'children of Abraham'" for the author of v. 124 – a view which echoes the aforementioned Christian argument. Shifting subsequently from the "bad" Abrahamic lineage (via Isaac) to the "good" one (via Ishmael) v. 128 portrays Abraham and his son Ishmael as forefathers of the Arabs – a motif which may, in turn, point to Christian missionary instruction in the Sinai and/or other neighbouring regions.[13] Interestingly enough, the reference in vv. 125 and 127 to their building of the

---

10 Notice the unambiguous reference to the Sons of Israel in v. 122.

11 See Carlos A. Segovia, "Discussing/subverting Paul: Polemical Re-readings and Competitive Supersessionist Misreadings of Pauline Inclusivism in Late Antiquity: A Case Study on the Apocalypse of Abraham, Justin Martyr, and the Qur'ān," in *Paul the Jew: A Conversation between Pauline and Second Temple Scholars*, ed. Gabriele Boccaccini and Carlos A. Segovia (Minneapolis: Fortress, 2015) 341–61.

12 Arthur J. Droge, *The Qur'ān: A New Annotated Translation* (Sheffield, UK, and Bristol, CT: Equinox, 2013) 13 n.149.

13 See Walter D. Ward, *The Mirage of the Saracen: Christians and Nomads in the Sinai Peninsula in Late Antiquity* (TCH 54; Oakland: University of California Press, 2015) 25–7.

"House" (البيت *al-bayt*, an undoubtedly elusive term which has nonetheless been traditionally identified with the Ka'ba) apparently draws on the Syriac "homiletic" literature on Genesis 22.[14] Again, the anti-Jewish rhetoric is patent in the argumentative style of vv. 135–40 and, tacitly, in v. 138, which reads: "God's *colour*! Who gives a better *colour* than God? It is him we worship!" (my emphasis). Obviously, صبغة الله *ṣibgat Allāh* ("God's colour") could represent a simple misreading of صنيعة الله *ṣanīʿat Allāh* ("God's favour"),[15] the latter expression ("God's *favour* [be upon us]! Who bestows a greater *favour* than God? It is him we worship!") matching perfectly, in turn, the claim made in v. 137 that the Jews should conform to those who truly worship God. The vindication of the quranic prophet in v. 129 is most remarkable too. Indeed, vv. 122–41 may be read as an intent to provide him (and hence his "community," as we read in v. 128) with a legitimate genealogy vis-à-vis the Jews.[16] Overall, therefore, vv. 122–41 display an unequivocal, albeit complex, anti-Jewish message, similar to that put forward in vv. 40–74, 75–82, 83–103, 104–10 of the same *sūra* (cf. the allusions to the "Children of Israel" in vv. 40, 47, 83, 122). Accordingly, Édouard-Marie Gallez takes the anti-Christian references in vv. 135 and 140 to be later interpolations.[17] Abraham's description as a حنيف *ḥanīf* in v. 135 also points to a Christian setting. Among the

---

14 See Joseph Witztum, "The Foundation of the House (Q 2:127)," *BSOAS* 72.1 (2009): 25–40. For an identification of *al-bayt*, the "House," with the Jerusalem temple, see Édouard-Marie Gallez, *Le messie et son prophète. Aux origines de l'Islam* (2 vols; Versailles: Éditions de Paris, 2005) 1:467–76.

15 See James A. Bellamy, "Some Proposed Emendations to the Text of the Koran," *JAOS* 113.4 (1993): 570–1 (reprinted in *What the Koran Really Says: Language, Text, and Commentary*, ed. Ibn Warraq [Amherst, NY: Prometheus Books, 2002] 503–5). See also idem, "Textual Criticism," in *Encyclopaedia of the Qur'ān*, ed. Jane Dammen McAuliffe (6 vols.; Leiden and Boston: Brill, 2001–6) 5:237–52, pp. 243–4, for a second alternative reading in lieu of *ṣibgat Allāh*, namely *kifāyat Allāh* ("God's sufficiency").

16 Cf. Edmund M. Beck, "Die Gestalt des Abraham am Wendepunkt der Entwicklung Muhammeds: Analyse von Sure 2, 118 (124)–135 (141)," *Le Muséon* 65 (1952): 73–94 (reprinted in *Der Koran*, ed. Rudi Paret [Darmstadt: Wissenschaftliche Buchgesellschaft, 1975] 111–33); Catherina Wenzel, "'Und als Ibrāhīm und Ismāʿīl die FunDammente des Hauses (der Ka'ba) legten' (Sure 2, 127): Abrahamsrezeption und Legitimät im Koran,"*ZRGG* 45.3 (2002): 193–209; Angelika Neuwirth, "The House of Abraham and the House of Amram: Genealogy, Patriarchal Authority, and Exegetical Professionalism," in *The Qur'ān in Context: Historical and Literary Investigations into the Qur'ānic Milieu*, ed. Angelika Neuwirth, Nicolai Sinai, and Michael Marx (Leiden and Boston: Brill, 2010) 499–531, pp. 501–3; Bertram Schmitz, "Das Spannungsverhältnis zwischen Judentum und Christentum als Grundlage des Entstehungsprozesses des Islams in der Interpretation von Vers 124 bis 141 der zweiten Sure," in *Der Koran und sein religiöses und kulturelles Umfeld*, ed. Tilman Nagel (Munich: Oldenbourg, 2010) 217–38.

17 Édouard-Marie Gallez, "'Gens du Livre' et Nazaréens dans le Coran: qui sont les premiers et à quel titre les seconds en font-ils partie?," *OC* 92 (2008): 174–86. The latter one (v. 140) is

numerous studies on the semantics of this term that have seen the light since Hartwig Hirschfeld had his *Beiträge zur Erklärung des Ḳorāns* published in 1886, the most complete ones are those by François de Blois and Gabriel Reynolds.[18] It is clear, from these and other studies, that originally *ḥanīf* did not mean "monotheist"; otherwise it would be totally unnecessary to label Abraham a *ḥanīf* and then immediately stress – as the Qur'ān systematically does (cf. Q 3:85) – that he was *not* an "idolater." As already noted by Theodor Nöldeke[19] (*Beiträge*, 30), the word *ḥanīf* likely adapts the Syriac ܚܢܦܐ *ḥanpā* (pl. ܚܢܦܐ *ḥanpē*) meaning "gentile," i.e. "non-Jew."[20]

As for the prophetic list in v. 136, it clearly divides into three segments: (*a*) Abraham + Ishmael + Isaac + Jacob | (*b*) the tribes of Israel | (*c*) Moses + Jesus followed by a more general reference to God's prophets. Now, mentioning Jesus in this way, i.e. alongside Moses (like in 2: 87), makes good sense given the anti-Jewish intent of the whole pericope. Therefore it is possible to read the first half of the concluding sentence in v. 136: "we make no difference between them and we are submissive to him" as meaning that Jesus should *not* be excluded from, but counted among, God's prophets. Q 4:150–1 reinforce this view, as they present as equivalent the notion of "making a distinction between God's prophets" and that of "believing only in some of them":

إِنَّ الَّذِينَ يَكْفُرُونَ بِاللَّهِ وَرُسُلِهِ وَيُرِيدُونَ أَنْ يُفَرِّقُوا بَيْنَ اللَّهِ وَرُسُلِهِ وَيَقُولُونَ نُؤْمِنُ بِبَعْضٍ وَنَكْفُرُ
بِبَعْضٍ وَيُرِيدُونَ أَنْ يَتَّخِذُوا بَيْنَ ذَٰلِكَ سَبِيلًا 4:150
أُولَٰئِكَ هُمُ الْكَافِرُونَ حَقًّا ۚ وَأَعْتَدْنَا لِلْكَافِرِينَ عَذَابًا مُهِينًا 151

4:150 Those who do not believe in God and his messengers and wish to make a distinction between God and his messengers say, "We believe in some of them, but we do not believe in others" – they wish to make divisions [there were no division should be made],

particularly obvious, as discussing the "Christian" origins (!) of the "Abraham, Ishmael, Isaac, Jacob, and the tribes [of Israel]" makes little if any sense.

18 François de Blois, "*Naṣrānī* (*Ναζωραῖος*) and *Ḥanīf* (*Ἐθνικός*): Studies on the Religious Vocabulary of Christianity and of Islam," *BSOAS* 65.1 (2002): 1–30; Gabriel Said Reynolds, *The Qur'ān and Its Biblical Subtext* (RSQ; London and New York: Routledge, 2010) 75–87. See also Geneviève Gobillot, "Hanîf,"in *Dictionnaire du Coran*, ed. Mohammad Ali Amir-Moezzi (Paris: Laffont, 2007) 381–4; Christoph Luxenberg, *The Syro-Aramaic Reading of the Koran: A Contribution to the Decoding of the Language of the Koran* (Berlin: Schiler, 2007) 55–7.

19 Theodor Nöldeke, *Neue Beiträge zur Semitischen Sprachwissenschaft* (Strassburg: Trüber, 1910; partial English translation: "On the Language of the Koran," In *Which Koran: Variants, Manuscripts, Linguistics*, ed. Ibn Warraq [Amherst, NY: Prometheus Books, 2011] 1–30, p. 30).

20 Cf. Mark 7:26 and Romans 1:16 in the Pəšīṭtā.

151 they are in truth the disbelievers; and we have prepared for the disbelievers a humiliating punishment.

To sum up then: 2:136 needs to be read like 3:84, save that in this case the vindicated figure is not quranic prophet, but Jesus.

Anti-Jewish Rhetoric, Anti-Christian Texts, and the Date of the Jesus Passages

Furthermore, the fact that, throughout the corpus, Jesus is repeatedly defended against the Jews is most remarkable indeed. Some texts even look Christian (rather than pro-Christian, as a more traditional approach would have them);[21] in other words, were they not found in the Qur'ān as they are, but be extant independently from it in, say, several parchment fragments lacking, they could be easily taken to be either excerpts of an otherwise lost Christian writing or fragments belonging to various Christian works of apologetic nature and interrelated content.

Q 3:50–2, 54, 55; 4:155–6; 5:78, 110–11, 112–15; 19:16–33 may help to substantiate this point. In what follows I shall only quote their most significant parts; see Chapter 2 for the complete text and the interpretation of each passage, which is preceded by a brief introductory text summarising its basic idea(s).

Q 3:50–2

Jesus tells the Jews that he brings them a sign from God, presents himself as confirming and updating the Torah, and asks his disciples to help him when he sees that the Jews do not believe in his mission

---

21 See e.g. David Marshall, "Christianity in the Qur'ān," in *Islamic Interpretations of Christianity*, ed. Lloyd Ridgeon (London and New York: Routledge) 3–29, p. 16, who surmises that Muḥammad first tried to gather theological support from some Christian group or groups, but then distanced himself from them after they rejected his teachings. Other authors contend instead that the Qur'ān refers to two specific Christian groups: the Abyssinians/Ethiopians and the Najranites, respectively. This, in fact, is the majority view among the post-quranic Muslim authors, who put forward a poor binary typology according to which those who converted to Islam (the Abyssinians) were good Christians, while those that did not (the Najranites) were bad Christians (see Haggai Mazuz, "Christians in the Qur'ān: Some Insights Derived from the Classical Exegetical Approach," *SO* 112 [2012]: 41–53). But there is no evidence to support this view, which is entirely biased and tells us more about the purpose of the later Muslim authors than about the exchanges between Muḥammad's own religious group and the Christian groups of 7th-century Arabia. It is as though the later Muslim authors intended to say to Christians living under Islamic rule: "Behold, a powerful Christian king and his court accepted Muḥammad as a true prophet, so follow their example!" Obviously, this is ideology, not history.

3:50 [Jesus said to the Jews,] "I have brought you a sign from your Lord ...
51 [I come to you] confirming the Torah [given to you] before me, and to allow you some things that were previously forbidden to you... ."
52 When Jesus saw their disbelief, he said, "Who are my helpers for God?" The disciples said, "We are God's helpers! We believe in God. Bear witness that we submit [to him"].

Q 3:54

The Jews plot against Jesus, but God plots against them

3:54 They [= the Jews] schemed [against Jesus], but God too schemed [against them] – God is the best of schemers.

Q 3:55

God raises Jesus to himself to deliver him from the Jews and promises to place Jesus's followers above them in the Day of Resurrection

55 [Remember] when God said, "Jesus!, I am going to take you and raise you to myself and purify you from those who disbelieve; and I will place those who follow you above the disbelievers until the Day of Resurrection ... ["]

Q 4:155–6

God withdraws his covenant from the Jews because of their disbelief and their slandering Mary

4:155 Because of their breaking of the covenant, and their disbelief in God's signs, and their killing of the prophets without any right, and their saying, "Our hearts are wrapped" – God has rather sealed them on account of their disbelief ...
156 ... and their saying against Mary a great slander,

Q 5:78

Jesus (and David, whose mention authenticates Jesus's messiahship) curse(s) the disbelieving Jews

5:78 Those of the Sons of Israel who disbelieved were cursed by the tongue of David and Jesus ...

Q 5:110–11

Jesus and Mary are favoured by God, and Jesus himself supported with the Holy Spirit so that he can spread God's word and perform various miracles (with God's permission); God, moreover, gives him the Torah and the Gospel and protects him against the Jews, who are (as it is often the case in the Qur'ān) portrayed as disbelievers – unlike Jesus's disciples, who bear witness to God

5:110 [Remember] when God said, "Jesus, son of Mary!, remember my favour upon you and upon your mother, when I supported you with the Holy Spirit [so that] you could speak to the people from the cradle, and in adulthood; and when I taught you the Writing, and wisdom, and the Torah, and the Gospel; and when you created the form of a bird out of clay with my permission, and you breathed into it and it became a [living] bird with my permission; and [when] you healed the blind and the leper with my permission; and when you brought forth the dead with my permission; when I restrained the Sons of Israel from [violently attacking] you – when you brought them clear signs, the disbelievers among them said, 'This is nothing but magic!';

111 and when I inspired the disciples [telling them], 'Believe in me and in my messenger!' – they said, 'We believe – bear witness that we are submissive[.]'[''"]

Q 5:112–15

Jesus's disciples ask him to demand from God what looks like a table for performing the eucharist

5:112 [Remember] when the disciples said, 'Jesus ... is your Lord able to send down for us a table from heaven?' He said, 'Fear God, if you believe [in him]!'

113 They said, 'We would like to eat from it to satisfy our hearts and know with certainty that you have spoken the truth to us, and [thus] be counted among its witnesses.'

114 Jesus ... said, 'Oh God! Our Lord! Send down for us a table from heaven, as a festival for [all of] us, from the first of us to the last of us and as a sign from you.'

115 God said, 'Yes, I will send it down for you. Whoever of you disbelieves after that – I shall punish him as I have never punished any other man.'

Q 19:16–24

Mary is comforted by the Holy Spirit, which assuming human form announces to her Jesus's birth; then it is the newborn Jesus who comforts his mother, telling her that she should not sorrow

19:16 And remember Mary in the Writing: when she withdrew from her family to an eastern place,

17 and she hided herself from them, we sent to her our Spirit, which took for her human. form

18 She said, "I take shelter with the Merciful from you, if you are fearful [of God]."

19 He said, "I am only a messenger of your Lord, sent to grant you a pure boy."

20 She said, "How shall I have a boy, when no man has touched me and I am not a prostitute."

21 He said, "Thus! Your Lord has said, 'It is easy for me. He will be a sign to the people an a mercy from us. It is a thing decreed.'"

22 So she conceived him and withdrew with him to a distant place.

23 The pains of childbirth drove there to the trunk of the palm-tree. She said, "I wish I were dead by now and forgotten!"
24 But, after giving birth, he [= Jesus] called out to her: "Do not sorrow! Your Lord has given you a pure child.["]

Q 19:27–33

Mary presents Jesus to her people, who suspect her; but then the newborn Jesus defends her and blesses himself in the name of God, whose servant and prophet he claims to be

19:27 She brought him to her people, carrying him. They said, "Mary! This is something really weird!
28 Sister of Aaron! Your father was not a bad man, nor was your mother a prostitute!"
29 But she pointed him [thus inviting them to address him]. They said, "How are we to speak to one who is [still] in the cradle, a [mere] child?"
30 He said, "I am God's servant. He has given me the Scripture and made me a prophet,
31 and blessed me wherever I am, and commended to me prayer and charity as long as I live,
32 as well as to respect my mother – he has not made me a tyrant or a miserable.
33 Peace be upon me the day I was born, and the day I die, and the day I will be raised alive."

Additionally, there is a good number of anti-Jewish texts in the Qur'ān that match the standards of Christian rhetoric. Three concrete examples will suffice to illustrate this:

(a) Killing God's prophets

The reference in 2:87 to the Jews as they who either bely or have God's prophets killed (cf. 2:61, 91; 3:21, 112, 181, 183; 4:155; 5:70) draws not only on the motif, but also the wording, in Matthew 12:3–5; 23:31–4; Luke 11:39–52; 13:34–5; Acts 7:51–3; 1 Thessalonians 2:14–16; Hebrews 11:37–8; and Diatessaron 33:44–7; 41:1–2.[22] Cf. too the attitude of the Jews in 17:7 before God's "second promise."

(b) Scriptural falsification

The notion of scriptural falsification is also key for understanding a core aspect of the anti-Jewish rhetoric of the Qur'ān (see e.g. 2:75–82) as well as its Christian

---

22 See further Emran Iqbal El-Badawi, *The Qur'ān and the Aramaic Gospel Traditions* (RSQ; London and New York: Routledge, 2014) 121–5. On the possible dependance of the the Qur'ān on the Diatessaron, see Jan M. F. Van Reeth, "L'Évangile du prophète," in *al-Kitāb: La sacralité du texte dans le monde de l'Islam. Actes du Symposium international tenu à Leuven et Louvain-la-Neuve du 29 mai au 1 juin 2002*, ed. Daniel De Smet, Godefroy Callatay, and Jan M. F. van Reeth (Brussels: SBEO, 2004) 155–74.

overtones. Comparing the Qur'ān to the writings of Aphrahat (d. c. 345), Ephraem the Syrian (d. 373), Isaac of Antioch (d. late 5th century), and Jacob of Serugh (d. 521) proves particularly eloquent in this respect. As Gabriel Reynolds observes, "[t]he Qur'an's concern with the failure of the Jews to read divine revelation properly is closely related to the conventional Christian anti-Jewish literature ... [and more specifically to] pre-Islamic Syriac Christian literature."[23] Furthermore, Emran El-Badawi suggests[24] that Matthew's and Luke's condemnation of the Jewish "scribes" (Syr. ܣܦܪܐ *sāfrē*), on the one hand, and, on the other hand, the quranic polemical association of "books" (أسفار *asfār*) with scribes, reflect a parallel rhetorical move and, hence, a parallel discursive strategy (cf. Matt 23; Luke 11:44; Diatessaron 40; Q 62:5).

(c) The "hardened hearts" of the Jews

Like Paul in Romans 9:18 and the author of Hebrews 3:8, 13, 15; 4:7, after mentioning the benefits bestowed by God on the Sons of Israel and underlining the role played by the Mosaic covenant as a symbol of Israel's election (in Q 2:40–73) the author of Q 2:74 depicts the obtuseness of the Jews before Christ by claiming that their "hearts" have been "hardened."

The Qur'ān's eschatology is likewise pervaded with Christian imagery. Compare, for instance, the reference to the "white (shining) faces" of the pious in the afterlife in Q 3:106–7 to the almost identical metaphor found in Matthew 28:2–3 and Diatessaron 52:48–51.[25] In turn, Q 2:210 contains an implicit allusion to the apocalyptic, messianic vision of the coming of the Son of Man with the clouds of heaven in Daniel 7:13–14; 4 Ezra 13:3; Mark 13:26–7; Matthew 24:30–1; Luke 21:27; and Diatessaron 42:22–3, although the Son of Man is here replaced by God himself (cf. Q 89:21–2) and his angels. El-Badawi persuasively argues that the Qur'ān parallels the New Testament version rather than Daniel's, due to the Qur'ān's reference to God's "angels,"[26] but he fails to mention 4 Ezra 13:3, where, like in Daniel 7:13–14, the angels go unmentioned.[27]

---

23 Gabriel Said Reynolds, "On the Qur'anic Accusation of Scriptural Falsification (*taḥrīf*) and Christian Anti-Jewish Polemic," *JAOS* 130.2 (2010): 189–202, p. 197.

24 See El-Badawi, *The Qur'ān and the Aramaic Gospel Traditions*, 128–30.

25 See once more El-Badawi, *The Qur'ān and the Aramaic Gospel Traditions*, 203–4.

26 El-Badawi, *The Qur'ān and the Aramaic Gospel Traditions*, 185–6.

27 On the Son of Man in the literature of Second Temple Judaism and the New Testament, George W. E. Nickelsburg and James C. VanderKam, *1 Enoch 2: A Commentary on the Book of 1 Enoch, Chapters 37–82*, ed. Klaus Baltzer (Hermeneia; Minneapolis: Fortress, 2012) 44–5, 62, 70–6; Lester L. Grabbe, "'Son of Man': Its Origin and Meaning in Second Temple Judaism," *in Enoch and the Synoptic Gospels: Reminiscences, Allusions, Intertextuality*, ed. Loren T. Stuckenbruck and Gabriele Boccaccini (Atlanta, GA: SBL, 2016) 169–98. See also Gabriele Boccaccini, ed., *Enoch and the*

Back to the accusations levelled against the Jews in Q 2:40–73, 75–82, 87, I would like to stress that their authors' straightforward anti-Judaism combines well with the defence of Jesus endorsed in the passages earlier supplied, i.e. 3:50–2, 54, 55; 4:155–6; 5:78, 110–11, 112–15; 19:16–24, 27–33. Put differently: criticising the Jews and defending Jesus function as the obverse and the reverse of one and the same ideology, and it is not possible to know beforehand which side the coin may show each time it falls. In fact, if one leaves aside the τ-, υ-, φ-, and χ-texts, most of which can be said to belong to a later stage in the development of the quranic corpus (a stage in which radical separation from Christianity, as witnessed for example in the inscriptions of the Dome of the Rock, was officially promoted),[28] most Jesus-texts have anti-Jewish overtones, for which reason I am willing to assign a single timeframe to their composition: *after* the arguably early texts (roughly, those comprised in *sūra*-s 75–114, plus 61:6)[29] that affirm that God is childless (which significantly never mention Jesus), and *before* the complete parting of the ways with Christianity put forward in such late anti-Christian texts as 4:172; 5:116–7; 9:30–1; 19:34–6. I propose to call such in-between period, Period 1 (P1), and to group in it, therefore, all Jesus passages except 4:171; 5:116–7; 9:30–1; 19:34–6, which – in contrast to all of them and to 4:172; 5:17, 72–5, the only three anti-Jesus passages contained in the Berlin Ms. Or. Fol. 4313 – I am therefore inclined to assign to a later time period, or Period 2 (P2). It is now necessary to find a historical setting suitable for both types of texts.

Their Setting and the Chronology of the Corpus

Ideological Stages, Redactional Layers, and Historical Periods

In my paper "A Messianic Controversy behind the Making of Muḥammad as the Last Prophet?,"[30] which I originally wrote in 2015, I argued for the existence of

---

Messiah Son of Man: Revisiting the Book of Parables (Grand Rapids, MI, and Cambridge: Eerdmans, 2007); Darrell L. Bock and James H. Charlesworth, eds., *Parables of Enoch: A Para-digm Shift* (London and New York: Bloomsbury, 2013).

28 Notice that 4:171–2 (together with 17:111) furnish the core of the message displayed on the Dome of the Rock Inscriptions, which date to the beginnings of 'Abd al-Malik's rule (692–705); see further Carlos A. Segovia, "Identity Politics and the Study of Islamic Origins: The Inscriptions of the Dome of the Rock as a Test Case," forthcoming in *Identity, Politics and the Study of Islam: Current Dilemmas in the Study of Religions*, ed. Matt Sheddy (CESIF; Sheffield, UK, and Bristol, CT: Equinox).

29 Chapter 5 below.

30 Carlos A. Segovia, "A Messianic Controversy behind the Making of Muḥammad as the Last Prophet?," forthcoming in *Early Islam: The Religious Milieu of Late Antiquity*, ed. Guillaume Dye (LAMINE; Chicago: Chicago Oriental Institute).

(1) Christian formulas (often with anti-Jewish overtones) mentioning Jesus, (2) pro-Christian compromise formulas, (3) anti-Christian polemical formulas, and (4) anti-Christian (as well as anti-Jewish) supersessionary formulas in the Qur'ān. Also, I distinguished between (*i*) an early-Muhamadan stage corresponding to the redactional layer of the Christian formulas; (*ii*) a late-Muhamadan-, or else post-Muhamadan, stage – if post-Muhamadan then possibly pre-Marwanid, and hence contemporary with the Arab overtake of the Near East – corresponding to that of the pro-Christian formulas; (*iii*) a post-Muhamadan, possibly early-Marwanid, stage corresponding to that of the anti-Christian polemical formulas; and, lastly, (*iv*) a post-Muhamadan, either early or late-Marwanid, stage corresponding to that of the anti-Christian supersessionary formulas.[31] This periodisation implied, then, defining *three* major periods in the making of Islam as a new religion, and hence simultaneously distinguishing between: (*a*) a still *basically-Christian* faith; (*b*) a period of *relative pro-Christian compromise* – roughly contemporary with Mu'āwiya's reign (661–80); and (*c*) the *struggle* for a *new* religious identity promoted by 'Abd al-Malik b. Marwān (r. 692–705) and almost fully achieved by his son and successor al-Walīd I (r. 705–15).

As it will become apparent, I hope, throughout the present essay, my current view is more nuanced, as I now believe the original and rather innovative Christology of the Qur'ān lacked any emphasis on Jesus's role and mission – its stress falls, instead, upon the *non*-human aspects of God's descended Word.[32] Thus I think the texts in the corpus which are favourable to Jesus reflect a conquest-, not a pre-conquest, setting.[33]

---

31 On the notion of redactional layers within the Qur'ān, see See Alfonse-Louis de Prémare, "Le Coran ou la fabrication de l'incréé," *Medium* 2.3 (2005): 3–30; Guillaume Dye, "Pourquoi et com-ment se fait un texte canonique. Quelques réflexions sur l'histoire du Coran," in *Hérésies: une con-struction d'identités religieuses*, ed. Christian Brouwer, Guillaume Dye, and Anja van Rompaey (PHR; Brussels: Éditions de l'Université de Bruxelles, 2015) 55–104. On the application of such notion to particular narratives, see e.g. Carlos A. Segovia, *The Quranic Noah and the Making of the Islamic Prophet: A Study of Intertextuality and Religious Identity Formation in Late Antiquity* (JCIT 4; Berlin and Boston: De Gruyter, 2015) 70–84.

32 See further Chapter 5.

33 This said, I maintain the view that there is in the Qur'ān (x) *elaboration* of, rather than *identification* with, a peripheral form of Christianity (which obviously implies more than, and differs from, a pro-Christian attitude); (y) eventual *sympathy* towards mainstream Christianity; and (z) a gradual *withdrawal* from Christianity that ranges from (z_1) polemics against it to (z_2) its rejection and replacement by something else. Also, I still think that (I) unclear dissemination of vague identity markers against a brewing background of common ideas and practices, (II) re-dissemination and re-semantisation of such markers along new ad hoc but still fuzzy lines or axes of crystallisation, and (III) the final promotion and consolidation of these denote the three phases through which all late-antique reli-gious identities (literally) "took shape" –

Besides, the aforementioned *b*-period looks to me as the most suitable for the incorporation of the *μ*-texts (and other related passages) into the Qur'ān. For some degree of sympathy towards more mainstream forms of Christianity (more mainstream vis-à-vis the peripheral variant displayed in the earliest quranic layers) and/or Christian communities, seems to have been the rule rather than the exception during Mu'āwiya's reign despite Mu'āwiya's occasional anti-Christian policy.[34] For his two military expeditions against Byzantium notwithstanding (the first one in 669, the second one in 674–7) Mu'āwiya, was proclaimed *amīr al-mu'minīn* ("Commander of the Faithful") in Jerusalem, married a Christian who gave him the son he would name his successor, appointed two Christians as his personal physician and court poet, and is said, moreover, to have visited the churches of the Holy Sepulchre and St Mary and to have invoked Christ's lordship to solve a dispute concerning the possession of Jesus's *sudarium*.[35] As Stephen Humphreys – employing perhaps too loosely the terms "Muslims," "religions," and "Islam," which represent formidable anachronisms – writes,

---

and that depicting formative Islam in a different way makes no sense and would require some counter-evidence that we simply lack.

34 See Chase F. Robinson, *'Abd al-Malik* (Oxford: Oneworld, 2005) 24–5. See also Robert G. Hoyland, *In God's Path: The Arab Conquests and the Creation of an Islamic Empire* (Oxford and New York: Oxford University Press, 2015) 108, 128–32, who moreover refers to Mu'āwiya's personal intervention in intra-Christian affairs. The period elapsing from Muḥammad's death to Mu'āwiya's ascension is particularly obscure to us despite its uniform presentation by the Muslim historiographers. The more we can say is that, after Muḥammad's death in 632 (if he did not himself lead the Arab conquest until 634, on which see Stephen J. Shoemaker, *The Death of a Prophet: The End of Muhammad's Life and the Beginnings of Islam* [DRLAR; Philadelphia: University of Pennsylvania Press, 2012] 18–27), his successors strove to achieve political supremacy in the Arabian peninsula, and that no authority lasted enough to lay the foundations of a cohesive Arab state. It is difficult to imagine, however, that they were all equally convinced by Muḥammad's message or loyal to Muḥammad's legacy (apparently, the Sufyanids were not if we are to assign some credibility to their opponents' claims). Nor did they all seem to have understood Muḥammad's teachings in the very same manner (allegedly, the Zubayrids and the Alids had very different views on what those teachings entailed). It is in light of this wavering indeterminacy that one must reinterpret the so-called early Muslim divisions and the rival leaderships of Mu'āwiya b. Abī Sufyān (and later Yazīd b. Mu'āwiya and 'Abd al-Malik b. Marwān) in Syria, 'Abd Allāh b. al-Zubayr (initially with 'Ā'iša bt. Abī Bakr and Ṭalḥa b. 'Ubayd Allāh) in the Ḥiǧāz, and 'Alī b. Abī Ṭālib (followed by his son al-Ḥusayn and then al-Muḫtar) in Iraq.

35 See R. Stephen Humphreys, *Mu'awiya ibn Abi Sufyan: From Arabia to Empire* (Oxford: Oneworld, 2006) 83–4; Roy Jackson, *Fifty Key Figures in Islam* (London and New York: Routledge, 2006) 21–5; Thomas O'Loughlin, *Adomnán and the Holy Places: The Perceptions of an Insular Monk on the Locations of the Biblical Drama* (London and New York: T & T Clark, 2007) 174.

> "We cannot not know exactly what his intentions were in performing these actions (assuming they actually happened) but there are two possibilities. First, on a political level, he assumed a key role of the Roman Emperor, making himself the advocate and guardian of the holy places of Jerusalem. Thus, he could present himself as the sovereign of both Christian and Muslims. Second, by publicly commemorating the life of the Prophet Jesus, he could underline the unbroken continuity between the two religions and show that Islam had come not to supplant Christianity but to fulfil it."[36]

In any event, this may well provide a background to narratives as important as those contained in Q 19:2–36 and 3:33–63, which, with their echoes of the Mariological liturgy of the Kathisma Church – whose architecture served too the model for the Dome of the Rock – seem to have a Palestinian setting.[37] Probably, this positive attitude towards mainstream Christianity developed parallel to the deterioration of the Arab-Jewish relations after the new Arab settlers were given land confiscated from the Jews, who, in turn, may have earlier helped them to gain control over the region. Transition from a positive to a negative view of the Arabs, as evinced if one compares the *Secrets of Rabbî Šim'ôn ben Yôḥây*, the *Jewish Apocalypse on the Umayyads*, and chs. 28 and 30 of the *Pirqê de-Rabbî 'Elî'ezer* to the *Story of the Ten Wise Jews* and *Targum Pseudo-Jonathan ad* Genesis 21:9–21,[38] clearly witnesses to this shift, which may well have taken place in the aftermath of 'Umar I's rule,[39] with Constans II acting as the new Byzantine emperor after Heraclius's reign, which was briefly followed by those of his two sons Constantine and Heraklonas.

---

36 Humphreys, *Mu'awiya ibn Abi Sufyan*, 84. "Ultimately," he adds, "Mu'awiya's real intentions are a mystery – which is perhaps the way he wanted it." But maybe we deem his behaviour puzzling or "mysterious" because we keep in mind the, again, anachronistic view that the pre-Marwanid Arab leaders were already Muslims, i.e. that they had a religion different, if not completely opposed to, Christianity; and as long as we continue working with this closed, entitative notions, we will hardly be able move beyond perplexity.

37 See Stephen J. Shoemaker, "Christmas in the Qur'ān: The Qur'ānic Account of Jesus' Nativity and Palestinian Local Tradition," *JSAI* 28 (2003): 11–39; Guillaume Dye, "Lieux saints communs, partagés ou confisqués: aux sources de quelques péricopes coraniques (Q 19: 16–33)," in *Partage du sacré: transferts, dévotions mixtes, rivalités interconfessionnelles*, ed. Isabelle Depret and Guillaume Dye (Brussels-Fernelmont:EME, 2012) 55–121; idem, "The Qur'ān and its Hypertextuality in Light of Redaction Criticism," forthcoming in *Early Islam: The Religious Milieu of Late Antiquity*, ed. Guillaume Dye (LAMINE; Chicago: Chicago Oriental Institute). Cf. too Mary's defence in Q 4:156. See also the comments on 23:50 in the preceding chapter.

38 See Carlos A. Segovia, "Friends, Enemies, or Hoped-for New Rulers? Reassessing the Early Jewish Sources Mentioning the Rise of Islam," forthcoming in *Jews and Judaism in Northern Arabia*, ed. Haggai Mazuz (BRLJ; Leiden and Boston: Brill).

39 See Tayeb El-Hibri, *Parable and Politics in Early Islamic History: The Rashidun Caliphs* (New York and Chichester, UK: Columbia University Press, 2010) 82–3.

In other words, the texts examined in the previous section reflect, on my reading, increasing social tension between Christians and Jews in mid- to late-7th-century Syria-Palestine – a tension that had raised sometime before, when in 602 Flavius Phocas Augustus had usurped the throne of Maurice, the Byzantine emperor. Riots erupted in several places of the Near East, especially Antioch, against Phocas's overt anti-Jewish policy. Yet the new emperor succeeded in suffocating the rebellion in 608. As a consequence, the Jews sought the alliance of the Persians, whose king Chosroes II, being Maurice's son-in-law, resolved to attack Byzantium to avenge his uncle's death. The Jews and the Persians fought side by side against the Byzantines, gained control over the whole region, had various churches and monasteries burnt, and took Jerusalem in 614. The view that these events would lead to the establishment of the Third Jewish Commonwealth started to circulate among the Jews, who saw themselves as the true heirs of the Maccabean revolt against Antiochus Epiphanes. As Elli Kohen writes in a remarkable monograph on the history of the Jews of Byzantium, "[t]here was even some attempt at Jewish proselytism."[40] However, things turned out quite differently from what they expected: "Not only was there no sign of Persian commitment to the rise of the Third Jewish Commonwealth, but oppressive taxes were imposed on Jews ... [and] many of the Palestinian Jews [were] carried to Persia."[41] In other words, their hopes ended in frustration.[42] In the meantime, Phocas had been deposed by Heraclius, who was crowned new emperor of the Byzantines in 610. At first, Heraclius could do nothing to stop the Persian conquest of the Fertile Crescent, but he managed to counter-attack the Persians in 622 and was able to recapture several crucial places between 624 and 627. In their disillusionment towards the Persians and fearing the consequences of a Byzantine victory, in 627 the Jews negotiated a treaty with Heraclius which ensured them immunity despite the injuries they had inflected on the Christians and granted the Emperor their financial support. And thus they felt relieved when Heraclius had the Persians subdued in 628. Yet the Emperor, persuaded by the ecclesiastical authorities of Palestine, did not keep his word. The edicts of Hadrian and Constantine were

---

40 Elli Kohen, *History of the Byzantine Jews: A Microcosmos in the Thousand Year Empire* (Lanham, MD: University Press of America, 2007) 37.

41 Kohen, *History of the Byzantine Jews*, 37.

42 See too Jacob Neusner, *A History of the Jews in Babylonia, V: Later Sasanian Times* (Leiden: Brill, 1970; reprinted in Eugene, OR: Wipf and Stock, 2008) 113–32; Peter Shäfer, *The History of the Jews in the Greco-Roman World* (London and New York: Routledge, 2003) 190–94; Seth Schwartz, *The Ancient Jews from Alexander to Muhammad* (KTAH; Cambridge and New York: Cambridge University Press, 2014) 149–51.

reissued and the Jews were expelled from Jerusalem or else forced to convert. In short, the Byzantines, once more, proved to be their enemies.[43]

By the time, then, when "the Arabs of *mḥmd*," as the Miaphysite chronicles of the 630s and 640s call them,[44] seized control of Syria-Palestine,[45] they came across this poignant tension and, despite some inevitable clashes, naturally sided with the social-religious group from whose help and support in matters of governance they could profit more.[46]

To be sure, the quranic corpus also contains a number of anti-Christian interpolations that should not be confused with its early texts' (e.g. Q 4:172; 5:17, 72–5; 112) questioning of the idea of God begetting a child, inasmuch as they pertain to a later, anti-Christian layer instead. Such interpolations do not always mention Jesus (I shall analyse in the next chapter one that does, though), yet they

---

43 For a discussion of the role played by the Jews of Palestine in the beginnings of the crisis, see Elliot S. Horowitz, *Reckless Rites: Purim and the Legacy of Jewish Violence* (Princeton, NJ: Princeton University Press, 2006) 237–47.

44 See Michael Philip Penn, *When Christians First Met Muslims: A Sourcebook of the Earliest Syriac Writings on Islam* (Berkeley and Los Angeles: University of California Press, 2015) 21–8. On the exact pronunciation of *mḥmd* (Maḥmid, Muḥammad?) see further Andreas Kaplony, "The Ortography and Pronunciation of Arabic Names and Terms in the Greek Petra, Nessana, Qurra and Senouthios Letters (Six to Eight Centuries ce)," *MLR* 22 (2015): 1–81; Ahmad al-Jallad, "The Arabic of the Islamic Conquests: Notes on Phonology and Morphology based on the Greek Transcriptions of the First Islamic Century," *BSOAS* 80.3 (2017): 419–39. On the terms *maḥmūd*, *aḥmad*, and *muḥammad*, see Chapter 5.

45 A scenario that was far from being completely new, as the region had long been under Arab rule in the service of Byzantium; see Greg Fisher, *Between Empires: Arabs, Romans, and Sasanians in Late Antiquity* (Oxford and New York: Oxford University Press, 2011). This may also contribute to explain the continuity in the archaeological record, on which see Gideon Avni, *The Byzantine–Islamic Transition in Palestine: An Archaeological Approach* (OSB; Oxford and New York: Oxford University Press, 2014).

46 If they were not initially encouraged by the Byzantines, and/or their Arab allies, to take control of some areas of the Fertile Crescent against the Persian advance in the region, that is; see in this respect Michael Lecker, "Were the Ghassānids and the Byzantines behind Muḥammad's Hijra," in *Les Jafnides. Des rois arabes au service de Byzance (VIe siècle de l'ère chrétienne) – Actes du colloque de Paris, 24–25 novembre 2008*, ed. Denis Genequand and Christian Julien Robin (OM 17; Paris: de Boccard, 2015) 277–93; Daniel A. Beck, *Evolution of the Early Qur'ān: From Anonymous Apocalypse to Charismatic Prophet* (ACDE 2; New York and Bern: Peter Lang, 2018) 1–78. On the possibility of a gradual Byzantine withdrawal from Syria-Palestine, see Yehuda D. Nevo and Judith Koren, *Crossroads to Islam: The Origins of the Arab Religion and the Arab State* (Amherst, NY: Prometheus Books, 2003). On the increasing importance of the Christian population for the Arab takeover of Syria-Palestine, Hoyland, *In God's Path*, 58.

often alter the meaning of the originally anti-Jewish texts into which they were introduced. An example of this kind is Q 5:51:

يَا أَيُّهَا الَّذِينَ آمَنُوا لَا تَتَّخِذُوا الْيَهُودَ وَالنَّصَارَىٰ أَوْلِيَاءَ ۘ بَعْضُهُمْ أَوْلِيَاءُ بَعْضٍ ۚ وَمَنْ يَتَوَلَّهُمْ مِنْكُمْ فَإِنَّهُ
مِنْهُمْ ۗ إِنَّ اللَّهَ لَا يَهْدِي الْقَوْمَ الظَّالِمِينَ 5:51

5:51 Believers! Do not take the Jews *and the Christians* as allies; they are one another's allies. Whoever takes them as allies becomes one of them; and God does not guide the evildoers.

Cf. 5:78 above and 82:

لَتَجِدَنَّ أَشَدَّ النَّاسِ عَدَاوَةً لِلَّذِينَ آمَنُوا الْيَهُودَ وَالَّذِينَ أَشْرَكُوا ۖ وَلَتَجِدَنَّ أَقْرَبَهُمْ مَوَدَّةً لِلَّذِينَ آمَنُوا الَّذِينَ
قَالُوا إِنَّا نَصَارَىٰ ۚ ذَٰلِكَ بِأَنَّ مِنْهُمْ قِسِّيسِينَ وَرُهْبَانًا وَأَنَّهُمْ لَا يَسْتَكْبِرُونَ 5:82

5:82 Surely you will find the Jews and the idolaters[47] to be the strongest enemies of the believers.[48] And surely [too] you will find that those who say "We are Christians" are the closest ones in affection to the believers, because there are priests and bishops among them and because they are not arrogant.

It is Q 5:78, 82, plus the Jesus narratives in *sūra*-s 3, 4, 5 and 19 (which often intertwine with the defence of Jesus's mother), as well as the hypothetical *Vorlage* of 5:51 ("Believers! Do not take the Jews as allies; they are one another's allies. Whoever takes them as allies is already one of them. And God does not guide the evildoers") that in my view contain the key to decipher the ideological climate of the years prior to 'Abd al-Malik's "reform" – which was actually much more than just a reform, since it happened to lay the *foundations* of Islam as a new political-religious *entity* in the late-antique Near East.[49] The positive reference to the bishops in 5:82, which would have been entirely unimaginable in the earliest quranic milieu,[50] is, to my mind, quite telling in this respect. As for the Adamic Christology arguably hinted at in Q 15:29; 21:91; 38:72; 66:12, it shows how inclined indeed some quranic authors living in the time of the Arab overtake of the

47 In allusion to the Jews themselves on account on their alleged past transgressions as described e.g. in Q 2:51, 54? On the notion of "idolatry" in the Qur'ān, see further Gerald R. Hawting, *The Idea of Idolatry and the Emergence of Islam: From Polemic to History* (Cambridge and New York: Cambridge University Press, 1999).

48 See also the comments on Q 9:31 in the next chapter.

49 On 'Abd al-Malik see Robinson, *'Abd al-Malik*. See also Segovia, "Identity Politics and Scholarship in the Study of Islamic Origins," and the Afterword to the present book.

50 See once more the next chapter.

Syria-Palestine and Iraq were to certain Christological views, even if they subtly adapted such views to their own particular mindset, which remained faithful to the major conviction of the earliest quranic theology – for which no human being could be appointed as God's son. It is therefore tempting to read their texts as their response to several anti-Christian Jewish writings circulating in the mid-7th-century Near East.

The P1 Jesus Passages as a Response to mid-7th-century Jewish Writings like *Sēfer Zərubbābel* and *Sēfer Tôlədôt Yēšû*?

The Qurān's vindication of Jesus basically focusses on three main themes: his conception and birth (in 3:45–9; 4:156; 19:16–33; 21:91; 66:12), his mission and deeds (in 2:87, 136, 253; 3:48–53, 84; 4:155, 163; 5:46, 78, 110–15; 6:85; 23:50; 33:7–8; 42:13; 43:57–64; 57:27; 61:6, 14), and his death and heavenly ascension (in 3:54–5, 4:157–9).[51] The ways in which such vindication is undertaken by the quranic authors vary from one passage to another, however; especially in the two first cases. Thus, for instance, in 2:87, 253 and 5:110 he is said to have the support of the Holy Spirit, while in 3:50 and again 5:110 he is additionally said to act with God's permission; both arguments attempt at legitimising his activity, but they are different from one another. Likewise, in 3:42–9 and 19:16–33 it is the defence of Mary's virginal conception, and hence the defence of Jesus's virginal birth, that is at stake, but whereas in 3:47 an angel explains to Mary that God can create a person by merely calling her into existence, the author of 19:24–6, 30–3 originally had Jesus himself comforting his mother and then made him defend her too against her accusers. Conversely, the vindication of Jesus's ascension to God is more uniform throughout the corpus (cf. 3:54–5, 4:157–9).

At some point, nevertheless, some quranic authors aimed at additionally defending Jesus in an altogether different way: by portraying him as a New Adam. In early Christian thought, sin had entered the history of mankind through the deeds of a single man: Adam, and therefore mankind could only be effectively redeemed from its sin through the deeds of another man, a New or Second

---

51 Notice, in contrast, that only 6 passages (4:171–2; 5:17, 72–5, 116–8; 9:30–1; 19:34–6) go against the belief on Jesus's divinity, thus witnessing to the discussion of mainstream Christian theology. Again, on my reading such passages re-instantiate an opposition already found in the earliest quranic layers, but which did not aim yet in these at the creation of a new religious identity – its purpose, instead, was to open a gap in a peripheral Christian world against the consolidation of a particular political-religious tendency (see the next Chapter).

Adam who could help mankind to restore its heavenly condition: Jesus-Christ.[52] Although the quranic authors of the mid-7th century refused to incorporate the soteriology inherent in this dual anthropological construct – perhaps they did not want to betray their predecessors, who a generation before them had not granted Jesus any particular role in the history of salvation, but polemicised instead against the soteriological prerogatives of the Christian authorities who had pledge to the decisions of the council of Chalcedon[53] – they sought to vindicate Jesus against his critics – the Jews – by comparing him to Adam, into whom God had breathed from his own Spirit (cf. 15:29; 38:72 and 21:91; 66:12). And in this they went further than the statement made in 3:59 apropos God's creation of Jesus by simply ordering him to be; for Adam's other most salient trait (namely, his superiority vis-à-vis the angels) can then be applied to Jesus as well. But let us take a closer look at the relevant passages.

Adam is mentioned in eighteen quranic pericopes: 2:30–9; 3:33–58; 6:95–9; 7:11–18, 26–30, 31–4, 35–53, 160–76, 189–90; 15:26–42; 17:61–5, 66–70; 18:45–50; 19:58–63; 20:115–23; 36:60–83; 38:67–88; 39:5–6.[54] The various themes evoked in them are Adam's creation,[55] Adam's fall,[56] Satan's punishment,[57] Adam's two sons Cain and Abel,[58] God's covenant with the sons of Adam,[59] and the comparison of

52 On the Pauline beginnings of this Adamic Christology, see James D. G. Dunn, *Christology in the Making: A New Testament Inquiry into the Origins of there Doctrine of the Incarnation* (2nd ed.; Grand Rapids, MI, and Cambridge, 1989) 98–128. On its Jewish roots, Crispin H. T. Fletcher-Louis, *All the Glory of Adam: Liturgical Anthropology in the Dead Sea Scrolls* (STDJ 42; Leiden and Boston: Brill, 2002); Nicholas A. Meyer, *Adam's Dust and Adam's Glory in the Hodayot and the Letters of Paul: Rethinking Anthropogony and Theology* (SNT 168; Leiden and Boston: Brill, 2016).

53 See chapters 4 and 5 below.

54 For a comprehensive picture of the quranic Adam, see J. Frederic McCurdy, Kaufmann Kohler, and Richard Gottheil, "Adam," in *The Jewish Encyclopedia*, ed. Isidore Singer et al. (12 vols.; New York: Funk and Wagnalls, 1906–12) 1:177–8; Cornelia Schöck, "Adam and Eve," in *Encyclopaedia of the Qur'ān*, ed. Jane Dammen McAuliffe (6 vols.; Leiden and Boston: Brill, 2001–6) 1:22–6, who, unfortunately, relies almost exclusively on the Islamic tradition when interpreting the Qur'ān, what leads her to systematically overlook the latter's biblical- and parabiblical subtexts; Roberto Tottoli, *Biblical Prophets in the Qur'ān and Muslim Literature*, trans. Michael Robertson (London and New York: Routledge, 2002) 18–20; Brannon Wheeler, "Adam," in *The Qur'an: An Encyclopedia*, ed. Oliver Leaman (London and New York: Routledge, 2006) 11–12; Morgan Guiraud, "Adam," in *Dictionnaire du Coran*, ed. Amir-Moezzi, 22–26.

55 In 7 narratives and a few isolated verses: $N1_1$ = Q 2:30–4; $N1_2$ = Q 7:11; $N1_3$ = Q 15:26–31; $N1_4$ = Q 17:61; $N1_5$ = Q 18:50; $N1_6$ = Q 20:115–16; $N1_7$ = Q 38:71–6 + Q 3:59; 6:98; 7:189–90; 39:6.

56 In 2 narratives: $N2_1$ = Q 2:35–9; $N2_2$ = Q 20:117–22.

57 In 4 narratives: $N3_1$ = Q 7:13–18; $N3_2$ = Q 15:32–42; $N3_3$ = Q 17:62–5; $N3_4$ = Q 38:77–85.

58 In a single narrative: N4 = Q 5:27–32.

59 In Q 3:33; 7:26–7, 31, 35, 172; 17:70; 19:58; 36:60–1.

Jesus with Adam.[60] Some details about the narratives on Adam's creation and fall, Satan's punishment, and their interwoven thematic segments are needed here:

- Vv. 30–9 in *Sūrat al-Baqara* (Q 2, "The Cow") combine two distinct narratives: one relative to Adam's creation ($N1_1$), comprising five verses (vv. 30–4) and eleven thematic segments (*B-M*); another one relative to Adam's fall ($N2_1$), comprising too five verses (vv. 35–9) but only seven thematic segments (*N-T*).[61] The events are presented thus: ($N1_1$) (*B*)[62] God informs the angels of his decision to appoint Adam as his representative on earth (v. 30). (*Γ*) The angels protest agains this decision (v. 30). (*Δ*) God accuses them of being ignorant (v. 30). (*E*) He teaches Adam the names of all things (v. 31) and then (*Z*) asks the angels about these (v. 31). (*H*) The angels admit their ignorance (v. 32). (*Θ*) God asks Adam to inform the angels of the names of all things (v. 33) and then (*I*) boasts himself of his wisdom before the angels (v. 33) (*K*) ordering them to worship Adam (v. 34). (*Λ*) They all do so, (*M*) save Iblīs who rebels (v. 34). ($N2_1$) (*N*) God allows Adam and his wife to inhabit the Garden (v. 35) but (*Ξ*) recommends them not to eat from one of its trees, for otherwise – he warns them – they will be among the evildoers (v. 35). (*O*) Satan (Arab. al-Šayṭān) makes them sin (v. 36) and (*Π*) God expels them from the Garden (v. 36). (*P*) Adam repents (v. 37), for God is merciful (v. 37). Then (*Σ*) God asks them to abandon the Garden but (*T*) announces that he will send a guide to mankind and that whoever follows it will not sorrow (v. 38), whereas those who deny God's signs will be severely punished in the afterlife (v. 39).[63]
- In contrast, vv. 11–18 in *Sūrat al-Aʿrāf* (Q 7, "The Heights") present a single narrative that, after mentioning ($N1_2$) (*A*) Adam's creation (v. 11), as well as (*K*) God's command to the angels (v. 11) which (*Λ*) they obey (v. 11), focusses instead on (*M*) Iblīs's rebellion (vv. 11–12) and (*Y*) his expulsion from the

60 In Q 3:59.

61 The names given to Satan in vv. 34 (إبليس Iblīs) and 36 (الشّيطان al-Šayṭān) are clear markers of these two narratives. On the term al-Šayṭān and its plausible Ethiopic background, see Manfred Kropp, "Der äthiopische Satan = *šayṭān* und seine koranischen Ausläufer; mit einer Bemerkung über verbales Steinigen," *OC* 89 (1995): 93–102; idem, "Beyond Single Words: Mā'ida – Shayṭān – jibt and ṭāghūt. Mechanisms of transmission into the Ethiopic (Gəʿəz) Bible and the Qur'ānic text," in *The Qur'ān in Its Historical Context*, ed. Gabriel Said Reynolds (RSQ; London and New York: Routledge, 2008) 204–16. Cf. Luxenberg, *The Syro-Aramaic Reading of the Koran*, 100–4, who argues instead that al-Šayṭān is a Syriac loanword. As for the name Iblīs, it draws on the Gk. διάβολος *diabolos* (likely through the Syriac ܕܝܒܠܘܣ *dīblūs* or ܕܝܐܒܘܠܘܣ *diyābūlūs*), which is frequently used in the Septuagint to translate the Heb. שָׂטָן *šāṭān* ("accuser"); cf. too Matthew 4:1 (see further Droge, *The Qur'ān*, 5, n.44).

62 Cf. *A* in Q 7:11; 15:26–9; 17:61; 38:71–2.

63 Cf. the theme of God's covenant with, and reiterated warnings to, the sons of Adam.

Garden (vv. 13–18) – hence on a third narrative ($N3_1$) in which, moreover, (*Φ*) Iblīs asks God to allow him time until the day of resurrection to chase men, lead them astray, and thereby prove that he is right in his mistrust (vv. 14–17), to which (*χ*) God in turn responds that in due time he will punish both Iblīs and his followers (v. 17).[64]

- Vv. 26–42 in *Sūrat al-Ḥiğr* (Q 15) merge N1 and N3, i.e. the story of Adam's creation (vv. 26–30) and that of Iblīs's rebellion (vv. 31–42): ($N1_3$) (*A*) God creates Adam (v. 26–9) and (*K*) commands the angels to worship him (v. 29), which (*Λ*) they do (v. 30) – all (*μ*) except Iblīs (v. 31). ($N3_2$) Then (*Φ*) Iblīs and God argue (vv. 32–42) like in Q 7:14–17, although the wording differs from one account to another; besides, in this case (*Ψ*) God responds to Iblīs that he will have no power whatsoever upon his faithful servants (vv. 41–2).
- Vv. 61–5 in *Sūrat al-Isrā'* (Q 17, "The Journey") mirror 15:26–42, as it comprises (again) segments *A* (v. 61), *K* (v. 61), *Λ* (v. 61), *M* (v. 61), *Φ* (vv. 62–5), and *Ψ* (vv. 63–5) – put differently, it consists of $N1_4$ + $N3_3$.
- V. 50 in *Sūrat al-Kahf* (Q 18, "The Cave") ($N1_5$) contains segments *K*, *Λ*, and *M*, and then displays a warning similar (albeit not identical) to that in Q 2:38–9, which may thus be labeled *T*'.
- Vv. 115–23 in *Sūrat Ṭā' Hā'* (Q 20) ($N1_6$ + $N2_2$) opens with an allusion to (*B*') God's covenant with Adam (v. 115) and then includes segments *K* (v. 116), *Λ* (v. 116), *M* (v. 116), (*Ξ*') God's warning to Adam and his wife concerning Iblīs (vv. 117–19) and (*O*') their transgression (vv. 120–1), (*P*') God's forgiving mercy towards Adam (v. 122), which does not prevent him from (*Σ*) expelling him and Eve from the Garden (v. 122), and (*T*'') God's instruction to mankind (v. 123).
- Lastly vv. 71–85 in *Sūrat Ṣād* (Q 38) ($N1_7$ + $N3_4$) reworks segments *A*/*B* (as in vv. 71–2 God announces the creation of Adam to the angels), *K* (v. 72), *Λ* (v. 73), *M* (v. 74–6), *Υ* (v. 77–8), *Φ* (vv. 79–83), and *X* (vv. 84–5).

The motif of the angels worshiping (literally, bowing down to) Adam, which is found in all N1 versions (cf. 2:34; 7:11; 15:29–30; 17:61; 18:50; 20:116; 38:72–3), is particularly interesting. First, it lacks – like God's covenant with Adam (in 20:115), Adam's repentance (in 2:37), and Satan's punishment (in 7:13–18; 15:32–42;

64 On Iblīs's portrayal and role in the Qur'ān, see Ida Zilio-Grandi, "Satan," in *Dictionnaire du Coran*, ed. Mohammad Ali Amir-Moezzi (Paris:Laffont, 2007) 790–3. See also Luxenberg's comparative analysis of *Sūrat al-Kawṯar* (Q 108) and 1 Peter 5:8–9 in *The Syro-Aramaic Reading of the Koran*, 292–300. On the Iblīs/al-Šayṭān (i.e. on N3), Karl-Friedrich Pohlmann, *Die Entstehung des Korans: Neue Erkenntnisse aus Sicht der historisch-kritischen Bibelwissenschaft* (3rd ed.; Darmstadt: WBG, 2015) 85–153.

17:62–5; 38:77–85) – any parallel in the biblical text.[65] Secondly, it is presented in the aforementioned quranic narratives in three different ways: (I) following Adam's instruction (in 2:34), (II) following God's breathing of his own spirit into Adam (in 15:29; 38:72), or (III) without any further qualification (in all other cases).

The most extensive study on the subject is Gabriel Reynolds's in his book *The Qur'ān and Its Biblical Subtext*.[66] "In part the Qur'ān uses this account as an etiology, to explain the devil's fall from heaven. Yet it also uses this account to make an anthropological point, to illustrate the high station of Adam, and thereby humanity," writes Reynolds.[67] Indeed. Still, I think there is something more in these narratives. But before pointing it out I should like to comment on the possible textual sources of the quranic motif of the angels worshiping Adam.

Abraham Geiger was in 1833 the first author to notice that the quranic motif of the angels bowing to Adam is reminiscent of two parabiblical, apocryphal writings: the *Life of Adam and Eve* (henceforth *LAE*) and the *Cave of Treasures* (*CT*).[68] The former is a 2nd–4th-century CE pseudepigraphical work inspired by Genesis 3, of which 2 different source versions are known to us: Greek and Latin, both combining testamentary and apocalyptic traits. The (shorter) Greek version recounts Adam's and Eve's death and burial; its author presents their mortal condition as an outcome of their sin but expresses faith in their resurrection. In addition, the Latin version narrates Adam's heavenly ascent and eschatological instructions to his son Seth. Similarities between *LAE* and several 1st-century Jewish writings like 4 Ezra and 2 Baruch, plus the lack of Christian soteriological elements in it, point to a plausible Jewish origin, although it was copied and preserved by Christian scribes in Greek, Latin, Slavonic, Armenian, and Georgian.[69] In turn, *CT* is

---

65 On Satan's punishment and Adam's repentance, see further Michael E. Stone, "The Fall of Satan and Adam's Penance: Three Notes on *The Books of Adam and Eve*," in *Literature on Adam and Eve: Collected Essays*, ed. Gary A. Anderson, Michael E. Stone, Johannes Tromp (SVTP 15; Leiden and Boston: Brill, 2000) 43–56; Gary A. Anderson, "The Exaltation of Adam and the Fall of Satan," in *ibid.*, 83–110.

66 Gabriel Said Reynolds, "Qur'ānic Case Studies [no.] 1: The prostration of the angels," in *The Qur'ān and Its Biblical Subtext* (RSQ; London and New York: Routledge, 2010) 39–54. Prior to Reynold's, the only relatively extensive study was that of Samuel M. Zwemer, "The Worship of Adam by Angels," *MW* 27 (1937): 115–27.

67 Reynolds, *The Qur'ān and Its Biblical Subtext*, 39.

68 Abraham Geiger, *Was hat Mohammed aus dem Judenthume aufgenommen?* (Bonn: Baaden, 1833); English translation by F. M. Young, *Judaism and Islam: A Prize Essay* (Madras: MDCSPCK Press, 1898) 77–8.

69 See Michael E. Stone, *A History of the Literature of Adam and Eve* (SBLEJL 3; Atlanta, GA: Scholars Press, 1992); Marinus de Jong and Johannes Tromp, *The Life of Adam and Eve and Related Literature* (Sheffield, UK: Sheffield Academic Press, 1997); Michael E. Stone and Gary A. Anderson, *A Synopsis of the Books of Adam and Eve* (SBLEJL 17; 2nd revised ed.; Atlanta, GA:

> "[a] popular and influential Syriac Christian retelling of Salvation history from Creation to Pentecost [that] describes Adam and Eve taking shelter in the eponymous cave after being driven from Eden, and adorning it with gold, myrrh and incense taken from the fringes of paradise. Part dwelling, part house of prayer, part tomb, the cave functions as a sacred place until the flood, when the relics and treasures gathered inside are taken into the ark. (Later the Magi present these treasures to the infant Jesus.) Adam's bones are buried at Golgotha, which is at the centre of the earth. It is at this spot where ... Abraham lays his son upon the altar and Jesus is crucified."[70]

Unlike *LAE*, *CT* "draws on earlier Jewish *and* Christian traditions. It reached its final form in the sixth century, and was transmitted in distinctive East and West Syriac recensions ... [though] translations survive in Coptic, Georgian, Arabic and Ethiopic."[71]

Various others authors have also underlined this twofold textual dependence.[72] Yet they seem to overlook one of the most salient features that diverges from one text to another: In *LAE* 13:2–14:2 God creates Adam in his likeness and, after breathing into him the breath of life, asks Michael to command the other angels to bow down to Adam. Conversely, in *CT* 2:10–24 God creates Adam in his likeness, but does not command the angels to bow down to him. Several creatures bow down to Adam when they hear him pronounce their names.[73] Then the

---

Scholars Press, 1999); Daphna Arbel, Robert J. Cousland, and Dietmar Neufeld, *And So They Went Out: The Lives of Adam and Eve as Cultural Transformative Story* (London and New York: T&T Clark, 2010).

70 Kristian Heal, "Cave of Treasures," in *The Routledge Encyclopedia of Ancient Mediterranean Religions*, ed. Eric Orlin, Lisbeth S. Fried, Jennifer Wright Knust, Michael L. Satlow, and Michael E. Pregill (London and New York: Routledge, 2015) 172.

71 Heal, "Cave of Treasures," 172 (my emphasis).

72 Including Heinrich Speyer in 1931, Samuel Zwemer in 1937, and Hartwig Hirschfeld in 1939; see the references provided in Tottoli, *Biblical Prophets in the Qur'ān and Muslim Literature*, 51 n.6. See also Reynolds, *The Qur'ān and Its Biblical Subtext*, 46–54; Droge, *The Qur'ān*, 5 n.43.

73 A third variant is given in the Coptic *Enthronement of Michael*, in which God commands Satan, therein depicted as the first-born, to venerate Adam (see Anderson, "The Exaltation of Adam and the Fall of Satan," 85–6). Jewish Rabbinic sources are, in contrast, less prone to expand on this motif – if they ever mention it, that is. Thus, whereas in *b. Sanhedrîn* 59b the angels prepare meat and wine for Adam, in *Genesis Rabba* 8:10, when they are about to worship Adam upon seeing his splendour, God shows them that he is just a man; and in *Pirqê de Rabbî 'Elî'ezer* (hereinafter *PRE*) 2, when all creatures bow down to Adam he asks them to bow with him to God instead. Yet *PRE* and the *Chronicles of Jerahmeel* present an intriguing parallel to Q 2:31–3, where Adam is able to name all creatures, while the angels are not. Besides, as noted by Reynolds (*The Qur'ān and Its Biblical Subtext*, 47) the angels' initial protest against God's creation of Adam is a typical Jewish exegetical motif resulting from the juxtaposition of Genesis 1:26–7 and Psalm 8:4 (see *b. Sanhedrîn* 38b).

angels bow down to him too when they hear God proclaim (about Adam): "I have made you king ... and I have made you ruler over all which I have created." Now, this difference is exactly the same one that we find between Q 15:29 and 38:72, on the one hand, and, on the other hand, Q 2:33–4, which read:

فَإِذَا سَوَّيْتُهُ وَنَفَخْتُ فِيهِ مِنْ رُوحِي فَقَعُوا لَهُ سَاجِدِينَ

When I have fashioned him and breathed into him of my spirit, bow down to him! (15:29; 38:72)

قَالَ يَا آدَمُ أَنْبِئْهُمْ بِأَسْمَائِهِمْ ؕ فَلَمَّا أَنْبَأَهُمْ بِأَسْمَائِهِمْ قَالَ أَلَمْ أَقُلْ لَكُمْ إِنِّي أَعْلَمُ غَيْبَ السَّمَاوَاتِ وَالْأَرْضِ
وَأَعْلَمُ مَا تُبْدُونَ وَمَا كُنْتُمْ تَكْتُمُونَ ❖ وَإِذْ قُلْنَا لِلْمَلَائِكَةِ اسْجُدُوا لِآدَمَ فَسَجَدُوا إِلَّا إِبْلِيسَ أَبَىٰ وَاسْتَكْبَرَ
وَكَانَ مِنَ الْكَافِرِينَ

(2:33) He said, "Adam, inform them of their names!" And when he had informed them of their names, He said, "Did not I tell you, 'I certainly know [the] unseen [things] on heaven and earth?' I know what you reveal and what you hide. (34) And [remember] when we said to the angels, "Bow down to Adam!," and they bowed, save Iblīs. He refused out of pride and became one of the disbelievers.

It is wrong to claim, therefore, that the quranic Adam story is closer to the narrative found in the *CT* than to that contained in *LAE*.[74] It all depends on the specific quranic narrative one takes into consideration ($N1_1$ or $N1_3$/$N1_7$, respectively).[75]

Yet there were arguably other writings also known to the quranic authors – writings which they presumably used too to elaborate a different narrative (N4) which is intimately connected to $N1_3$/$N1_7$, but not to $N1_1$. For, as Reynolds aptly observes,[76] the wording in Q 15:29 and 38:72 is reproduced almost verbatim in two other quranic passages, namely 21:91 and 66:12:

وَالَّتِي أَحْصَنَتْ فَرْجَهَا فَنَفَخْنَا فِيهَا مِنْ رُوحِنَا وَجَعَلْنَاهَا وَابْنَهَا آيَةً لِلْعَالَمِينَ

And she [= Mary] who guarded her private chastity – we breathed into her of our spirit, and made her and her son a sign for all men. (21:91)

---

74 *Pace* Reynolds, *The Qur'ān and Its Biblical Subtext*, 49.
75 In my opinion, it is clear too that *CT* strongly influenced Ibn Isḥāq's work, which Ibn Hišām would later transform into Muḥammad's "biography" but originally amounted, first and foremost, to an ambitious rewriting of the biblical *Heilsgeschichte* from the perspective of the new Arabian prophet understood as a substitute for Jesus and identified with the "receiver" of the quranic revelation. See Gordon Darnell Newby, *The Making of the Last prophet: A Reconstruction of the Earliest Biography of Muhammad* (Columbia: University of South Carolina Press, 1989).
76 Reynolds, *The Qur'ān and Its Biblical Subtext*, 53.

وَمَرْيَمَ ابْنَتَ عِمْرَانَ الَّتِي أَحْصَنَتْ فَرْجَهَا فَنَفَخْنَا فِيهِ مِنْ رُوحِنَا وَصَدَّقَتْ بِكَلِمَاتِ رَبِّهَا وَكُتُبِهِ وَكَانَتْ مِنَ الْقَانِتِينَ

> And Mary, daughter of ʿImrān, who guarded her chastity – we breathed into him of our spirit, and she accepted the words of her Lord and his writings, and became one of the obedient. (66:12)

Yet Reynolds skips over the odd morphology in 66:12: فيه *fīhi* ("into *him*," ه *-hi* being a 3rd-person-singular masculine pronoun) instead of فيها *fīhā* ("into *her*" like in Q 21:91, which displays the 3rd-person-singular feminine pronoun هَا *-hā*).[77] Droge, in contrast, correctly perceives such feature to be of significance: "*fīhi* could refer to Jesus,"[78] which is actually very plausible given 4:171 ("... the Messiah, Jesus son of Mary, is God's messenger and his Word, which he conveyed to Mary, and a spirit from him ... ") and 19:17 ("... we sent to her our Spirit which assumed for her the likeness of a man ... ").[79]

Moreover, 3:59 draws, as Reynolds notices too,[80] an explicit analogy between Adam and Jesus:

إِنَّ مَثَلَ عِيسَىٰ عِنْدَ اللَّهِ كَمَثَلِ آدَمَ ۖ خَلَقَهُ مِنْ تُرَابٍ ثُمَّ قَالَ لَهُ كُنْ فَيَكُونُ

> Indeed, the appearance of Jesus before God is like the appearance of Adam, whom he created from the dust. He said to him, "Be!," and he became.

This verse, in turn, echoes the wording displayed in 3:47, where Mary questions her pregnancy and capacity to give birth and is comforted by Gabriel:

قَالَتْ رَبِّ أَنَّىٰ يَكُونُ لِي وَلَدٌ وَلَمْ يَمْسَسْنِي بَشَرٌ ۖ قَالَ كَذَٰلِكِ اللَّهُ يَخْلُقُ مَا يَشَاءُ ۚ إِذَا قَضَىٰ أَمْرًا فَإِنَّمَا يَقُولُ لَهُ كُنْ فَيَكُونُ

---

77 Interestingly, pronouns shift too (from feminine plural to masculine plural) in 2:31:

وَعَلَّمَ آدَمَ الْأَسْمَاءَ كُلَّهَا ثُمَّ عَرَضَهُمْ عَلَى الْمَلَائِكَةِ فَقَالَ أَنْبِئُونِي بِأَسْمَاءِ هَٰؤُلَاءِ إِنْ كُنْتُمْ صَادِقِينَ

> And he taught Adam the names – all of them (*kullahā*). Then he presented them (*ʿaraḍa-hum)* to the angels and said, "Inform me of the names of these, if you are truthful."

78 Droge, *The Qurʾān*, 393 n.25.

79 See once more Droge, *The Qurʾān*, 393 n.25. Cf. Luke 1:35. Pretending that in 19:17 that which assumes the likeness of a man is an angel, makes little sense, therefore.

80 Reynolds, *The Qurʾān and Its Biblical Subtext*, 52–4.

> She said, "My Lord, how shall I have a child, when no man has touched me?" He said, "Thus: God creates whatever he wills. When he decrees something, he simply says to it, 'Be!,' and it becomes."

Traditionally, 3:59 is interpreted (in accordance with 2:116; 3:79–80; 4:171–2; 5:17, 72–5, 116–17; 6:101; 9:30–1; 10:68; 17:111; 18:4, 102; 19:35, 88–94; 23:91; 39:4; 43:81; 72:3; 112) as a denial of Jesus's divine status – i.e. as meaning "the likeness of Jesus with God is like that of Adam," etc. But this verse can be also interpreted as displaying an anti-Jewish argument in an attempt to counter Jewish suspicions of, and accusations against, Mary's miraculous conception.[81] Now, if the latter view is correct – and hence of 15:29; 38:72 and 21:91; 66:12, with their similar treatment of Adam and Jesus, are somehow related – then one may inquire[82] whether Hebrews 1:6 and Jacob of Serugh's *Homilies against the Jews* (notice the title!) were also known to the authors of 15:29; 21:91; 38:72; and 66:12, since those writings abound in the specific symbolic correlation of Adam and Jesus echoed in the Qur'ān.[83]

---

81 Reynolds, *The Qur'ān and Its Biblical Subtext*, 53–4. Cf. 4:156 and Mary's defence in 19:16–33, of which 3:42–57 represents but a textual variant. See in this respect Luxenberg, *The Syro-Aramaic Reading of the Koran*, 127–42. See also Guillaume Dye, "The Qur'ān and Its Hypertextuality in Light of Redaction Criticism," paper presented at the 1st Nangeroni Meeting of the Early Islamic Studies Seminar, Milan, June 15–19, 2015, forthcoming in *Early Islam: The Sectarian Milieu of Late Antiquity*, ed. Guillaume Dye (LAMINE; Chicago: Chicago Oriental Institute, 2017), who persuasively makes the case for a Palestinian background. As for the timeframe in which such accusations might have taken place (perhaps during Phocas's [602–10] or, alternatively, Heraclius's [610–41] reign?), see the overall picture provided above and my upcoming paper "Friends, Enemies, or Hoped-for New Rulers? Reassessing the Early Jewish Sources Mentioning the Rise of Islam," forthcoming in *Jews and Judaism in Northern Arabia*, ed. Haggai Mazuz (BRLJ; Leiden and Boston: Brill).

82 As Reynolds insightfully does (*The Qur'ān and Its Biblical Subtext*, 48–50, 52).

83 See Jacob of Serugh, *Homilies against the Jews*, *PO* 174; Reynolds, *The Qur'ān and Its Biblical Subtext*, 53, provides a fair English trans. of the relevant verses and a few pertinent cross-references, including Philippians 2:10, Origen's *Homilies on Genesis and Exodus* 12, and Tertullian's *De Resurrectione Carnis* 6. A Syrian background for these exchanges remains the most plausible hypothesis, though. "It is something of a truism among scholars of Syriac," writes Sidney Griffith, "to say that the more deeply one is familiar with the works of the major writers of the classical period, especially the composers of liturgically significant, homiletic texts such as those written by Ephraem the Syrian (c. 306–73), Narsai of Edessa and Nisibis (c. 399–502), or Jacob of Serugh (c. 451–521), the more one hears echoes of many of the standard themes and characteristic turns of phrase at various points in the discourse of the Arabic Qur'ān" (Sidney H. Griffith, "Christian Lore and the Arabic Qur'ān: The 'Companions of the Cave' in *Sūrat al-Kahf* and in Syriac Christian Tradition," in *The Qur'ān in Its Historical Context*, ed. Reynolds, 109–37, p. 109). See also Alphonse Mingana, "Syriac Influence on the Style of the Ḳur'ān," *BJRL* 11 (1927): 77–98; JohnBowman, "The Debt of Islam to Monophysite Syrian Christianity," *NTT* 19

Whatever the case, the Adamic-Christian overtones in 15:29; 21:91; 38:72; and 66:12 depart from the innovative theology of the early quranic authors.[84] That is to say, they represent a new concern for highlighting Jesus's more-than-respectable status. Arguably they can be deemed the product (drawing perhaps on 19:17?) of the *contact* with mid-7th-century Palestine Christianity *contra* Jewish accusations against Jesus.

In fact, as David Olster writes, "[t]he Arab invasions inspired the Christians to write anti-Jewish texts [just as much as] they inspired the Jews to write anti-Christian texts."[85] The Palestinian Jewish apocalypse of the first quarter of the 7th century known as *Sēfer Zərubbābel*, whose author describes the Anti-Christ *'Armîlûs* – whom he moreover identifies with Heraclius – as born from the sexual intercourse between Satan and a statue of Mary, is an eloquent sample of the later category.[86] Similarly, the *Sēfer Tôlədôt Yēšû*, likely written too in 7th-century Palestine, polemicises *inter alia* against the specific aspects of Jesus's life (roughly his birth, activity, and death) whose defence the quranic authors

(1964–5):177–201; Gunther Lüling, *Über den Ur-Qur'ān: Ansätze zur Rekonstruktion vorislamischer christlicher Strophenlieder im Qur'ān* (Erlangen: Lüling, 1974); Luxenberg, *The Syro-Aramaic Reading of the Koran*; Claude Gilliot "Reconsidering the Authorship of the Qur'ān: Is the Qur'ān Partly the Fruit of a Progressive and Collective Work," in *The Qur'ān in Its Historical Context*, ed. Reynolds, 88–108; Karl-Heinz Ohlig and Gerd R. Puin, eds., *The Hidden Origins of Islam: New Research into Its Early History* (Amherst, NY: Prometheus Books, 2010); Joseph Witztum, "Joseph among the Ishmaelites: Q 12 in Light of Syriac Sources," in *New Perspectives on the Qur'ān: The Qur'ān in Its Historical Context 2*, ed. Gabriel Said Reynolds (RSQ; London and New York: Routledge, 2011) 425–48; idem, "The Syriac Milieu of the Qur'*ān: The Recasting of Biblical Narratives,*" PhD dissertation (Princeton University, 2011); El-Badawi, *The Qur'ān and the Aramaic Gospel Traditions*. On the possible use of Jacob's *Homilies* in the quranic narratives, see further Segovia, *The Quranic Noah and the Making of the Islamic Prophet*, 89.

84 See the Chapter 5.

85 David M. Olster, *Roman Defeat, Christian Response, and the Literary Construction of the Jew* (Philadelphia: University of Pennsylvania Press, 2015) 175.

86 See David Biale, "Counter-History and Jewish Polemics against Christianity: The *Sefer Toldot Yeshu* and the *Sefer Zerubavel*," *JSS* 6 (1999): 130–45; Alexei Sivertsev, *Judaism and Imperial Ideology in Late Antiquity* (Cambridge and New York: Cambridge University Press, 2011) 155. See also John C. Reeves, "Sefer Zerubbabel: The prophetic Vision of Zerubbabel ben Shealtiel," in *Old Testament Pseudepigrapha: More Noncanonical Scriptures*, ed. Richard Bauckham, James R. Davila, and Alexander Payanotov (Grand Rapids, MI, and Cambridge: Eerdmans, 2013) 448–66. On Heraclius possible defence in the Qur'ān, Glen W. Bowersock,*Empires in Collision in Late Antiquity* (Waltham, MA: Brandeis University Press and Historical Society of Israel, 2012) 56, 60–4. See also Kevin van Bladel, "The Alexander Legend in the Qur'ān 18:83–102," in *The Qur'ān in Its Historical Context*, ed. Reynolds, 175–203;Tommaso Tesei, "The Prophecy of Ḏū-l-Qarnayn and the Origins of the Qur'ānic Corpus," *MA* (2013–14): 273–90; and n.46 above.

recurrently undertake in their writings.[87] All pieces of the puzzle therefore match one another offering the view of an intended rapprochement between the new Arab elite and their new Christian subjects – possibly, again, under Mu'āwiya.

The P2 Jesus Passages and the Making of a New Religious Identity

Conversely, the purpose of 4:171; 5:116–7; 9:30–1; 19:34–6 is to reject Jesus's divinity. In my view, these texts can be tentatively dated to 'Abd al-Malik's time (692–705), which is also the period in which the word "Islam" appears for the first time in an official inscription – namely, the Dome of the Rock in Jerusalem.[88]

Indeed, 4:171 is reproduced verbatim in the Dome of the Rock, whose texts are usually understood to reflect/quote earlier *quranic* formulas. I am not completely against this latter view, but I ultimately find it too speculative, as there simply is no evidence to support the notion that *all* the content of these texts is earlier than the inscriptions – whether we like it or not, the sole evidence we have about some of them is that they are found inside the Dome of the Rock itself. Projecting back onto such inscriptions the idea of a pre-Marwanid Qur'ān (with some perceptible variances in the wording at most) is certainly possible, but there is no proof whatsoever to assist this widespread claim. As Alfred-Louis de Prémare writes,

> A historian studying these texts might envisage three hypotheses concerning the content of the inscriptions ... which have parallels within the Qur'ān:
> 1. the texts were composed directly for the [monument] in question, and were reused later, with some slight modifications, in the final composition of the Qur'ānic text;
> 2. they represent fragments that were scattered, attesting to the existence of a sort of Ur-Qur'ān, still being drafted, selected, and assembled, some of which at the same time could have been used in the inscriptions on the monuments;
> 3. they were actual "quotations" taken from a fully formed Qur'ān that is the one we now have today.

---

87 See again Biale, "Counter-History and Jewish Polemics against Christianity"; Robert E. Van Voorst, *Jesus Outside the New Testament: An Introduction to Ancient Evidence* (Grand Rapids, MI, and Cambridge: Eerdmans, 2000) 122–9; Peter Schäfer, Michael Meerson, and Yaakov Deutsch, eds.,*Toledot Yeshu ("The Life Story of Jesus") Revisited: A Princeton Conference* (TSAJ 143; Tübingen: Mohr Siebeck, 2011); Michael Meerson and Peter Schäfer, in collaboration with Yaakov Deutsch, David Grossberg, Abigail Manekin, and Adina Yoffie, *Toledot Yeshu: The Life Story of Jesus* (2 vols.; TSAJ 159; Tübingen: Mohr Siebeck, 2014).

88 On the Dome of the Rock, see the Afterword.

> ... [N]one of these hypotheses seems sufficient to prevail over the others ... [Yet] it seems to me ... that one can exclude the third [one]. It is in Jerusalem, in any case, in the place that stood as the symbol of eastern Christianity, where the Islamic anti-trinitarian and Christological polemic, as expressed in the inscriptions in the Dome of the Rock, has its true *sitz im leben.*[89]

Thus I take 5:116–7; 19:34–6 to come, too, from this period, in which the making of a new religious identity vis-à-vis Christianity was implemented by the Umayyads in the person of ʿAbd al-Malik b. Marwān. Undeniably, ʿAbd al-Malik 's inscriptions present some rather outstanding rhetorical ambivalences,[90] but his project is visibly uniform in spite of these. If, from the 630s to the early 690s, different Arab leaders had claimed to be heirs to Muḥammad's polity in the Ḥiǧāz, Syria, and Iraq, it is indeed only in the early 690s that a new, unified Arab state with its capital in Syria was fully established at last. Put differently: it was only with ʿAbd al-Malik and that the foundations of an Arab state were laid, which in turn paved the way to the emergence of Islam as a new religion – the official religion of that particular Arab state.

In fact, ʿAbd al-Malik is usually depicted as a reformer. He reformed law, theology, and ritual, as well as the administration and the army. He also transformed the coinage by removing all previous Christian imagery from the coins themselves and by adding on every minted one a formulaic reference to Muḥammad. Likewise, he had numerous milestones incorporating such reference placed all over his kingdom. Furthermore, he rebuilt the Kaʿba and established Mecca, together with Jerusalem, as a compelling religious symbol for all his subjects. He delivered sermons and letters to make his authority all the more effective among them. Most likely, he had the Qur'ān (a collection of writings of miscellaneous nature) collected for the first time and expanded.[91] And last but not least, he had

89 Alfred-Louis de Prémare, "ʿAbd al-Malik b. Marwān and the Process of the Qur'ān's Composition," in *The Hidden Origins of Islam: New Research into Its Early History*, ed. Karl-Heinz Ohlig and Gerd-R. Puin (Armherst, NY: Prometheus Books, 2010) 189–221, p. 193. Unlike de Prémare, Joachim Gnilka (*Die Nazarener und der Koran: eine Spurensuche* [Freiburg: Herder, 2007] 142–8) conventionally takes the inscriptions to be the oldest available testimony of the Qur'ān. Also while he views Judaism as the major religious influence behind emergent Islam, and the latter as a fully-formed religion by 692, he does not totally discard Luxenberg's proposal to read them as pre-Muhammadan Christian-oriented texts (see further Christoph Luxenberg, "A New Interpretation of the Arabic Inscription in Jerusalem's Dome of the Rock," in *The Hidden Origins of Islam*, ed. Karl-Heinz Ohlig and Gerd-R. Puin [Amherst, NY: Prometheus Books, 2010] 125–51).

90 See further Segovia, "Identity Politics and Scholarship in the Study of Islamic Origins."

91 A word on the earliest quranic manuscripts and their problematic dating may be helpful at this juncture. The palaeographic dating of BNF Arabe 328 to the 670s (on which see François Déroche, *La transmission écrite du Coran dans les débuts de l'islam: Le codex Parisino- petropolitanus*

the Dome of the Rock built in Jerusalem as the official emblem of his rulership – an emblem that, in a carefully-studied anti-Christian political manoeuvre,[92] questions mainstream Christian belief and displays a Muhamadan creed whose only known precedent is a Zubayrid confessional formula of the mid-680s.[93] This theological questioning, which echoes and consolidates the criticism formulated against Jesus's divine sonship in Q 4:172; 5:17, 72–5; 112, is what we find in Q 4:171; 5:116–7; 9:30–1; 19:34–6. Arguably, the need to make it explicit can be explained as a reaction to former attempts to build a bridge between the religion of the new Arab elites and mainstream Christianity – the very bridge, perhaps, that Mu'āwiya had earlier tried to secure.

Transition

The difference between the two historical periods examined in this chapter – those of Mu'āwiya (P1) and 'Abd al-Malik (P2) – therefore explains, on my reading, the existence of two different Jesus-centred Christologies in the quranic corpus: one sympathetic towards mainstream Christian dogma, or at least sympathetic to the latter's anti-Jewish premises and Adamic trimings, that remains silent on the issues of Jesus's sonship and incarnation (C2); the other one opposed to Christian belief without however rejecting Jesus as the Word of God, a spirit from him,

[Leiden and Boston: Brill, 2009]) lacks the necessary carbon-14 support. In turn, the C-14 dating of the Ṣan'ā' palimpsest has provided extravagant results: 388–588, 433–599, 543–643, and 578–669, for which reason it is not possible to establish the date of its composition. As for the manuscript fragments in Tübingen and Leiden, due caution is also needed despite the claim that they fully confirm the possibility of dating a few fragments (of which precise document?) between the 650s and the 700s, as two additional timeframes (650s–710s and 750s–760s, respectively) have also been identified as possible regarding their dating. See further Alba Fedeli, "Is the Dating of Qur'ānic Manuscripts still a Problem?," forthcoming in *Early Islam: The Sectarian Milieu of Late Antiquity*, ed. Guillaume Dye (LAMINE; Chicago: Chicago Oriental Institute). I, of course, am aware that Ms. Or. Fol. 4313 in Berlin, containing (only) Q 4:172 and 5:17, 72–5, has been dated back to 602–52 with a 95% of probability. Even if I am not fully convinced by the implications usually drawn from this rather wide result, I therefore take such passages (like Q 112 for that matter) to likely predate those that I have assigned to 'Abd al-Malik's times. The possibility that 'Abd al-Malik attempted at consolidating previous theological views is, as I have written, something very plausible.

92 Frank Van der Velden, "Die Felsendominschrift als Ende einer christologischen Konvergenztextökumene im Koran," *Oriens Christianus* 95 (2011): 213–46.

93 Jeremy Johns,"Archaeology and the History of Early Islam: The First Seventy Years," *JESHO* 46.4 (2003): 411–36; Robert G. Hoyland, "New Documentary Texts and the Early Islamic State," *BSOAS* 69.3 (2006): 395–416, pp. 396–7.

and his messenger (C3). Yet the two independent series of texts that validate this contrast present a common trait: they are both late in historical terms – likely, post-conquest fragments. As we will see in the next two chapters, however, the early Qur'ān also contains a Christology (C1) that shares important aspects with C3 – against which C2 thus represents a relative deviation – while being, at least initially, altogether different from it in turn. Such Christology's most salient marker is the complete absence of the figure of Jesus from it – in other words, its non-Jesus-centred nature. In the two next chapters I shall explore its conditions of possibility and its content. This, of course, means that we will need to move backwards from the point we have reached in this chapter. Readers fond of conventional narrative logic (*à la* Hollywood) might find this temporal twist unnecessarily demanding. Yet I am persuaded that, as Jean-Luc Godard famously said, a story should have a beginning, a middle, and an end, but not necessarily in that order.

4 Moving Backwards: A Peripheral South-Arabian Christology?

The Withdrawal from Byzantium's Political and Religious Control in 6th-Century Yemen – and the Arabian Peninsula

The Making of a Christian Yemen in the 6th Century

Before paying attention to the Qur'ān's early Christology, however, we should glimpse into 6th- and 7th-century South-Arabia and Iraq. First, I will try to show that withdrawal from Byzantium's indirect control in political and religious matters defined the situation in Yemen and thereby the Arabian Peninsula – in addition to other important regions of the Near East – on the eve of Islam.

Around 525 or 531, Kaleb,[1] king of Aksūm (ancient Ethiopia), defeated the self-proclaimed (in 521 or 522) Jewish king of Ḥimyar (pre-Islamic Yemen) Yūsuf As'ar Yaṯ'ar,[2] who following his rise to power had the Aksumite garrison in Ẓafār (the Himyarite capital) killed, Ẓafār's church destroyed, the coastal regions of the Red Sea facing Aksūm seized, and the Miaphysite community of Nağrān (the main Christian spot in the south-west of the Arabian Peninsula, next to the modern frontier between Saudi Arabia and Yemen) massacred. Thus Aksumite authority, which had gained prominence in the region in the 500s and the 510s, and Christianity with it (after a *longue durée* of Jewish supremacy), were imposed in Ḥimyar – an event from which Byzantium benefited, for it implied controlling with the help of a victorious ally the trade routes through the eastern and western shores of the Read Sea against its own rival empire: Persia.[3]

Yet Kaleb did not annex Ḥimyar. Instead, he maintained the Himyarite throne and placed on it a Himyarite prince called Sumyafa' Ašwa'.[4] Very likely, the latter was of Jewish origin but had converted to Christianity after Kaleb's successful campaign in Ḥimyar. Be that as it may, two extant, if fragmentary, official

1 Unvocalised Gəʿəz ከለበ፡አለ፡አጸበሐ KLB ʼL ʼṢBḤ (vocalised Kaleb Ǝllä Aṣbəḥa); Greek Ἑλλησθεαῖος Hellestheaios.
2 Sab. 𐩺𐩥𐩪𐩰 | 𐩱𐩪𐩱𐩧 | 𐩺𐩻𐩱𐩧 YWS^{1}F ʼS^{1}ʼR YṮʼR; Arab. ذو نواس ḏū Nuwās; Gk. Δουναας Dounaas.
3 On Ethiopia, Ḥimyar, Byzantium, and Persia between the 4th and the 7th centuries, see further Bowersock, *Empires in Collision in Late Antiquity*.
4 Sabaic 𐩪𐩣𐩺𐩰𐩲 | 𐩱𐩦𐩥𐩲 SMYFʿ ʼŠWʿ; Gk. Ἐσιμιφαῖος Esimiphaios.

https://doi.org/10.1515/9783110599688-004

inscriptions in Sabaic bear witness to his Christian faith, namely Istanbul 7608 bis,[5] and Wellcome A 103664.[6]

Istanbul 7608 bis consists of 16 lines. It stars with a fragmentary trinitarian thanksgiving formula that mentions Sumyafaʿ Ašwaʿ and the king of Aksūm (ll. 1–3), as well as the latter's military success in Ḥimyar (ll. 3–8).[7] Next figures a list with the names and the tribes of those who helped him (ll. 9–15), Sumyafaʿ Ašwaʿ included (l. 11). It concludes with a two-part *basmala* mentioning God (*Raḥmānān*) and his Son Christ, the victorious (l. 16).

In turn, Wellcome A 103664 consists of 17 lines. Its first four lines cannot be conveniently interpreted, as they are too poorly preserved. L. 5 seemingly contains a two-part thanksgiving formula, similar to that found in l. 16 of Istanbul 7608 bis. Ll. 5–9 allude to the king and his acceptance of Aksumite authority. Ll. 10–17 provide a list of names akin to that found in ll. 9–15 of Istanbul 7608 bis; and an additional reference to Sumyafaʿ Ašwaʿ is made in l. 16 within that list, following a succinct allusion to warfare and destruction (l. 15).

As Iwona Gajda aptly puts it, "pour la première fois dans l'histoire de l'Arabie du Sud, des formules religieuses chrétiennes apparaissent dans un texte officiel."[8]

The formulas in question are those found in l. 1 and l. 16 of the first inscription (henceforth formulas no. 1 and 2)[9]:

No. 1	**Istanbul 7608 bis, l. 1**
𐩥𐩣𐩬]𐩰𐩪 | 𐩤𐩵𐩪 W-MN]FS¹ QDS¹	and (the)] Holy [Spi]rit

No. 2	**Istanbul 7608 bis, l. 16**
𐩪𐩣 | 𐩧𐩢𐩣𐩬𐩬 | 𐩥𐩨𐩬𐩠𐩥 | 𐩫𐩧𐩯𐩩𐩯 | 𐩶𐩡𐩨𐩬 S¹M RḤMNN W-BN-HW KRS³TS³ ĠLBN	(in the) name of *Raḥmānān* <= the Merciful> and his son Christ(, the) victorious

5 http://dasi.humnet.unipi.it/index.php?id=dasi_prj_epi&prjId=1&corId=0&colId=0&navId=800877863&recId=2410.

6 http://dasi.humnet.unipi.it/index.php?id=dasi_prj_epi&prjId=1&corId=0&colId=0&navId=800877863&recId=2459.

7 On this type of formulas, see Iwona Gajda, *Le royaume de Ḥimyar à l'époque monothéiste. L'histoire de l'Arabie du Sud ancienne de la fin du IVᵉ siècle de l'ère chrétienne jusqu'a l'avènement de l'Islam* (MAIBL 40; Paris: Académie des Inscriptions et Belles-Lettres, 2009) 226–31.

8 Gajda, *Le royaume de Ḥimyar à l'époque monothéiste*, 115.

9 I give the transliteration provided by the CSAI team at the University of Pisa, directed by Alessandra Avanzini: http://dasi.humnet.unipi.it/index.php?id=42&prjId=1&corId=0&colId=0&navId=800877863&rl=yes.

and in l. 5 of the second inscription (henceforth formula no. 3):

No. 3	Wellcome A 103664, l. 5
𐩧𐩢𐩣𐩬𐩬 | 𐩥𐩨]	
RḤMNN W-B[	*Raḥmānān* and (his) S[on

No. 1 looks like the last segment of a, thus only partly preserved, mainstream trinitarian formula ("God, his Son, and the Holy Spirit"). Conversely, no. 2 does not need to be read in the same way, as it could simply mention God and his Son (see Abrəha's formula below)[10]; and the same applies to no. 3, which echoes No. 2. In any event, the Ethiopic influence is perceptible (despite the inclusion of the divine name 𐩧𐩢𐩣𐩬𐩬 RḤMNN) in the wording of the first formula: Ethiopic መንፈስ ፡ ቅዱስ *Mänfäs Qəddus* → (Sabaic) 𐩣𐩬𐩰𐩦 | 𐩤𐩵𐩦 MNFS¹ QDS¹.[11]

But there is an even more salient feature in these formulas, more specifically in nos. 2 and 3. In addition to being mentioned by his name in no. 2 (𐩫𐩧𐩯𐩩𐩯 KRS³TS³= Χριστός *Christos*), Christ is described as God's "Son" (𐩨𐩬𐩠𐩥 BN-HW ["his son"]) in formulas nos. 2 and 3. This, again, matches the normal Christian formula "God (the Father) and his Son" and the usual Ethiopic *basmala*.[12] However, Sumyafaʿ Ašwaʿ's inscriptions represent, as we shall see, the last occurrence of this particular formula ("God and his Son") in the official Christian inscriptions of late-antique South Arabia – an issue, in my view, which hitherto has not been paid enough attention.

Reflections on Abrəha's Enigmatic Christology

Sumyafaʿ Ašwaʿ's reign was short-lived, nevertheless. Around 535, his army commander, Abrəha,[13] deposed him and assumed the throne of Ḥimyar. Upon receiving this news, Kaleb sent two military expeditions against Abrəha, but the new self-proclaimed king managed to negotiate an agreement with Kaleb's soldiers the first time, and then crushed Kaleb's second expedition.

---

10 *Pace* Gajda, who considers it "[u]ne second formule trinitaire" (*Le royaume de Ḥimyar à l'époque monothéiste*, 115).

11 Gajda, *Le royaume de Ḥimyar à l'époque monothéiste*, 115.

12 Manfred Kropp, "»Im Namen Gottes, (d. i.) des gnädigen (und) B/(b)armherzigen«. Die muslimische Basmala: Neue Ansätze zu ihrer Erklärung," *OC* 97 (2013–14): 190–201, p. 195.

13 Unvocalised Geʿez አበረሀ; Sabaic 𐩱𐩨𐩧𐩠; Arab. أبرهة.

Judging from what we know of his reign between the 540s and the 550s,[14] Abrəha brought stability to Ḥimyar and successfully extended his rule to several neighbouring regions of the Arabian peninsula including Saba', ḏū Raydān, Ḥaḍramawt, Yamanat, Ṭawd and Tihāma. More interestingly, he refused to act as a vassal king of Aksūm, as can be fairly deduced from the way in which his official inscriptions display his "will to maintain, if not to restore, the brilliance of the cradle of South Arabian civilisation and thus to consolidate a contested legitimacy by acting as an indigenous sovereign."[15] He died c. 565 (allegedly after a frustrated expedition against Mecca) and was succeeded by his two sons Aksūm and Masrūq, who ruled successively until the mid-570s[16]; then his dynasty came to an end and the Christian kingdom of Ḥimyar collapsed with the help of Persia.[17]

Among other minor inscriptions of that period, we have several official inscriptions by Abrəha himself, in particular for our purposes here CIH 541[18] and DAI GDN 2002–20,[19] both from 548, and Ry 506[20] from 552.

CIH 541 is the longest of Abrəha's extant inscriptions and consists of 136 lines. It opens with a trinitarian thanksgiving formula (ll. 1–3) followed by a reference to Abraha's name (l. 4), titles (ll. 4–6), and dominions (ll. 6–8).[21] It then

14 Gajda, *Le royaume de Ḥimyar à l'époque monothéiste*, 118–49; Christian Julien Robin, "Arabia and Ethiopia," in *The Oxford Handbook of Late Antiquity*, ed. Scott Fitzgerald Johnson (Oxford and New York: Oxford University Press, 2012) 247–332, pp. 284–8.

15 Robin, "Arabia and Ethiopia," 285; cf. Gajda, *Le royaume de Ḥimyar à l'époque monothéiste*, 119.

16 I.e. shortly after the date traditionally assigned to Muḥammad's birth.

17 On Abrəha's expedition against Mecca and its supposed allusion in *sūra* 105 of the Qur'ān ("The Elephant"), see Robin "Arabia and Ethiopia," 285–8. On the problems inherent in Q 105, its plausible biblical subtext, and its possible anti-Persian background, Alfred Louis de Prémare, "'Il voulut détruire le Temple'. L'attaque de la Ka'ba par les rois yéménites avant l'islam: Abḫār et Histoire," *JA* 288 (2000): 261–7; Daniel A. Beck, *Evolution of the Early Qur'ān: From Anonymous Apocalypse to Charismatic Prophet* (ACDE 2; New York and Bern: Peter Lang, 2018) 1–78.

18 http://dasi.humnet.unipi.it/index.php?id=dasi_prj_epi&prjId=1&corId=0&colId=0&navId=389874095&recId=2382.

19 http://dasi.humnet.unipi.it/index.php?id=dasi_prj_epi&prjId=1&corId=0&colId=0&navId=800877863&recId=2391.

20 http://dasi.humnet.unipi.it/index.php?id=dasi_prj_epi&prjId=1&corId=0&colId=0&navId=800877863&recId=2447.

21 As Manfred Kropp wrote to me in a private communication of July 24, 2015, 𐩸𐩨𐩺𐩣𐩬 ZBYMN *in* ll. 4–6 (𐩸𐩺𐩨𐩣𐩬 ZYBMN through metathesis in Ry 506 l. 1)= "the one in (i.e. the Lord of) 𐩺(𐩨)𐩣𐩬 Y(B)MN," can hardly be a reference to Yemen, inasmuch as *ymn* for Ḥimyar/Yemen is attested neither in Sabaic nor in Ethiopic (cf. Gajda, *Le royaume de Ḥimyar à l'époque monothéiste*, 120). He perspicaciously suggested to me, therefore, that 𐩺(𐩨)𐩣𐩬 Y(B)MN (as also 𐩺𐩣𐩬𐩩 YMNT in CIH 541 l. 7; DAI GDN 2002–20 l. 10; and Ry 506 l. 2) may be interpreted as alluding to the Yamāma in central Arabia, which Abrəha conquered in the time when he had CIH 541

reports a rebellion that the king suffocated (ll. 10–55) prior to having the inscription set up (l. 9). This report is followed by another one mentioning the king's repair of the Ma'rib dam (ll. 55–61), which is alluded to again in ll. 68–71; the celebration of a mass in its church (ll. 65–7); and a plague (ll. 72–5). Next we find more details about the king's military campaigns in Arabia (ll. 76–80); the indication that he returned to Ma'rib after them (ll. 80–7); and a report concerning the subsequent organisation of a diplomatic conference in which delegations from Ethiopia, Byzantium, Persia, and the Arab vassal kingdoms of the Romans and the Sassanians participated (ll. 87–92). Some supplementary information on the plague mentioned in ll. 72–5, the rebuilding of the Ma'rib dam, and the mass alluded to in ll. 65–7, is then given in ll. 92–117, as well as a detailed list of provisions (ll. 118–36).

DAI GDN 2002–20 must be linked to CIH 541 (they belong to the same building and are more or less contemporary) and consists of 41 lines. It starts with a thanksgiving formula similar, if longer, to that found in CIH 451 ll. 1–3, but which lacks any reference to the Holy Spirit (ll. 1–4); it mentions too the king's name and his dominions (ll. 5–12). The rest of the inscription consists of extensive report on the restoration of the Ma'rib dam (ll. 13–41) that echoes the one provided in CIH 541 ll.

Finally, Ry 506 consists of only 9 lines. It opens with an abridged thanksgiving formula that resembles that found in DAI GDN 2002–20 ll. 1–4, although it is visibly shorter (l. 1), and which mentions once more the king's name (l. 1) and his dominions (ll. 1–2). Then his military campaigns in central Arabia are referred to (ll. 2–8). Lastly, we find another thanksgiving formula, now mentioning God alone and the date (552) when the inscription was set up (l. 9).

In this case we find three different religious formulas, one in ll. 1–3 of the first inscription (henceforth formula no. 4):

---

and DAI GDN 2002–20 set up and thus could be expected to be listed among the king's dominions in both inscriptions, which are roughly contemporary with one another. On Abrəha's conquests see further Christian Julian Robin, "Abraha et la reconquête de l'Arabie déserte: un réexamen de l'inscription Ryckmans 506 = Murayghan 1," *JSAI* 39 (2012): 1–93; idem, "Arabia and Ethiopia," 284–8; idem, "Note d'information. Soixante-dix ans avant l'islam: L'Arabie toute entière dominée par un roi chrétien," *CRAI* 2012.1 (2012): 525–53; idem, "À propos de Ymnt et Ymn : « nord » et « sud », « droite » et « gauche », dans les inscriptions de l'Arabie antique," in *Entre Carthage et l'Arabie heureuse. Mélanges offerts à François Bron*, ed. Françoise Briquel-Chatonnet, Catherine Fauveaud, and Iwona Gajda (OM 12; Paris: De Boccard, 2013) 119–40.

No. 4	**CIH 541, ll. 1–3**
𐩨𐩭𐩺𐩡 | 𐩥[𐩧]𐩵𐩱 | 𐩥𐩧𐩢–	
𐩣𐩩 | 𐩧𐩢𐩣𐩬𐩬 | 𐩥𐩣𐩪–	
𐩢𐩠𐩥 | 𐩥𐩧𐩢 | [𐩤]𐩵𐩪	
B-ḪYL W-[R]Dʾ W-RḤ—	With the power(,) {and} the [a]id and the mer-
MT RḤMNN W-MS^1—	cy of *Raḥmānān*(,) {and} his Messi-
Ḥ-HW W-RḤ [Q]DS^1	ah and the Holy [Gho]st

another one in l. 1–4 of the second inscription (henceforth formula no. 5):

No. 5	**DAI GDN 2002–20, ll. 1–4**
𐩨𐩭𐩺𐩡 | 𐩥𐩬(𐩮)[𐩧]	
𐩥𐩧𐩵𐩱 | 𐩧𐩢𐩣𐩬𐩬	
𐩣𐩧𐩱 | 𐩪𐩣𐩺𐩬	
𐩥𐩣𐩪𐩢𐩠(𐩥)	
B-ḪYL W-N(Ṣ)[R]	With the power(,) {and} the he(l)[p]
W-RDʾ RḤMNN	and the support of *Raḥmānān*,
MRʾ S^{1}MYN	Lord of the heavens(,)
W-MS^{1}Ḥ-H(W)	and hi(s) Messiah

and another one in l. 1 of the third inscription (henceforth formula no. 6):

No. 6	**Ry 506, l. 1**
𐩨𐩭𐩺𐩡 | 𐩧𐩢𐩣𐩬𐩬 | 𐩥𐩣𐩪𐩢𐩠𐩥	
B-ḪYL RḤMNN W-MS^{1}Ḥ-HW	With the power of *Raḥmānān* and his Messiah

Despite some slight variations in their three consecutive segments that may be summarised as follows:

Wording	**Components**
Segment 1	
No. 4: With the power, the aid and the mercy	A + B + C
No. 5: With the power, the help and the support	A + D = B' + E = C'
No. 6: With the power	A

Wording	Components
Segment 2	
No. 4: of *Raḥmānān*	E
No. 5: of *Raḥmānān*, Lord of the heavens	E + F
No. 6: of *Raḥmānān*	E
Segment 3	
No. 4: his Messiah and the Holy Spirit	G + H
No. 5: and his Messiah	G
No. 6: and his Messiah	G

the three formulas run parallel (S1: A ± B/B' + C/C' | S2: E ± F | S3: G ± H), although only no. 4 can be said to convey a trinitarian message.

Now, three features are particularly noteworthy in comparison to Sumyafa' Ašwa''s aforementioned formulas: Firstly, a different choice regarding the opening words of the thanksgiving formulas:

Sumyafa' Ašwa':	In the name of
Abrəha:	With the power + the aid/help and the mercy/ support of

Secondly, the different wording displayed in the reference to the Holy Spirit:

Sumyafa' Ašwa':	𐩣𐩬𐩰𐩪 | 𐩤𐩵𐩪	MNFS^{1} QDS^{1}
Abrəha:	𐩧𐩢 | 𐩤𐩵𐩪	RḤ QDS^{1}

which denotes Syriac, rather than Ethiopian, influence in the latter case,[22] and hence bear witness to a clear *shift* in Abrəha's linguistic and cultural policy – aiming perhaps at affirming his political independence from Aksūm. Lastly, the wording relative to Jesus and Jesus's relation to God is also different:

Sumyafa' Ašwa', no. 2:	*Raḥmānān* <u>and his son</u> Christ, the victorious
Sumyafa' Ašwa':, no. 3:	*Raḥmānān* <u>and his Son</u>
Abrəha, nos. 4, 5, 6:	*Raḥmānān* <u>and his Messiah</u>

22 Cf. the Syriac term for the Holy Spirit: ܪܘܚܐ ܕܩܘܕܫܐ *rūḥā d-qūdšā* (from which the quranic روح القدس *rūḥ al-qudus* derives too). See further Alfred F. L. Beeston, "Foreign Loanwords in Sabaic," in *Arabia Felix. Beiträge zur Sprache und Kultur des vorislamischen Arabien. Festschrift Walter M. Müller zum 60. Geburtstag*, ed. Norbert Nebes (Wiesbaden: Harrassowitz, 1994) 39–45, p. 42; Gajda, *Le royaume de Ḥimyar à l'époque monothéiste*, 121; Robin "Note d'information," 540.

Peripheral Christianity and Formative Islam

Why did Abrəha choose the term 𐩣𐩪𐩢 MS^{1}Ḥ ("Messiah") – which is unattested elsewhere in the whole corpus of ancient South-Arabian inscriptions (ASA) to name Jesus? Several explanations have been provided so far. In 1960, Alfred Beeston – who was also the first to notice this quite remarkable fact – suggested that Abrəha might have inclined himself towards Eastern Diphysitism (i.e. towards the Christology of the East-Syrian Church) out of his distaste for Kaleb – for Aksūm was, like West Syria and Egypt, mostly Miaphysite.[23] In turn, Irfaṇ Shahîd contended that Abrəha probably converted to the Chalcedonian faith (which sustained a moderate Diphysite Christology compared to that of the Church of the East)[24] in order to obtain support from Byzantium.[25] More recently, Iwona Gajda has discussed Beeston's (and implicitly Shahîd's) view(s) and proposed an alternative one: "Abraha précise bien qui sont le Père et le Fils: « Raḥmānān et son Messie ». Il s'agit probablement d'un usage local"[26]; "[i]l ne nous paraît pas possible d'avancer une [autre] hypothèse en se fondant sur les données dont nous disposons."[27] Conversely, Christian Robin highlights the apparent Jewish-Christian nature of Abrəha's formula.[28] Lastly, Jonn Block argues that "it is not inconceivable that Abrəha allowed ambiguity in his presentation of the faith in order to gain Byzantine support for his action against the Persians, but an official conversion from Monophysitism to Nestorianism is very unlikely. It is more likely that Byzantium still had Monophysite leanings, and was on friendly terms with Abyssinia. Beeston's conviction on the matter seems lower than that of Shahîd, who proposes the possibility that Abrəha changed his faith from Monophysite to Chalcedonian."[29]

I take Shahîd's interpretation to be too far-reaching, as there is no evidence to support it. If emphasising Jesus's humanity might have proved effective in attempting to establish friendly relations with Byzantium, one may question, however, whether the term MS^{1}Ḥ could bear witness to Abrəha's eventual conversion from Miaphysitism to the Chalcedonian faith. Gajda's "local-usage" hypothesis has no evidence to support it either – for, as I have underlined, Abrəha's formula is unattested elsewhere in the ASA corpus; notice, moreover, that, *pace* Gajda, Abrəha

23 Alfred F. L. Beeston, "Abraha," in *EI* (Leiden: Brill, and Paris: A. Maisonneuve, 1960) 1:105–6, p. 105.
24 See Chapter 1, n.26 above. See also the next chapter.
25 Irfan Shahîd, "Byzantium in South Arabia," *DOP* 33 (1979): 23–94, p. 31.
26 Gajda, *Le royaume de Ḥimyar à l'époque monothéiste*, 122.
27 Gajda, *Le royaume de Ḥimyar à l'époque monothéiste*, 122 n.456.
28 Robin "Note d'information," 540.
29 C. Jonn Block, *The Qur'ān in Christian-Muslim Dialogue: Historical and Modern Interpretations* (RSQ; London and New York: Routledge, 2014) 21.

does not make clear "qui sont le Père *et le Fils*" (my emphasis), for he actually does *not* explicitly call the Messiah the "Son," even if formula no. 4, which is also the longest and perhaps the most important one, presents an apparent – but no more than that, therefore – trinitarian outlook. In turn, Robin's interpretation overlooks the problems inherent in the adjective "Jewish-Christian," on which much and good has been written in the past years.[30] As for Beeston's hypothesis, I think it cannot be immediately dismissed, but it certainly needs to be nuanced – I shall now try to explain how.

Invocations of Jesus in late-antique Christianity normally mention "God (the Father) and his Son Christ." Yet East Diphysites, who held that Christ was God's Son (like the Miaphysites and the Chalcedonians), are known to have emphasised (against the Miaphysites and even more than the Chalcedonians themselves) Jesus's human nature. Thus the well-known East-Syrian description of Mary as Χριστοτόκος *Christotokos* (i.e. "Mother of the Messiah") rather than Θεοτόκος *Theotokos* ("Mother of God"). Let me be clear: the formula "God and his Messiah" has a relatively weak scriptural basis[31] and is not attested in the corpus of late-antique East-Syrian literature; but it may be said to implicitly *fit* within the Diphysite mindset.[32] Besides, East-Diphysite Christians apparently lived in Yemen during Abrəha's reign.[33] Hence it is not totally unreasonable to ask whether Abrəha tried to distance himself from Aksūm by endorsing an East-Syrian-oriented Christology.

But it could also be that Abrəha – who obviously was and presented himself as a Christian king – simply tried to avoid any sharp provocation against the Jews of Ḥimyar, a land that for several centuries had witnessed to an ongoing religious

---

30 See further Chapter 1, n.33 above.

31 I am grateful to Antonio Piñero (private communication of July 19, 2015) for checking the whole NT corpus so as to determine if there is a single scriptural passage that may be adduced against this view – the only two occurrences being Luke 9:20 and Acts 3:18.

32 Cf. too Arius's salutation to Eusebius of Nicomedia "on account of God and his Messiah" (*NPNF1* 3:41), which shows that Arians (and possibly Anomoeans later on, whose presence in 4th-century South Arabia is documented in the work of Philostorgius) shared a similar caution against the assimilation of God and Jesus – the Christological differences between Arianism/Anomoeanism and Eastern Diphysitism notwithstanding, that is.

33 See Robin, "Arabia and Ethiopia," 282–3, who bases his report in the *Chronicle of Seert*. See for discussion Philip Wood, *The Chronicle of Seert: Christian Historical Imagination in Late Antique Iraq* (OECS; Oxford and New York: Oxford University Press, 2013) 249–53. Even if the author(s) of the *Chronicle of Seert*, "by claiming precedence in Najran, ... may have ... sought to emphasise their own role as intermediaries with the Muslim authorities" (Wood, *The Chronicle of Seert*, 253), there is in my view no need to completely dismiss their report as an *ad hoc* construction, since the presence of East Syrians in Nağrān is mentioned in both the *Book of the Himyarites* 13 and the *Martyrium Arethae* 2.6. See also Alois Grillmeier, *Christ in Christian Tradition*, English translation by O. C. Dean Jr. (2 vols.; Louisville, KY: Westminster John Knox. 1975–96) 2:321.

conflict (indirectly promoted by Byzantium and Persia) between Christians and Jews, and which he attempted to rule in his own way.[34] Had Abrəha intended not to offend his Jewish subjects, he could have done so by evoking God alone (instead of God plus his Messiah = Jesus); indeed, *Raḥmānān* was (also) the south-Arabian Jewish name for God. Yet referring to Jesus as the Messiah would be less provoking for them than describing him as God's divine Son, anyway.

In fact, these two hypotheses need not contradict themselves, as apparently Diphysites and Jews did not collide in antiquity as often as Miaphysites and Jews happened to. Thus Adam Becker[35] contends that among the late-antique Christian literature not even a single extant anti-Jewish text can be attributed to the Diphysites. It is true, as Philip Wood pointed to me in a private communication of August 26, 2015, that Ephraem, whose anti-Judaism is quite manifest,[36] was part of the inheritance of all Syriac speakers, be they East- or West Syrians, and hence that they all shared a more-or-less-straightforward anti-Jewish attitude from the very beginning – even if for the East-Syrian Christians the Zoroastrians often played the role of the Pharisees in the way they mapped the Gospels onto contemporary events, which meant that in practice the Jews drew less fire among them. Yet the tension between the Diphysites and the Jews was less pointed in comparison to the prevalent situation among the Miaphysites, and in my opinion this fact cannot be overlooked. But if both hypotheses may complement one another, it is perhaps wise to assign a bigger role to the possibility pointed to in the latter one, as some kind of *Realpolitik* towards the Jews may well have helped Abrəha to successfully lay the foundations of an autonomous and cohesive rule.

Whatever the case, Abrəha's innovative Christological formula evinces that South-Arabian Christians in the 6th century were not unfamiliar with the representation of Jesus as God's "Messiah" instead of "Son" – a feature that, curiously, we find again in the Qur'ān.[37] Besides, if 𐩺(𐩨)𐩣𐩬 / 𐩺𐩣𐩬𐩩 Y(B)MN/YMNT

34 This hypothesis was suggested to me by Guillaume Dye in a private communication of July 13, 2015.

35 Adam H. Becker, "Beyond the Spatial and Temporal *Limes*: Questioning the 'Parting of the Ways' Outside the Roman Empire," in *The Ways that Never Parted: Jews and Christians in Late Antiquity and the Early Middle Ages*, ed. Annette Yoshiko Reed and Adam H. Becker (TSAJ 95; Tübingen: Mohr Siebeck, 2003) 373–92, p. 387.

36 See further Christine Shepardson, *Anti-Judaism and Christian Orthodoxy: Ephrem's Hymns in Fourth-Century Syria* (NAPSPMS 20; Washington, DC: Catholic University of America Press, 2008).

37 See Chapter 2 above. The fact that Abrəha's formula ("*Raḥmānān* and his Messiah") is paralleled in the quranic corpus (which often refers to God as "*al-Raḥmān*" and to Jesus as the "Messiah (son of Mary)" has not escaped Robin's attention ("Arabia and Ethiopia," 540). See also Irfan Shahîd, "Islam and *Oriens Christianus*: Makka 610–622 AD," in *The Encounter of Eastern Christianity with Early Islam*, ed. Emmanouela Grypeou, Mark N. Swanson, and David Thomas

in CIH 541, DAI GDN 2002–20, and Ry 506 can be interpreted as alluding to the Yamāma, as I have suggested following Manfred Kropp, there is good reason to presume that Abrəha did not only conquer, but also had his particular form of Christianity spread in central Arabia. Most likely too, his peculiar type of Christianity also reached Yaṯrib in the Ḥiǧāz.[38] And perhaps even Mecca, which had commercial ties with the Yamāma in pre-Islamic times.[39] Furthermore, the Yamāma was the region where, according to the later Muslim sources, Musaylima "the liar," i.e. Muḥammad's main rival prophet (who, the legend goes, was called "al-Raḥmān" after his Lord's name) preached his own monotheistic message – and where the battle between Musaylima and his followers, on the one hand, and, on the other hand, those of Muḥammad led by Abū Bakr, took place in 632 (Musaylima himself being killed in the battlefield at a place that would later come to be known as the "Garden of Death"). Of course, it is extremely difficult to establish with accuracy, as Al Makin aptly observes,[40] the differences between Musaylima's and the quranic prophet's religious views – since they both preached in the name of the same God and thus spoke the same theological language, used similar rhetorics, and even had their own shrines and their own Qur'ān-s.[41] Needless to say, the Muslim sources authenticate Muḥammad's religion as divinely inspired and dismiss Musaylima's as being radically false, but this binary opposition obviously serves a legitimationist purpose and conveys a theological, rather than historical, argument. It is then fair to ask whether Musaylima's and the quranic prophet's religious views may have been similarly influenced by Abrəha's. Compare the apparent quranic parallels to the latter's Christology, which I have already mentioned, as well as Musaylima's presumed reference[42] to the parable of the "mustard seed" in Matthew 13:31–2; 17:20; Mark 4:30–2; and

(Leiden and Boston: Brill. 2006) 9–31, pp. 20–21, who, albeit he adduces no evidence thereof, interprets the quranic phrase "Jesus son of Mary" as a Diphysite expression circulating in Mecca in Muḥammad's lifetime; as well as Frank van der Velden's interpretation of Q 5:116 in "Kotexte im Konvergenzstrang – die Bedeutung textkritischer Varianten und christlicher Bezugstexte für die Redaktion von Sure 61 und Sure 5,110–119," *OC* 92 (2008): 130–73.

38 Robin, "Note d'information."

39 Al Makin, "Sharing the Concept of God among Trading Prophets: Reading the Poems Attributed to Umayya b. Abī Ṣalt," in *Religions and Trade: Religious Formation, Transformation and Cross-Cultural Exchange between East and West*, ed. Peter Wick and Volker Rabens (DHR 5; Leiden and Boston: Brill, 2014) 283–305, p. 290.

40 Al Makin, *Representing the Enemy: Musaylima in Muslim Literature* (EUS 106; Frankfurt and New York: Peter Lang, 2008) 219–31.

41 The parallelisms between Musaylima's stanzas and the so-called "Meccan" *sūra*-s of the Qur'ān are particularly noteworthy. See Al Makin, *Representing the Enemy*, 219–23.

42 *Apud* al-Ṭabarī, *Tārīḫ al-Rusul wa-l-Mulūk*, ed. Muḥammad Abū l-Faḍl Ibrāhim (10 vols.; Cairo: Dār al-Ma'ārif, 1960–9) 3:272.

Luke 13:18–19; 17:6: in particular, the wording in Musaylima's presumed stanza: فلو أنّها حبّة خردل *fa-law annahā ḥubbat ḫardala* ... ("*if* it were *only* mustard seed ...") is noteworthy, as it matches the Old Syriac version of Matthew and Luke, whereas *'lw* is lost in the Pəšīṭtā[43]; and one of the manuscripts of the Old Syriac gospels (namely, Syrus Sinaiticus) omits the words οὐκ ἐγίνωσκεν αὐτὴν ἕως *ouk eginōsken autēn heōs* ("but had no intercourse with her," in reference to Joseph, and to Mary) in Matthew 1:25,[44] therefore implicitly presenting Jesus as humanly born of his mother – which somehow matches, once more, the Christology of the Qur'ān.

Moreover, as evinced by his word choice concerning the "Holy Spirit," Abrəha opened the doors of Yemen – and likely those of the Arabian Peninsula as well – to Syrian cultural and religious influence. In this manner he established the premises for a new, *peripheral* type of Christianity somehow acceptable perhaps to the majoritarian Jewish population of Yemen and in which, apparently too, non-Chalcedonian elements could simultaneously penetrate. Moreover, Abrəha's domains included most of the Arabian Peninsula, probably through the intermediation of the Hujrids, whose kingdom was apparently vassal to Ḥimyar in the same way the Arab kingdoms of the Jafnids in North-Western Arabia and the Nasrids in Iraq were vassal to Byzantium and Persia, respectively[45]; while of the Hujrids we know that they were in contact with the Nasrids of Ḥīrā in present-day Iraq, who, in turn, in the mid-6th century had a monastery built in their capital upon request of a Christian Hujrid princess,[46] that they regularly traded with Mecca, and that by the late 6th century they officially converted to Eastern Diphysitism.[47] In the following section I will actually suggest that it was in Iraq, rather than the Ḥiǧāz, that the anonymous quranic prophet began his career.[48] Besides, one should not

43 F. Crawford Burkitt, *Evangelion da-Mepharreshe: The Curetonian Version of the Four Gospels, with the readings of the Sinai Palimpsest* (2 vols.; Cambridge: Cambridge University Press, 1904) 2:77–8.

44 Burkitt, *Evangelion da-Mepharreshe*, 2:261.

45 See further Christian Julien Robin, "Le royaume Ḥujride, dit « royaume de Kinda », entre Ḥimyar et Byzance," *CRSAIBL* 140.2 (1996): 665–714, pp. 692–5.

46 Robin, "Le royaume Ḥujride, dit « royaume de Kinda », entre Ḥimyar et Byzance," 695.

47 On the Nasrids of Ḥīrā (Arab. al-Ḥīra) and their connections to Mecca, see Isabel Toral-Niehoff, "The 'Ibād of al-Ḥīra: An Arab Christian Community in Late Antique Iraq," in *The Qur'ān in Context: Historical and Literary Investigations into the Qur'ānic Milieu*, ed. Angelika Neuwirth, Nicolai Sinai, and Michael Marx (Leiden and Boston: Brill, 2010) 323–47.

48 See further Carlos A. Segovia, "Messalianism, Binitarianism, and the East-Syrian Background of the Qur'ān," forthcoming in *Remapping Emergent Islam: Texts, Social Contexts, and Ideological Trajectories*, ed. Carlos A. Segovia (SWLAEMA; Amsterdam: Amsterdam University Press; idem, "Asceticism and the Early Quranic Milieu: A Symptomatic Reading of Q 17:79, 43:36, 73:1–8, 74:43, 76:26, and 108" (forthcoming); Gilles Courtieu and Carlos A. Segovia, "Bābil, Makka and Ṭā'if, or

lose sight, as Daniel Beck insightfully wrote to me in a private communication of February 16, 2017, that "Byzantine theological and imperial influence collapsed simultaneously across all the Arabian regions as 'heretical' Christologies emerged and the Persian threat intensified"; and that against such background "the rise of innovative 'Syriac' Christology" like that endorsed by Abrəha may be viewed as "a development linked to the rise of anti-imperial (or at least autonomous) proto-Arab identity."

East Syria and Iraq, or Christianity beyond the Limes of the Byzantine Empire

Evidently, the more we look to the east the more chances we have to find a type of Christianity susceptible of being described as *peripheral*. In particular, East Syria and Iraq were beyond Byzantine control and home to a type of Christianity that was not just non-Chalcedonian, but also radically alien (in fact opposed) to the dogma established in Ephesus twenty years before the Council of Chalcedon: namely, that to Jesus's human and divine "natures" (Syr. ܟܝܢ̈ܐ *kyanē*, sing. ܟܝܢܐ *kyanā*) corresponds a single "individual manifestation" (Syr. ܩܢܘܡܐ *qnōmā*, pl. ܩܢܘܡ̈ܐ *qnōmē*). The struggle of the Church of the East to defend the view that the human and the divine cannot be assimilated does not merely imply that Jesus's human nature must be fully taken into consideration against all claims to dissolve Christ into his divine nature, for otherwise salvation would be intrinsically inaccessible to humankind[49]: it echoes too the core belief of pre-Nicene Christianity that the man in which God's Word chose to dwell and God's Word as such cannot be assimilated.[50] Thus the accusation raised by the opponents of

(always) Ctesiphon(-Seleucia)? New Insights into the Iranian Setting of the Earliest Quranic Milieu" (provisional title), to be presented to the 3rd Nangeroni Meeting of the Early Islamic Studies Seminar (EISS), Milan, June 2019.

49 So Jaroslav Pelikan, *The Christian Tradition: A History of the Development of Doctrine* (2 vols.; Chicago and London: University of Chicago Press, 1971–4) 2:46, and Dietmar W. Winkler, "The Age of the Sassanians (until 651)," in *The Church of the East: A Concise History*, ed. Wilhelm Baum and Dietmar W. Winkler (London and New York: RoutledgeCurzon, 2000) 7–41, pp. 22–3 – as though the theological concerns of the Church of the East were those of the Latin Church, on which see Hans Urs von Balthasar, *Katolisch. Aspekte des Mysteriums* (Einsiedeln: Johannes Verlag, 1975). See for discussion Henry Corbin, *Le Paradoxe du monothéisme* (Paris: L'Herne, 1981) 152, who speaks of a "monophysisme à rebours [où] c'nest plus le divine qui absorbs l'homme, c'est l'homme qui absorbe … le divin."

50 Corbin, *Le Paradoxe du monothéisme*, 151.

the Church of the East that its Christology entailed a dual sonship: one divine, the other one human – in the like of Valentinus's gnosticism and that of the Ebionites and the Elkasaites (the Jewish-Christians that many scholars have in vain tried to connect Muḥammad to!).[51] Now, in the 2nd and 3rd centuries (at the time in which Christianity was persecuted in the Roman empire, that is) East Syria, Iraq, and South-Western Iran were the regions where Marcion and Bardaiṣān (the similarities of whose views with those of Valentinian gnosticism have often been evoked) as well as Mānī (who had began his career as an Elkasaite) preached their own interpretation(s) of Christianity.[52] Formed institutionally in the second half of the 3rd century, the Church of the East remained permeable to their shaping influence despite its attempts at ecumenism. Thus the canons of Nicaea (which had become effective in the West around 362) were officially accepted by the East-Syrian Church only in 410 and through the adaptation/rewording of the Nicene Creed according to local views; and yet in 424 the Church of the East would become fully independent from the other (Western) churches. Moreover, as late as the mid-6th century the debate around Nicaea's profession of faith was still well alive, if we are to judge by the issues discussed at the synod of 554. And even though modern scholars – in an attempt to rescue it from its isolation – tend to emphasise its non-Nestorianism and hence its "orthodoxy,"[53] the fact remains that throughout the 5th century Nestorius's Christology received

---

51 Corbin, *Le Paradoxe du monothéisme*, 139.

52 Labelling it "heretical" would make little sense, for "proto-orthodox" Christianity represented but a particular tradition which was, moreover, later than most gnostic currents. On Marcion, see Judith M. Lieu, *Marcion and the Making of a Heretic: God and Scripture in the Second Century* (Cambridge and New York: Cambridge University Press, 2015). On Bardaiṣān, Han J. V. Drijvers, *Bardaiṣān of Edessa* (SSN 6; Assen: Van Gorkum & Co., 1966; reprinted in Piscataway, NJ: Gorgias Press, 2012). On Mānī, Michel Tardieu, *Le Manichéism* (Paris: Presses Universities de France, 1981; English translation by M. B. DeBevoise, with an Introduction by Paul Mirecki: *Manichaeism* (Chicago: University of Illinois Press, 2008); Timothy Pettipiece, "Manichaeism at the Crossroads of Jewish, Christian and Muslim Traditions," in *Patristic Studies in the Twenty-First Century: Proceedings of an International Conference to Mark the 50th Anniversary of the International Association of Patristic Studies*, ed. Brouria Bitton-Ashkelony, Theodore de Bruyn, and Carol Harrison (Turnhout, BE: Breopols, 2015) 299–313.

53 See e.g. Sebastian P. Brock, "The Christology of the Church of the East in the Synods of the Fifth to Early Seventh Centuries," in *Aksum-Thyateira: A Festschrift for Archbishop of Thyateira and Great Britain*, ed. George D. Dragas (London: Thyateira House 1985) 125–42. Brock's understandable willingness to recover the East-Syrian Church from its oblivion leads him, nonetheless, to present its Christology in a overtly "pro-orthodox" fashion, and hence to overlook its many nuances. Thus he systematically pays attention to the resolutions adopted in the synods instead of pondering the relevance and the scope of the often upsetting theological problems addressed in them.

considerable support within the East-Syrian Church – Nestorius's views being inherently favourable to the development of an Angelomorphic Christology of the type one often finds in pre-Nicene Christianity, Manichaeism (whose proximity to "Messalianism" cannot be ignored) included.[54] And the fact is that one finds a number of extremely significant Manichaean and Messalian markers – as well as an inequivocal if encrypted reference to Ctesiphon-Seleucia, the Sasanian capital in Iraq – in the earliest quranic layers.[55] Lastly, the elaboration, around 612, of a conceptually precise and institutionally authoritative Christology by Babai the Great did not entirely rule out within the East-Syrian Church the coexistence of Diphysites, peripheral-, and pre-Nicene Christians.[56] It is

---

54 See once more Corbin, *Le Paradoxe du monothéisme*, 133–61; Charles A. Gieschen, *Angelomorphic Christology: Antecedents and Early Evidence* (Leiden and Boston: Brill, 1998); Jarl E. Fossum, *The Name of God and the Angel of the Lord: Samaritan and Jewish Concepts of Intermediation and the Origins of Gnosticism* (WUNT 36; Tübingen: Mohr Siebeck, 1985); Werner Sundermann, "CHRISTIANITY v. Christ in Manicheism," in *Encyclopædia Iranica*, 5.5 (1991): 335–39; available online at http://www.iranicaonline.org/articles/christianity-v. See also Sebastian P. Brock, "The Church of the East Up to the Sixth Century and Its Absence from Councils in the Roman Empire," in *Syriac Dialogue: The First Non-Official Consultation on Dialogue within the Syrian Tradition, with Focus on the Theology of the Church of the East*, ed. Alfred Stirnemann and Gerhard Wilflinger (Vienna: Pro-Oriente, 1996) 68–85; Winkler, "The Age of the Sassanians (until 651)"; Gerrit J. Reinik, "Tradition and the Formation of the 'Nestorian' Identity in Sixth- to Seventh-Century Iraq," in *Religious Origins of Nations? The Christian Communities of the Middle East*, ed. R. Bas ter Haar Romeny (Leiden and Boston: Brill, 2010) 217–50; Jan M. F. Van Reeth, "Melchisédech le Prophète éternel selon Jean d'Apamée et le monarchianisme musulman," *OC* 96 (2012): 31 n.164, 32, 35; Timothy Pettipiece, "Parallel Paths: Tracing Manichaean Footprints along the Syriac *Book of Steps*," in *Breaking the Mind: New Studies in the Syriac* Book of Steps, ed. Christian S. Heal and Robert A. Kitchen (CUASEC; Washington, DC: Catholic University of America, 2014) 32–40. Also, Carlos A. Segovia, "Messalianism, Binitarianism, and the East-Syrian Bacground of the Qur'ān," forthcoming in *Remapping Emergent Islam: Texts, Social Contexts, and Ideological Trajectories*, ed. Carlos A. Segovia (SWLAEMA; Amsterdam: Amsterdam University Press); idem, "Asceticism and the Early Quranic Milieu: A Symptomatic Reading of Q 17:79, 43:36, 73:1–8, 74:43, 76:26, and 108" (forthcoming).

55 See Beck, *Evolution of the Early Qur'ān*; idem, "The Astral Messenger, The Lunar Redemption, The Solar Salvation: Manichaean Cosmic Soteriology in the Qur'ān's Archaic Surahs (Q 84, Q 75, Q 54), forthcoming in *Remapping Emergent Islam*, ed. Segovia; Segovia, "Messalianism, Binitarianism, and the East-Syrian Background of the Qur'ān"; idem, "Asceticism and the Early Quranic Milieu"; Courtieu and Segovia, "Bābil, Makka and Ṭā'if, or (always) Ctesiphon(-Seleucia)?"

56 See further Philip Wood, "Christianity in the Arabian Peninsula," forthcoming in *Early Islam: The Sectarian Milieu of Late Antiquity*, ed. Guillaume Dye (LAMINE; Chicago: Chicago Oriental Institute), whose references to the *Acta Arethae*, Išōʿyahb I, and Thomas of Marga are particularly helpful in this respect. In turn, an attempt to link the emergence of Islam to the development of

therefore fair to ask whether some peripheral (including Arab) groups (those settled around Ḥīrā, for instance?)[57] might have striven to uphold an even more clear *Engelchristologie* by stressing Jesus's human condition. Be that as it may, during Abrəha's reign or shortly after the Ḥiǧāz in the Arabian Peninsula and Ḥīrā in Sasanian Iraq had their commercial ties strengthened, and this likely favoured the spread of East-Syrian religious views and notions in all this area.[58] Presumably, direct Persian control of Yemen between the 570s and 630s had this scenario reinforced.

Monks, Bishops, and the Plausible Anti-Chalcedonian Setting of Q 9:31, 34

Misunderstood Terms and Redactional Layers in Q 9:30–1

I, moreover, should now like to make the point that, despite the support implicitly granted to Heraclius in Q 18:83–102; 30:2–5,[59] (pro-) Chalcedonian christianity was alien to the quranic authors and possibly the direct target of their criticisms (on the wake of Chosroes II's military expedition against Byzantium and his suppression of the East-Syrian Catholicate?) in, at least, two relevant plus elsewhere unmatched passages now found in *Sūrat al-Tawba* (Q 9, "Repentance"), namely vv. 30–1 and 34.

Paulicianism in the 7th-century Near East has recently been made by Peter von Sivers, "Christology and Prophetology in the Early Umayyad Arab Empire," in *Die Entstehung einer Weltreligion III*, ed. Markus Gross and Karl-Heinz Ohlig, (ISFIK 7; Berlin: Schiler, 2014), 255–85, to whom I am grateful for drawing my attention to the uneven development of East-Syrian Christianity in the early 7th century.

57 See Isabel Toral-Niehoff, "The 'Ibād of al-Ḥīra"; idem, "Late Antique Iran and the Arabs: The Case of al-Hira," *JPS* 6 (2013): 115–26; Greg Fisher and Philip Wood, "Writing the History of the 'Persian Arabs': The Pre-Islamic Perspective on the 'Naṣrids' of al-Ḥīrah," *IS* 49.2 (2016): 247–90.

58 See again Toral-Niehoff, "The 'Ibād of al-Ḥīra." See also Michel Tardieu, "L'arrivée des Manichéens à Al-Hîra," in *La Syrie de Byzance à l'Islam. VIIe–VIIIe siècles*, ed. Pierre Canivet and Jean-Paul Rey-Coquais (Damascus: IFD, 1992) 15–24; and now too Gilles Courtieu and Carlos A. Segovia, "Bābil, Makka and Ṭā'if, or (always) Ctesiphon(-Seleucia)? New Insights into the Iranian Setting of the Earliest Quranic Milieu," (forthcoming).

59 See further Kevin van Bladel, "The Alexander Legend in the Qur'ān 18:83–102," in *The Qur'ān in Its Historical Context*, ed. Gabriel Said Reynolds (RSQ; London and New York: Routledge, 2008), 175–203;Tommaso Tesei, "The Prophecy of Ḏū-l-Qarnayn and the Origins of the Qur'ānic Corpus," *MA* (2013–14): 273–90; Glen W. Bowersock, *Empires in Collision in Late Antiquity* (Waltham, MA: Brandeis University Press and Historical Society of Israel, 2012) 53–78.

Q 9:30–1 read thus:

وَقَالَتِ الْيَهُودُ عُزَيْرٌ ابْنُ اللَّهِ وَقَالَتِ النَّصَارَى الْمَسِيحُ ابْنُ اللَّهِ ۖ ذَٰلِكَ قَوْلُهُمْ بِأَفْوَاهِهِمْ ۖ يُضَاهِئُونَ
قَوْلَ الَّذِينَ كَفَرُوا مِنْ قَبْلُ ۚ قَاتَلَهُمُ اللَّهُ ۚ أَنَّىٰ يُؤْفَكُونَ 9:30

اتَّخَذُوا أَحْبَارَهُمْ وَرُهْبَانَهُمْ أَرْبَابًا مِنْ دُونِ اللَّهِ وَالْمَسِيحَ ابْنَ مَرْيَمَ وَمَا أُمِرُوا إِلَّا لِيَعْبُدُوا إِلَٰهًا وَاحِدًا ۖ
لَا إِلَٰهَ إِلَّا هُوَ ۚ سُبْحَانَهُ عَمَّا يُشْرِكُونَ 31

9:30 The Jews say, "'Uzayr is the son of God," and the Christians say, "The Messiah is the Son of God." This is what they utter with their mouths. They reproduce the words of those who disbelieved before [them]. [May] God fight them. How is it that they are [so] deluded?

31 They have taken their chief-rabbis and their bishops as lords besides God, and [also] the Messiah, Jesus son of Mary, while they have only been commanded to worship one God – there is no God but him. Glory be to him above all what they associate [to him]![60]

In my view, these two verses present *three* successive redactional strata: (I) the *first* one consists in Q 9:31's *Vorlage*; (II) the *second* one, in a later addition incorporated into it which slightly modified its original meaning; and (III) the *third* one, in Q 9:31's expansion after (i.e. drawing on) II, plus Q 9:30. Alternatively, it may be that II and III are part of the same layer, in which case there would be *two* instead of three strata behind the current text of Q 9:30–1. Be that as it may, my interest in this much debated passage[61] arises from the fact that Q 9:31's *Vorlage*, with its reference to the "bishops," is susceptible of being read as an anti-Chalcedonian formula. Before explaining why, however, it is necessary to clarify the nouns listed in the opening sentence of the verse.

The Qur'ān mentions six times, be it separately or all together, the terms ربّانيّون *rabbāniyyūn*, أحبار *aḥbār*, قسّيسون *qissīsūn*, and رهبان *ruhbān*. The most common English equivalents to such Arabic terms are:

rabbāniyyūn = rabbis
aḥbār = scribes
qissīsūn = priests
ruhbān = monks

60 On the name 'Uzayr, see the comments on 9:30 in Chapter 2. On the terms أخبار *aḥbār* ("chief-rabbis") and رهبان *ruhbān* ("bishops"), see below.

61 See Mun'im Sirry, *Scriptural Polemics: The Qur'ān and Other Religions* (Oxford and New York: Oxford University Press, 2014) 48–50.

This equivalence is somewhat problematic, but let us accept for now that "scribes" and "monks" are, respectively, good equivalents to *aḥbār* and *ruhbān* – in addition to being the most widespread ones, that is.

In Q 5:82 (which I have already quoted in the previous chapter) we read that Christians are the nearest people in affection to the "believers" (مؤمنون *mu'minūn*) because there are *qissīsūn* and *ruhbān* among them.[62] In 5:44 a good point is likewise made about the *rabbāniyyūn* and *aḥbār* as witnesses to the giving of the Torah. Things suddenly change in 57:27; 5:63; 9:31, 34, however. 57:27 states that "monasticism" (رهبانيّة *rahbāniyya*) – or perhaps something else, as we shall see – is not observed with due observance amongst the Christians, whereas 5:63 depicts many of the *rabbāniyyūn* and *aḥbār* as transgressors and sinners. Lastly, 9:31 accuses the Jews and the Christians of taking their *aḥbār* and *ruhbān* as "lords" (أرباب *arbāb*) besides God, while 9:34 contends that many of them steal money from people.

Thus we apparently have the following diagram:

Quranic attitude towards →	**Christian "priests" & "monks"**	**Jewish "scribes" & Christian "monks"**	**"Rabbis" & Jewish "scribes"**
+	5:82 Christians are the nearest people to the believers, because there are "**priests**" (*qissīsūn*) and "**monks**" (*ruhbān*) among them		5:44 A good point is made about the "**rabbis**" (*rabbāniyyūn*) and the Jewish "**scribes**" (*aḥbār*) as witnesses to the giving of the Torah
±	57:27 "**Monasticism**" (*rahbāniyya*) is not been observed with due observance		

62 The word for "affection" is مودّة *mawadda*. On the term *mu'minūn*, see Fred M. Donner, "From Believers to Muslims: Confessional Self-identity in the Early Islamic Community," *Al-Abhath* 50–1 (2002–2003): 9–53; idem, *Muhammad and the Believers: At the Origins of Islam* (Cambridge, MA, and London: Harvard University Press, 2010). For a criticism of Donner's interpretation of Muḥammad's community, see Patricia Crone, "Among the Believers," *Tablet*, August 10, 2010, http://www.tabletmag.com/jewish-news-and-politics/42023/amongst-the-believers).

(Continued)

Quranic attitude towards →	Christian "priests" & "monks"	Jewish "scribes" & Christian "monks"	"Rabbis" & Jewish "scribes"
–		9:31 The Jews have taken their "**scribes**" (*aḥbār*), and the Christians their "**monks**" (*ruhbān*) and the Messiah (*al-masīḥ*), as lords (*arbāb*) besides God	5:63 Many "**rabbis**" (*rabbāniyyūn*) and Jewish "**scribes**" (*aḥbār*) ought to be regarded as sinners and transgressors
		9:34 Many Jewish "**scribes**" (*aḥbār*) and Christian "**monks**" (*ruhbān*) steal money from the people	

Yet things are quite more complex than they seem to be.

First, it is interesting to observe the different ways in which the Jewish religious authorities are alluded to in these passages. In 5:44, 63 they are labeled *rabbāniyyūn* and *aḥbār*; the first of these two terms belongs to the verbal root *r.b.b.* (to "preside above") and is used in 3:146 as a synonym for "religious scholars" in general, whereas in 3:79 it denotes instead the true "worshipers of the Lord." In turn, the term *aḥbār* derives from the root *ḥ.b.r.* (to find "delight" in something; cf. 30:15; 43:70) and it is exclusively used in the quranic corpus to name the Jewish religious authorities. Conversely, in Q 9:31, 34 the Jewish authorities are only referred to as *aḥbār*. This may be due to the fact that, unlike *aḥbār*, the noun *rabbāniyyūn* falls, morphologically and phonetically speaking, too close to the noun (also from the root *r.b.b.*) *arbāb* or "lords" – their mutual identification being one of the points that the author of 9:31 wants to disprove. Yet *rabbāniyyūn* and *aḥbār* do not need be taken as denoting two different types of (Jewish) religious authority but one, even though a distinction in rank may be traced between them; in short, my contention is that both terms are used to designate the "rabbis."[63]

63 As Holger Zellentin writes, "[t]he terms '*ḥbry*' in the Aramaic plural or '*ḥbrym*' in the Hebrew plural designate a number of people. In the Talmudic period, these can be 'colleagues' of equal

The terms *qissīsūn* and *ruhbān* also have their own little peculiarities. To begin with, the plural noun *qissīsūn* is a hapax, and most likely an adaptation from either the Gəʾəz noun ቀሲሳን *qasisān* (sing. ቀሲስ *qasis*)[64] or the Syriac ܩܫܝܫܐ *qašīšē* (sing. ܩܫܐ *qašā*), both Semitic nouns meaning "priests." As for the noun *ruhbān*, it is – as I have earlier suggested – commonly translated by the English noun "monks." Yet neither of the two verbal roots from whence the Arabic noun may be said to derive imply the notion of "monasticism" – which additionally complicates the translation of *rahbāniyya* (another quranic hapax!) by the latter concept. *r.h.b.*, the first of such roots, conveys the notion of "fearing [God]" (cf. 2:40; 7:116, 154; 8:60; 16:51; 21:90; 28:32; 59:13) – in this case *ruhbān* would be better translated as "fearful ones" in the sense of "God-fearers." As for the second root from which *ruhbān* may derive, it is (despite the middle *h*) the aforementioned *r.b.b.* – in which case *ruhbān* should be translated as "leaders" (cf. the Syriac ܪܘܪܒܢܐ)[65]; or, to put it in more forceful terms: as "bishops."[66] By the same token, then, *rahbāniyya* should be translated as "episcopacy"; its interpretation as designating "monasticism" is, in fact, post-quranic.[67]

---

rank or the member of an elusive group within the rabbinic movement who paid special attention to purity and the payment of the tithe. In post-Talmudic times, the *ḥbr* is a member of the Palestinian rabbinic academy or a communal leader honored by the rabbis through this title; in Babylonia the term even designates one of the leaders of the rabbinic academy" (Holger M. Zellentin, "*Aḥbār* and *Ruhbān*: Religious Leaders in the Qur'ān in Dialogue with Christian and Rabbinic Literature," in *Qur'ānic Studies Today*,ed. Angelika Neuwirth and Michael A. Sells [RSQ; London and New York: Routledge, 2016] 258–89, p. 267).

64 Wolf Leslau, *Comparative Dictionary of Ge'ez (Classical Ethiopic), Ge'ez-English / English-Ge'ez, with an index of the Semitic Roots* (Wiesbaden: Harrassowitz, 2006) 85.

65 See Abraham Geiger, *Was hat Mohammed aus dem Judenthume aufgenommen?* (Bonn: Baaden, 1833) 50–1; François de Blois, "*Naṣrānī* (*Ναζωραῖος*) and *Ḥanīf* (*Ἐθνικός*): Studies on the Religious Vocabulary of Christianity and of Islam," *BSOAS* 65.1 (2002): 9; Zellentin, "*Aḥbār* and *Ruhbān*," 272.

66 The possibility that the quranic *ruhbān* is an adaptation of the Syr. *rwrbn'* (from the root *r.b.b.*) by dissimilation of *rr* to *rh* to make it fit (instead) a *r.h.b.* pattern, however, escapes de Blois ("*Naṣrānī* and *Ḥanīf*," 9) and Zellentin ("*Aḥbār* and *Ruhbān*," 290, n.35), who argue that both roots represent separate derivative options. In turn, Geiger (*Mohammed*, 50–1) translates *ruhbān* as "clerics," thus implicitly assimilating *ruhbān* and *qissīsūn*; for a critical appraisal of this position, see below.

67 Emran El-Badawi, "From 'Clergy' to 'Celibacy': The Development of *Rahbānīyya* between the Qur'ān, Ḥadīth and Church Canon," *Al-Bayān* 11.1 (2013): 1–14. See also Beck, *Evolution of the Early Qur'ān*, 273–334, who rightly translates *ruhbān* as "bishops." Cf. Geoffrey Parrinder, *Jesus in the Qur'an* (London: Faber and Faber; New York: Barnes and Noble, 1965; reprinted in London: Oneworld, 2014) 157, who finds a possible allusion to the cult of saints in Q 9:31: "it is well known that legends and devotions grew up around the lives of some of the Christian martyrs and

There are two important additional reasons, moreover, to identify *ruhbān* with bishops and *rahbāniyya* with episcopacy.

First, the reference to the latter term in 57:27 takes place within a brief section (namely, 57:25–27) whose criticism on the way in which the *rahbāniyya* is observed immediately follows a long pericope on avarice, charity, and the fair spending of money in God's cause (57:7–24). Put together, then, these two notions match the accusation in Q 9:34 that many *rahbāniyya* steal money from people. Now, it is difficult in this context to equate *rahbāniyya* with monasticism and *rahbāniyya* with monks. Identifying the latter with "bishops" makes much more sense – as also does the understanding that *rahbāniyya* designates "episcopacy," not monasticism. For it is not the monks,[68] but the bishops in their condition of "overseers" of the (Christian) community – which is how they are portrayed in 57:27[69] – who may, eventually, unfairly take money from the people, as the author of 9:34 furthermore denounces. If similar abuses take place under their jurisdiction, one may infer, they are the ones to blame, as well.[70]

Secondly, translating *ruhbān* by bishops matches better their comparison to the *aḥbār* in 9:34. As Zellentin insightfully observes, "after accusing the *aḥbār*, the rabbinic officials, of wrongfully eating up the people's wealth, the Qur'ān in turn accuses the *ruhbān* of doing so. It seems, then, that the *ruhbān* held a position of esteem and monetary compensation in the Christian community akin to that of the *aḥbār* in the rabbinic community. This suggests that the *ruhbān* were the overseers of the Christian community ... just as the *aḥbār* were superior to the regular rabbis in the case of the Jewish community."[71] To be precise, the author of 9:34 does not accuse the *ruhbān* of eating up the people's wealth after having accused the a*ḥbār* of doing so; he accuses them of eating up the people's wealth simultaneously, albeit he mentions them successively ("many of the a*ḥbār* and the *ruhbān* eat up the wealth of the people wrongfully" [9:34b]). Yet this does not affect Zellentin's argument, which I find ultimately compelling.

---

ascetics." Cf. too Sidney H. Griffith, "Monasticism and Monks," in *Encyclopaedia of the Qur'ān*, ed. Jane Damen McAuliffe (6 vols.; Leiden and Boston: Brill, 2001–6) 3:406.

68 The same reasoning can be applied to clerics in general, *pace* Geiger (see n.9 above).

69 On the semantics of the term *ri'āyatihā* ("observance," "oversight") in 57:27, see further Zellentin, "*Aḥbār* and *Ruhbān*," 272.

70 Of course, the Messalian fragments of the early Qur'ān get additional meaningfulness in this context; see further Segovia, "Messalianism, Binitarianism, and the East-Syrian Background of the Qur'ān."

71 "With regard to the parallel relationship between the rabbis and their overseers, the *aḥbār*, it therefore seems probable that *ruhbān* may well be the overseers over the *qissīsīn*," he adds (Zellentin, "*Aḥbār* and *Ruhbān*," 273).

If this interpretation is correct, it should be noticed, moreover, that the author of v. 9:34 may have merged two sources: Matthew 23; Mark 12:49; and Luke 11:44; 20:47 with their criticism against the scribes and Pharisees who out of greed steal from widows, on the one hand, and, on the other hand, *Didascalia Apostolorum* 7 with its warning on bishops as regards the distribution of wealth within the Church.[72]

Pro-Chalcedonian Bishops and Anti-Chalcedonian Monks?

As Phil Booth shows, the criticism of bishops was common in anti-Chalcedonian, especially Miaphysite, monastic circles,[73] so one does not actually need to presume – as Zellentin does – an influence of the *Didascalia* on the quranic authors, who may have simply used a formula that was current, therefore, among the Miaphysite Christians of the Near East, including the Arabs of Palestine and the Roman *provincia Arabia* east of the Jordan, who were in their majority Miaphysites. Thus, for instance, Chalcedonians are designated in John Rufus's *Plerophoriae* as "the party of the bishops,"[74] as in their majority these had given way before the canons approved at Chalcedon in 451.

There are several possibilities, then:

(*a*) either Q 9:31, 34 were originally composed in the Ḥiǧāz, in which case we ought to surmise that the term "bishops," applied to the pro-Chalcedonian hierarchy of the Church, was widespread not only among the Arabs of Palestine and the Roman *provincia Arabia* – in fact, Rufus himself was a native of the latter province[75] – but also among their southern neighbours, the Arabs

---

72 El-Badawi, "From 'Clergy' to 'Celibacy,'" 5, 7–8. On the hypothetical influence of the *Didascalia* (and especially its 4th-century Syriac version) on the Qur'ān, see Holger M. Zellentin, *The Qur'ān's Legal Culture: The Didascalia Apostolorum as a Point of Departure* (Tübingen: Mohr Siebeck, 2013).

73 Phil Booth, *Crisis of Empire: Doctrine and Dissent at the End of Late Antiquity* (Berkeley and London: University of California Press, 2014) 8, 9, 38, 40.

74 Booth, *Crisis of Empire*, 40 n.160. See further Jan-Eric Steppa, *John Rufus and the World Vision of Anti-Chalcedonian Culture* (GDACS 1; Piscataway, NJ: Gorgias Press, 2002).

75 On the spread of anti-Chalcedonian Christianity in these regions, see Aryeh Kofsky, "Peter the Iberian: Pilgrimage, Monasticism, and Ecclesiastical Politics in Byzantine Palestine," *LA* 47 (1997): 209–22; Cornelia B. Horn, "A Chapter in the Pre-History of the Christological Controversies in Arabic: Readings from the Works of John Rufus," *POr* 30 (2005): 133–56; idem, *Asceticism and Christological Controversy in Fifth-Century Palestine: The Career of Peter the Iberian* (OECS; Oxford and New York: Oxford University Press, 2006) 106–111.

of the Ḥiǧāz and Yemen – whose sympathy towards some anti-Chalcedonian, Miaphysite views cannot be *a priori* ruled out[76]; or

(*b*) 9:31, 34 are late Palestinian texts[77] that use the term "bishops" to designate the pro-Chalcedonian hierarchy as it was current among the Miaphysites of the Levant; or

(*c*) 9:31, 34 represent something altogether different: something whose meaning needs to be deciphered, and whose intent must be accordingly reassessed, from a quite different perspective.

For despite the quranic use of polemical notions like "repentance"[78] and "conversion to the truth,"[79] on which Miaphysite monks and missionaries eventually put their emphasis[80] in their effort to establish a spiritual hierarchy "opposed to the 'outer' hierarchy of the Church, especially the leaders and bishops ... [whom they viewed] as corrupted ... [due to their] acceptance of the decisions of Chalcedon,"[81] the criticism of the "bishops" undertaken in 9:31 and 34 may also be read against the background of the monastic crisis that took place in the *Church of the East* in the early 7th century, during which accusations of "Messalianism" (a term likely denoting a diffuse but undeniably existent and somewhat anarchic phenomenon)[82] were made against non-conformist monastic groups similar perhaps to that behind Q 17:79, 43:36, 73:1-8, 74:43, 76:26, and 108, with their stress on the benefits of prayer.[83] This, in my view, is a the most plausible hypothesis – one that takes us back to Iraq, therefore.

---

76 On which see the previous section. Being Arabia (in the broad sense of the term) a peripheral region, the fact that the Arabs of the Peninsula were open, as I have argued, to East Diphysite influence does not necessarily preclude the possibility that they were simultaneously exposed to West-Syrian Myaphisite ideas.

77 See the division offered in the previous chapter.

78 E.g. in Q 9:104; 30:31; 38:44; 39:17; 50:33; 68:32, etc.

79 E.g. in Q 2:42; 3:71; 10:35; 17:80; 38:84; 43:78, etc.

80 See Horn, *Asceticism and Christological Controversy in Fifth-Century Palestine*, 107, 146.

81 Horn, *Asceticism and Christological Controversy in Fifth-Century Palestine*, 120.

82 See my discussion of Brouria Bitton-Ashkelony, "'Neither Beginning nor End': The Messalian Imaginaire and Syriac Asceticism," *Adamantius* 19 (2013): 222–39 in "Asceticism and the Early Quranic Milieu."

83 See once more Segovia, "Asceticism and the Early Quranic Milieu." For an overview of the crisis, see Alberto Camplani, "The Revival of Persian Monasticism (Sixth to Seventh Centuries): Church Structures, Theological Academy, and Reformed Monks," in *Foundations of Power and Conflicts of Authority in Late-Antique Monasticism*, ed. A. Camplani and G. Filoramo (OLA 157; Leuven: Peeters, 2007) 277–95.

Besides, we now have a diagram visibly different from the one earlier displayed:

Quranic attitude towards →	**Christian "priests" & "bishops"**	**Jewish "rabbis" & Christian "bishops"**	**"Rabbis"**
+	5:82 Christians are the nearest people to the believers, because there are "**priests**" (*qissīsūn*) and "**bishops**" (*ruhbān*) among them		5:44 A good point is made about the "**rabbis**" (*rabbāniyyūn* + *aḥbār*) as witnesses to the giving of the Torah
±	57:27 "**Episcopacy**" (*rahbāniyya*) is not been observed with due observance		
–		9:31 The Jews have taken their "**rabbis**" (*aḥbār*), and the Christians their "**bishops**" (*ruhbān*) and the Messiah (*al-masīḥ*), as lords (*arbāb*) besides God	5:63 Many "**rabbis**"- (*rabbāniyyūn* + *aḥbār*) ought to be regarded as sinners and transgressors
		9:34 Many "**rabbis**" (*aḥbār*) and Christian "**bishops**" (*ruhbān*) steal money from the people	

The criticism of the ecclesiastical authorities is therefore patent in 9:31, 34. It is thus difficult to interpret in such context 5:82, with its positive allusion to the "bishops": perhaps its author meant other bishops, or perhaps 5:82 dates to Muʿāwiya's times, when, as we have seen in the precedent chapter, attempts to establish good relations with their Christian subjects of Syria-Palestine – and, one may legitimately deduce, their ecclesiastical representatives – were made by the post-conquest Arab political elite.

My conjecture then is that 9:31's *Vorlage* might be rather early, while the interpolation incorporated into it and v. 30 – with their analogies with 4:171–2; 5:17,

72–5, 116–7; 19:34–6– may come from a later period. Anyway, it is worth taking a look at both verses, as they show that anti-clerical polemics were vital for the quranic authors.

The Philological Crux in v. 9:31a – and v. 9:30

The standard vocalisation of 9:31a reads:

ٱتَّخَذُوٓا۟ أَحْبَارَهُمْ وَرُهْبَـٰنَهُمْ أَرْبَابًا مِّن دُونِ ٱللَّهِ وَٱلْمَسِيحَ

ittaḫaḏū aḥbārahum wa-ruhbānahum arbāb[an] *min dūni llāhi wa-l-masīḥa*
They have taken their rabbis and their bishops as lords besides God, and the Messiah

i.e. "They (the Jews) have taken their rabbis and [they (the Christians) have taken] their bishops as lords besides God, as well as the Messiah." There is no comma after the word "God" in the Arabic text, but I have used it in the English translation so as to highlight, with a brief pause, the unequal grammatical case of the consecutive terms "God" (genitive ending *-i*) and "Messiah" (accusative ending *-a*). The nouns "rabbis," "bishops," and "lords" are all in the accusative, as well; therefore, it is easy to connect all such terms and to understand that the direct object of the verb, i.e. those taken as "lords" by the Jews and the Christians, are the rabbis, the bishops and Jesus, respectively. Yet the expression "and the Messiah" is oddly placed at the end of the sentence, which is anything but logical in grammatical terms and seems to imply, furthermore, that both groups alike (i.e. the Jews and the Christians) regard the Messiah as "lord" besides God – an awkward statement concerning the Jews, to be sure!

Was it to illustrate this absurd claim that 9:30, with its puzzling allusion to ʻUzayr/Ezra being viewed as the Son of God by the Jews, was added and strategically placed before 9:31a? This would imply that 9:30 postdates both 9:31a and its *Vorlage*, and that it was incorporated to the corpus (or else to the pre-quranic document originally containing 9:31a + 9:31b) to clarify the otherwise obscure point made by the author of 9:31a, in accordance with the thesis displayed in 9:31b. Also, it would explain the purpose of 9:30, whose reference to ʻUzayr/Ezra has caused so many interpretative problems to Muslim and Western scholars alike.[84] Put differently: even if no Jewish group had ever transformed Ezra (or any other relevant religious figure for that matter, with the exception of Enoch

84 See Mun'im Sirry, *Scriptural Polemics: The Qur'ān and Other Religions* (Oxford and New York: Oxford University Press, 2014) 48–50.

in 1 Enoch 71:14) into the Son of God, they had to be accused of doing so by the author of 9:30 in order to make sense of the convoluted argument in 9:31a, which implicitly attributes to the Jews and the Christians alike the belief in the lordship of the Messiah.

Five Hypotheses in Search of Q 9:31's *Vorlage*

1. A first way out of the philological crux in 9:31a consists in placing the phrase "and the Messiah" after the reference to "their bishops":

ٱتَّخَذُوٓا۟ أَحْبَارَهُمْ وَرُهْبَـٰنَهُمْ وَٱلْمَسِيحَ أَرْبَابًا مِّن دُونِ ٱللَّهِ

ittaḫaḏū aḥbārahum wa-ruhbānahum wa-l-masīḥa arbāban min dūni llāhi
They have taken their rabbis, their bishops and the Messiah as lords besides God

i.e. "They (the Jews) have taken their rabbis and [they (the Christians) have taken] their bishops and the Messiah as lords besides God." In fact, this is the way in which most people unconsciously read this verse. In short, someone (a copyist or an editor) misplaced the expression "and the Messiah," which should be conveniently relocated, therefore.

This looks like a very simple option, yet it implies altering the *rasm* or consonantal skeleton of the quranic text – and hence a major change in the latter.

But there are other additional options.

2. One is to interpret "and the Messiah" as a later addition to a *Vorlage* which may have been as follows:

ٱتَّخَذُوٓا۟ أَحْبَارَهُمْ وَرُهْبَـٰنَهُمْ أَرْبَابًا مِّن دُونِ ٱللَّهِ

ittaḫaḏū aḥbārahum wa-ruhbānahum arbāb^{an} min dūni llāhi
They have taken their rabbis and their bishops as lords besides God

On this hypothesis, an editor added the expression "and the Messiah" so as to expand the *Vorlage*'s criticism of the bishops' authority (which amounts to a practical issue) into the questioning of the mainstream Christian belief that Christ himself is the "Lord," which is a completely different kind of issue.[85] Accordingly,

85 Additions of the type *wa* ... ("and ...") are well documented in the "Uthmanic" codex and in particular Q 9, e.g. *ad* Q 9:74, which reads "punishment in this world *and in the hereafter*" (my emphasis), whereas the San'ā' palimpsest (DAI 01–27.1) has instead "punishment in this world" (stop). I am indebted to Daniel Beck for pointing this fact to me in a private communication of

the expression "and the Messiah" in the accusative and 9:31b would belong to the same redactional layer. I find this possibility to be the most compelling one.

3. Another option, however, is to read "the Messiah," like "God," in the genitive instead of the accusative, as the conjunctive و *wa-* ("and") would normally demand:

> اتَّخَذُوٓاْ أَحْبَارَهُمْ وَرُهْبَـٰنَهُمْ أَرْبَاباً مِّنْ دُونِ ٱللهِ وَٱلْمَسِيحِ
>
> *ʾttaḫaḏū aḥbārahum wa-ruhbānahum arbāb^an^ min dūni llāhi wa-l-masīḥi*
>
> *They have taken their rabbis and their bishops as lords besides God and the Messiah*

i.e. "They (the Jews) have taken their rabbis and [they (some Christians) have taken] their bishops as lords besides God and his Messiah." In so far as the Quranic *rasm* lacks any diacritical marks, changing the final *-a* in *al-masīḥ* into an *-i* (and hence reading *al-masīḥi* in the genitive instead of *al-masīḥa* in the accusative) seems to be a reasonable option despite its extravagance. Besides, this option, in addition to being entirely coherent from a logical and grammatical viewpoint, presents, unlike option no. 1, the advantage of not requiring a shift in the *rasm*, and, unlike option no. 2, the advantage of not demanding the suppression of one of its segments.

It should be observed, moreover, that the above-reconstructed expression "God and the Messiah" in the genitive (i.e. "God and his Messiah") formally matches the official Yemenite Christological formula of the second half of the 6th century, to which I shall return in the next section, as well as a pre-Islamic *talbiya* (prayer) recorded in Muqātil b. Sulaymān's *Tafsīr* (mid-8th century) which reads:

> لا شريك لك \ إلا شريكا هو لك \ تملكه وما ملك
>
> *lʾ šryk lk / illʾ šryk hw lk / tmlkh w-mʾ mlk*
>
> *lā šarīka lak / illā šarīk^an^ huwa lak / tamlikuhu wa-mā malak*
>
> *You have no partner / except the partner that you have; / You possess him and all that is his*

and that could furthermore reflect a pre-Islamic Arabic adaptation of the Nicene Creed drawing on 1 Corinthians 15:27–8.[86]

Still, there are two other options.

June 25, 2016. For the the San'ā' palimpsest, see Behnam Sadeghi and Mohsen Goudarzi, "Ṣan'ā' 1 and the Origins of the Qur'ān," *IJHCME* 87 (2012): 1–129.

86 On which see Manfred Kropp, "Tripartite, but Anti-Trinitarian Formulas in the Qur'ānic Corpus, Possibly Pre-Qur'ānic," in *New Perspectives on the Qur'ān: The Qur'ān in Its Historical Context 2*, ed. Gabriel Said Reynolds (RSQ; London & New York: Routledge, 2011) 247–64, esp. pp. 262–3.

4. One is to surmise that the original text behind 9:31a was as follows:

ٱتَّخَذُوٓاْ أَحْبَارَهُمْ أَرْبَابًا مِّن دُونِ ٱللَّهِ وَٱلْمَسِيحِ

ʾttaḫaḏū aḥbārahum arbāb^an min dūni llāhi wa-l-masīḥi
They have taken their rabbis as lords besides God and the/his Messiah

i.e. one may drop the phrase "and their bishops" as a later addition whilst reading, once more, "the Messiah" in the genitive, in which case a purely Christian, anti-Jewish text would emerge before one's eyes.

5. The other option is to fancy a more complex *Vorlage*, like this one:

ٱتَّخَذُوٓاْ أَحْبَارَهُمْ أَرْبَابًا مِّن دُونِ ٱللَّهِ وَٱتَّخَذُوٓاْ رُهْبَنَهُمْ أَرْبَابًا مِّن دُونِ ٱلْمَسِيحِ

ʾttaḫaḏū aḥbārahum arbāb^an min dūni llāhi wa ʾttaḫaḏū ruhbānahum arbāb^an min dūni l-masīḥi
They have taken their rabbis as lords besides God, and they have taken their bishops as lords besides the Messiah

i.e. "Just as the Jews have taken their rabbis as lords besides God, so too some Christians have taken their bishops as lords besides his Messiah."

The ideology of 9:31's *Vorlage* varies too from one option to another:

1 must be read as an anti-Jewish- and anti-Christian polemical text whose purpose is to denounce either Christian authority or an excess in its exercise, and Christian belief. I have earlier explain why I do not find this textual reconstruction compelling (it implies a major change in the *rasm*).

In turn, 2 ought to be read as an anti-Jewish- and anti-/intra-Christian polemical text whose author's intent is to denounce either Christian authority or an excess in its exercise. Reading it as intra-Christian- instead of anti-Christian is thus perfectly possible; and in such case one would need to acknowledge the author's purpose as being anticlerical in the first place – or else polemical against the hierarchy of a rival Christian group (e.g. Chalcedonian or pro-Chalcedonian).

As for 3, it needs to be read as an anti-Jewish- and intra-Christian polemical text against Christian authority or an excess in its exercise; or, perhaps again, against a rival Christian group. Yet the frequency of additions of the type "and the Messiah" in Q 9 militates in favour of the preceding hypothesis instead.

Conversely, 4 should be read as a Christian, anti-Jewish text. There are numerous passages of this kind in the quranic corpus, but none of them goes as far as to proclaim Jesus's divine sonship. Thus its interpretation in this sense looks problematic.

Lastly, 5 partly resembles 3, whose ideology it echoes in a much more complex way. Yet such complexity looks somewhat artificial, for which reason this reconstruction can be, I think, discarded as well.

In conclusion, it is obvious that 9:31 confronts the reader with a number of problems that can no longer be ignored – and more than likely that 9:31 and 34 witness to the struggle against the hierarchy of the Church, possibly pro-Chalcedonian.

5 From the Qur'ān's Early Christology to the Elaboration of the Muhamadan *Kerygma*

A Sketch of the Early Qur'ān Christology (Q 75–107)

Introducing a Systematically Overlooked but Crucial Topic

In his recent and extremely suggestive – in fact groundbreaking – book, Daniel Beck argues that if the ecclesiastical authorities, in particular the pro-Chalcedonian bishops and the priests loyal to them, were the target of the quranic authors, then the best way to undermine their authority was to eliminate their alleged institutional role by rejecting the very basis on which their delegated authority was grounded: the sacraments as a means to salvation; and the best way to make this fully effective, he adds, was to deny Jesus's divine sonship and his role in the economy of salvation, so as to disprove the very notion of soteriological mediation. Hence repentance and conversion to God (understood as the leitmotif of all previous revelations),[1] plus an intense eschatological expectation before an event initially deemed imminent[2] and the subsequent observance of ethical purity (with all its implications, ascesis included), became the sole soteriological referents of the Qur'ān's early community, he concludes.[3]

Yet the rejection of Jesus's role in the economy of salvation – which is never explicitly stated but seems an obvious component of the earliest quranic texts, may additionally be interpreted as witnessing to the existence, and thereby the survival, of a peripheral *Engelchristologie* whose theological background, key notions, and *Wirkungsgeschichte* Henry Corbin first throughout his vast inspiring work,[4]

1 Cf. Roberto Tottoli, *I profeti biblici nella tradizione islamica* (Brescia: Paideia, 1999); English translation by Michael Robertson: *Biblical Prophets in the Qur'ān and Muslim Literature* (RSQ; London and New York: Routledge, 2002) 7–11.

2 See Stephen J. Shoemaker, *The Death of a Prophet: The End of Muhammad's Life and the Beginnings of Islam* (DRLAR; Philadelphia: University of Pennsylvania Press, 2012) 118–96.

3 See Daniel A. Beck, *Evolution of the Early Qur'ān*: From Anonymous Apocalypse to Charismatic Prophet (ACDE 2; New York and Bern: Peter Lang, 2018) 79–108, 273–334. I am grateful to him for sharing an early draft of his book with me prior to its publication. "Rejection of the soteriological premise [centred on the notion of a crucified God,]" Beck further underlines, "was shared by Manichaeans, Nestorians, and ... Julianists alike," whose Christologies echoed one another and were derivative of that "soteriological negation" (private communication of February 16, 2017).

4 See e.g. Henry Corbin, *Le Paradoxe du monothéisme* (Paris: L'Herne, 1981) 133–61.

https://doi.org/10.1515/9783110599688-005

and more recently Jan Van Reeth in a remarkable paper,[5] have explained and deciphered, and which may somehow be described as anti-Nicene, anti-Ephesian, and anti-Chalcedonian at the very same time (in allusion to the Church councils of 325, 431, and 451, respectively) – a Christology that, in my hypothesis, was gradually *erased* until it was finally *subverted* in the two next quranic redactional layers, being then replaced by the combination of a more strict *monotheism* and what I propose to call the Muhamadan *kerygma*; and yet a Christology whose memory the proto-Shiite tradition – as Ali Amir-Moezzi indirectly but convincingly shows – apparently preserved. Accordingly, in this chapter I will try to present its core notions, textual basis, and development – and to examine the fundamental implications of this systematically overlooked issue. If the Jesus passages contained in the quranic corpus are the key to unraveling the latter's post-conquest chronology, the Christological passages found in its earliest layers are the key to deciphering the Qur'ān's original sectarian milieu.

A Heavenly Messenger that Speaks Directly to Mankind and Refers to God as "He" – but Who Is One with God

It is generally believed that the Qur'ān combines three interrelated features: divine speech, an angelic speaker as its deliverer, and a human prophet as its recipient. Perceptibly, however, there are various passages, stylistically different from one another, to which this scheme cannot be applied – e.g. Q 1, which rather looks like a prayer; the verses mentioning Muḥammad by his name, i.e. 3:144, 33:40, 47:2, 48:29, in which the people is addressed directly and the quranic prophet the object, instead of the addresser, of the (divine?) speech; or 112, which displays a brief monotheistic confessional formula. Yet there is an even bigger exception to the aforementioned alleged rule: in one of the *earliest* quranic layers comprising chapters 75–93, 95–6, 99–104, 107 of the corpus,[6] *there is no human messenger at*

5 Van Reeth, "Melchisédech le Prophète éternel selon Jean d'Apamée et le monarchianisme musulman," *OC* 96 (2012): 8–46.

6 *Sūra*-s 75–93, 95–6, 99–104, 107 are usually assigned to the "Meccan I" stratum of the Qur'ān, whereas Q 98 is normally assigned to its "Medinan" stratum (see further Theodor Nöldeke, *Geschichte des Qorāns* [Göttingen: Dieterich, 1860] 73; Theodor Nöldeke and Friedrich Schwally,*Geschichte des Qorāns* [2nd ed.; 2 vols.; Leipzig: Weicher, 1909–19] 1:91). See my criticism of Räisänen in Chapter 1, where I explain why I do not take this classification – and more broadly the view that *all* the Qur'ān goes back to Muḥammad – to be valid. Still, I do think it has some basis, in the sense that these *sūra*-s may well constitute very early texts if one considers their visionary style, alien to the socio-political concerns characteristic of the later quranic layers and much more condensed than the apocalyptic style displayed in *sūra*-s 52 and 56, with which they

all except in a few verses: 81:22–8; 87:1–13; 88:21–3,[7] which I shall analyse in the next section. Instead, *what one finds in these early quranic chapters is* (A_2) a *divine "messenger"* (رسول *rasūl*) *who* (A_3) *speaksdirectlyto the people about their judgement to come and* (A_5) *is "one" with God – for even though* (A_1) he *speaks in "I" form and* (A_4) *refers to God as "He,"* (A_1) he *often refers to God and himself as "We."*[8]

To provide the reader an eloquent example of this idea, I will focus on a limited number of verses: 75:1–30; 76:2–4; 79:15–33; 81:19–21); yet I will provide the necessary parallels (all of them pertaining to *sūra*-s 75–114) in due course.

The first set of verses that call for attention are vv. 1–19 in *Sūrat al-Qiyāma* (Q 75, "The Resurrection"):

(A_1) **Q 75:1–19**

لَا أُقْسِمُ بِيَوْمِ الْقِيَامَةِ 75:1
وَلَا أُقْسِمُ بِالنَّفْسِ اللَّوَّامَةِ 2
أَيَحْسَبُ الْإِنْسَانُ أَلَّنْ نَجْمَعَ عِظَامَهُ 3
بَلَىٰ قَادِرِينَ عَلَىٰ أَنْ نُسَوِّيَ بَنَانَهُ 4
بَلْ يُرِيدُ الْإِنْسَانُ لِيَفْجُرَ أَمَامَهُ 5
يَسْأَلُ أَيَّانَ يَوْمُ الْقِيَامَةِ 6

nevertheless present a number of parallelisms. They differ too from *sūra*-s 94, 97–8, 105–6, 108–14, which may be very old too, but whose styles are different as well. On the stylistic peculiarities of Q 52–3, 56, 69, 74–75, 77–9, 81–6, 88–93, 95, 99–101, 103–6, 108, and the possibility that form an independent layer within the corpus, see Tommaso Tesei, "The Qur'ān(s) in Contex(s)", unpublished, available online at https://www.academia.edu/s/435c3a5a16/the-qur'ans-in-contexts. On *sūra* 94, Daniel A. Beck, *Evolution of the Early Qur'ān*, 215–72.

7 Although a human figure might be said to sometimes play the liminal role of a "medium," on which see Manfred Kropp's incisive comments *ad* Q 85 in *The Qur'an Seminar Commentary / Le Qur'an Seminar: A Collaborative Study of 59 Qur'an Passages / Commentaires collaborative de 50 passages coraniques*, ed. Mehdi Azaiez, Gabriel Said Reynolds, Tommaso Tesei, and Hamza M. Zafer (Berlin and Boston: De Gruyter, 2016) 408–9.

8 Overall, I follow Beck's "genealogy of the messenger function" in his book where he hypothesises on the plausible reason underlying the juxtaposition of "I" and "We" speeches in Q 75–114, speaks of (*a*) "God's cosmic *Rasūl*" thereof and apropos Q 81 (cf. my A-texts); (*b*) "the human *rasūl* [who,] wrapped in glory and divinized by his purity, stands into his Lord's presence as the *Rūḥ* descends upon him" in Q 73–4 (cf. my B- and C-texts and my differentiation between three processes: the introducing the human *rasūl*, his defence, and his exaltation); (*c*) the "noble human *rasūl*" who seemingly replaces the "cosmic *rasūl*" in Q 69 (cf. my D-texts); (*d*) his "opponents" who "compromise the truth because of their worldly ambition" in Q 68 (cf. my B-texts); (e) the two direct "encounters" between the human *rasūl* and God in Q 53 (cf. my D-texts); and (*f*) the "glorification of the human *rasūl*" in Q 17 (cf. again my C-texts). Formally, therefore, our differences basically affect our grouping of certain texts.

فَإِذَا بَرِقَ الْبَصَرُ 7
وَخَسَفَ الْقَمَرُ 8
وَجُمِعَ الشَّمْسُ وَالْقَمَرُ 9
يَقُولُ الْإِنْسَانُ يَوْمَئِذٍ أَيْنَ الْمَفَرُّ 10
كَلَّا لَا وَزَرَ 11
إِلَىٰ رَبِّكَ يَوْمَئِذٍ الْمُسْتَقَرُّ 12
يُنَبَّأُ الْإِنْسَانُ يَوْمَئِذٍ بِمَا قَدَّمَ وَأَخَّرَ 13
بَلِ الْإِنْسَانُ عَلَىٰ نَفْسِهِ بَصِيرَةٌ 14
وَلَوْ أَلْقَىٰ مَعَاذِيرَهُ 15
لَا تُحَرِّكْ بِهِ لِسَانَكَ لِتَعْجَلَ بِهِ 16
إِنَّ عَلَيْنَا جَمْعَهُ وَقُرْآنَهُ 17
فَإِذَا قَرَأْنَاهُ فَاتَّبِعْ قُرْآنَهُ 18
ثُمَّ إِنَّ عَلَيْنَا بَيَانَهُ 19

75:1 Nay! *I* swear by the Day of Resurrection!
2 And nay! *I* swear by the accusing soul!
3 Do men think that *we* shall not assemble their bones?[9]
4 Well – *we* are [even] able to fashion their fingers [again]!
5 Yet men like to gush about what awaits them.
6 They ask, "When will the Day of Resurrection come?"
7 When the sight is dazed,
8 and the moon becomes dark,
9 and the sun and the moon are joined together –
10 on that day they will ask, "Where is the way out [of this]?"
11 But nay! There will be no refuge [then]!
12 To *your* Lord that day *you* [all] shall return.[10]
13 On that day men will be informed of what they have sent forth and kept back.
14 Nay! [All] men will bear witness against their deeds[11]
15 regardless of the excuses they may offer.
16 [But] do not move your tongue so as to hasten it,
17 as on *us* depends its collection and its recitation.[12]
18 When *we* recite it, follow its recitation
19 [and] then [be] sure [that] on *us* depends its explanation.

9 Lit., "Does man think that we shall not assemble his bones?," in the singular; so too vv. 4–15, though all mankind is alluded to in this way – therefore my use of the plural form in vv. 3–15.
10 Lit., "To your Lord on that day will be your dwelling place."
11 Lit., "[Every] man will be witnesses against himself."
12 I.e. the collection of such signs and the recitation of such message.

This strongly eschatological text, which resembles many others in *sūra*-s 75–93, 95–6, 99–104, and 107, presents, like 90:1–4, the interest of the grammatical-person shift (from "I" to "We") in v. 3. There is, however, no clue in the text itself as to the identity of the "I" speaker in vv. 1–2, who therefore can be interpreted to be either human or super-human (i.e. a human- or, alternatively, a heavenly being); cf. 81:15–18; 90:1, 3, though 77:38–9; 86:16; and 92:14 patently point to a heavenly origin. Conversely, the "We" speaker in vv. 3–4, does seem to be of heavenly nature, as he refers as "We" to her/him and to someone else who, together with her/him, will "gather" mankind's bones and is, moreover, able to "fashion" their fingers again – these clearly being an allusion to God's creation and re-creation (i.e. resurrection) of mankind. It is 81:19–21 that gives us her/his identity

(A_2) **Q 81:19–21**

إِنَّهُ لَقَوْلُ رَسُولٍ كَرِيمٍ 81:19
ذِي قُوَّةٍ عِنْدَ ذِي الْعَرْشِ مَكِينٍ 20
مُطَاعٍ ثَمَّ أَمِينٍ 21

81: 19 Certainly this is the speech of *a noble messenger,*
20 *full of power,* [who is] *secure with the Holder of the Throne –*
21 *one to be obeyed and trustworthy.*

The wording in these two verses from *Sūrat al-Tawkīr* (Q 81, "The Shrouding") suggests a *heavenly being* – a heavenly speaker, according to A_1 and A_2 (cf. 86:1–3). But, as we shall see, the *heavenly messenger* thus introduced must not be merely thought of as the "angel of revelation"; for he does not only communicate God's words. Her/his role is much more important indeed. As for the possibility that vv. 20–1 represent an interpolation aiming at transforming an original theophany (in v. 19) into an angelophany,[13] the allusion to a "messenger" in v. 19 rules it out, I think – for in the Qur'ān God can hardly be understood to be a messenger, even if he sometimes seems to communicate his words to the quranic prophet without an angelic intermediator. Deciding whether an angelophany implies a theophany is another matter, though; and one to which I shall further return.

It is, moreover, interesting to notice that the heavenly messenger speaks here *directly* to the people, i.e. without a human intermediator. Vv. 20–1 in

13 On which see Arthur J. Droge, *The Qur'ān: A New Annotated Translation* (Sheffield, UK, and Bristol, CT: Equinox, 2013) 423 n.15.

Sūrat al-Qiyāma (Q 75) make this clear enough. In them, the heavenly messenger addresses in the plural those who love this short-lived world and neglect the hereafter:

(A3) **Q 75:20–30**

كَلَّا بَلْ تُحِبُّونَ الْعَاجِلَةَ 75:20
وَتَذَرُونَ الْآخِرَةَ 21
وُجُوهٌ يَوْمَئِذٍ نَاضِرَةٌ 22
إِلَىٰ رَبِّهَا نَاظِرَةٌ 23
وَوُجُوهٌ يَوْمَئِذٍ بَاسِرَةٌ 24
تَظُنُّ أَنْ يُفْعَلَ بِهَا فَاقِرَةٌ 25
كَلَّا إِذَا بَلَغَتِ التَّرَاقِيَ 26
وَقِيلَ مَنْ ۜ رَاقٍ 27
وَظَنَّ أَنَّهُ الْفِرَاقُ 28
وَالْتَفَّتِ السَّاقُ بِالسَّاقِ 29
إِلَىٰ رَبِّكَ يَوْمَئِذٍ الْمَسَاقُ 30

75:20 But no! *You* love this world
21 and neglect the hereafter!
22 On that Day some faces will be radiant
23 looking to their Lord
24 while other will be scowling
25 thinking about the calamity that shall reach them.
26 But no! When it reaches the collarbones
27 and it is said [by the angels], "Who shall cure [this one]?,"
28 and it is certain for him that the [time to] depart has come,
29 when the legs are tangled with one another,
30 the [only] drive on that Day will be to *your* Lord.

Cf. 77:20, 27, 38–9; 78:18, 30; 79:27, 33; 81:22, 26, 28–9;82:9–10, 12, 17–18; 84:24; 89:17–20; 102:1–8; 109:1–6 and those verses that may be read as addressing all believers: 77:14; 79:15; 82:6–8; 84:6; 85:12–17; 89:6; 89:27–8; 90:2, 12; 92:14; 93:3–9; 94:1–4; 96:1, 3, 9–13, 19; 99:5; 101:10; 105:1; 107:1; 108:1–3; 110:2–3.

Besides, if, on the one hand, the heavenly messenger repeatedly marks off his *subordination* to God by referring to him as "he," on the other hand he refers to God and himself as "We," thus reinforcing the notion of a *shared plural yet univocal identity* (of God and his theophanic form[s]). An example of the former notion can be found in vv. 15–26 and 27–33 of *Sūrat al-Nāzi'āt* (Q 79, "Those Who Pull Out"):

(A4) **Q 79:15–33**

هَلْ أَتَاكَ حَدِيثُ مُوسَىٰ 79:15
إِذْ نَادَاهُ رَبُّهُ بِالْوَادِ الْمُقَدَّسِ طُوًى 16
اذْهَبْ إِلَىٰ فِرْعَوْنَ إِنَّهُ طَغَىٰ 17
فَقُلْ هَلْ لَكَ إِلَىٰ أَنْ تَزَكَّىٰ 18
وَأَهْدِيَكَ إِلَىٰ رَبِّكَ فَتَخْشَىٰ 19
فَأَرَاهُ الْآيَةَ الْكُبْرَىٰ 20
فَكَذَّبَ وَعَصَىٰ 21
ثُمَّ أَدْبَرَ يَسْعَىٰ 22
فَحَشَرَ فَنَادَىٰ 23
فَقَالَ أَنَا رَبُّكُمُ الْأَعْلَىٰ 24
فَأَخَذَهُ اللَّهُ نَكَالَ الْآخِرَةِ وَالْأُولَىٰ 25
إِنَّ فِي ذَٰلِكَ لَعِبْرَةً لِمَنْ يَخْشَىٰ 26
أَأَنْتُمْ أَشَدُّ خَلْقًا أَمِ السَّمَاءُ ۚ بَنَاهَا 27
رَفَعَ سَمْكَهَا فَسَوَّاهَا 28
وَأَغْطَشَ لَيْلَهَا وَأَخْرَجَ ضُحَاهَا 29
وَالْأَرْضَ بَعْدَ ذَٰلِكَ دَحَاهَا 30
أَخْرَجَ مِنْهَا مَاءَهَا وَمَرْعَاهَا 31
وَالْجِبَالَ أَرْسَاهَا 32
مَتَاعًا لَكُمْ وَلِأَنْعَامِكُمْ 33

79:15 Has the story of Moses come to you,
16 when his Lord called him in the holy valley of Ṭuwā and said [to him],
17 "Go to Pharaoh, for surely he has transgressed,
18 and tell him, 'Do you want to purify yourself?,'
19 and, 'I will guide you to your Lord, so that you may then fear [him]'"?
20 He showed him a great sign,
21 but he denied it and disobeyed.
22 Then he turned away in haste
23 and called and gathered his people
24 and said, "I am your Lord, the Most High!";
25 so *God* seized him with a punishment in [both] the next life and this life.[14]
26 Surely there is in [all] this is a lesson for those who fear [God]!
27 Are you a stronger than the sky?[15] *He* built it;
28 *he* raised its roof and fashioned it,
29 and [then] darkened its night and brought forth its brightness;

---

14 Lit., "with a punishment of the last and the first."
15 Lit., "Are you a stronger creation or the sky?"

30 and then *he* had the earth spread out,
31 *he* brought forth from it its water and its pasture;
32 and the mountains *he* made them firm –
33 a provision for you and your livestock.

Cf. 75:38; 79:25, 27–32; 80:18–23; 85:13–16; 87:1–5, 7; 88:24; 89:6,13–14, 28; 93:6–8; 95:8; 96:1–5, 8, 14; 99:5; 100:11; 1 05:1–5. Instead, an example of the "We" speech by which the heavenly messenger presents himself as being close to God can be found in vv. 2–4 of *Sūrat al-Insān* (Q 76, "The Human"):

(A5) **Q 76:2–4**

إِنَّا خَلَقْنَا الْإِنْسَانَ مِنْ نُطْفَةٍ أَمْشَاجٍ نَبْتَلِيهِ فَجَعَلْنَاهُ سَمِيعًا بَصِيرًا 76:2
إِنَّا هَدَيْنَاهُ السَّبِيلَ إِمَّا شَاكِرًا وَإِمَّا كَفُورًا 3
إِنَّا أَعْتَدْنَا لِلْكَافِرِينَ سَلَاسِلَ وَأَغْلَالًا وَسَعِيرًا 4

76: 2 Indeed *we* created man from a drop, a mixture – *we* test him[16] – and *we* gave him hearing and sight.
3 *We* guided him to the [straight] path, [to see] whether [he would be] thankful or ungrateful [to us].
4 And surely *we* have prepared for the disbelievers chains, and fetters, and a blazing [Fire].

Cf. 77:16–27, 38; 78:6–16, 28–30; 80:25–32; 87:6; 88:25–6; 89:29–30; 90:4, 10, 19; 92:7, 10, 12–13; 94:1–4; 95:4–5; 96:15, 18; 97:1; 108:1. Notice too the pronominal alternation in 87:1–5 ("he"), 6 ("We"), 7 ("he"), 8 ("We"); 88:24–5, etc.

***Excursus 1*: Traces of an Angelomorphic Christology?**

A brief excursus is in order here. Daniel Boyarin has aptly underlined that *binitarianism*, i.e. the notion, as the rabbis would have it, that there are "two powers in heaven," far from being a Christian invention, and far from being the reason for the parting of the ways between Christianity and Rabbinic Judaism, was an acceptable and indeed widespread Jewish belief in the Second Temple period.[17]

---

16 This phrase would fit better at the beginning of the next verse: "we test him. We guided him ... ," etc.

17 See further Daniel Boyarin, "The Gospel of the *Memra*: Jewish Binitarianism and the Prologue to John," *HTR* 94.3 (2001): 243–85; idem, *Border Lines: The Partition of Judaeo-Christianity* (DRLAR; Philadelphia: University of Pennsylvania Press, 2004); idem, *The Jewish Gospels: The Story of the Jewish Christ*, with a Foreword by Jack Miles (New York: The New Press, 2012).

Moreover, he points to the survival of a pre-Jewish Israelite religious stratum characterised by the dynamic coexistence of the Canaanite god 'El and YHWH in the role of Israel's Ba'al behind the unfolding of such a binitarian scheme into the pair formed by YHWH and his Messiah.[18]

Now, it must be observed that, in the apocalyptic literature of Second Temple Judaism,[19] God's Messiah is frequently portrayed as an angel.[20] Regardless of this, he is assigned different functions – an eschatological function, to be sure, but also a priestly function and a teaching function among others – as well as different identities.[21] In fact, as I have written elsewhere,

> [a] given figure may be ... modelled upon another one whose specific characters it readapts, whereas other figures develop some features not included in any previous model ... A twofold hybrid procedure can be documented as well: adoption (reinterpretation) and innovation (which can sometimes depend on a former reinterpretation) may well converge at times. Be that as it may, one must quite often deal with either explicit or implicit "transpositions."[22]

Needless to say, emergent Christianity fits perfectly into this creative web. Yet identifying Jesus with God's incarnated Son sent by the Father for the redemption of mankind's sins obscures the general picture, as it reduces the entire film of early Christian messianology to a single photogram. And this is the problem. For early Christianity developed other competing thoughts as well. In particular for our purposes here, a Christology in which – contrary to Paul's and the Church's Jesus-Christocentrism, which although different from one another[23]

---

18 Boyarin, *The Jewish Gospels*, 35–52. On the religion of ancient Israel, see Mark S. Smith's seminal work *The Early History of God: Yahweh and the Other Deities in Ancient Israel* (2nd ed.; Grand Rapids, MI, and Cambridge: Eerdmans, 2001).

19 On which see John J. Collins, *The Apocalyptic Imagination: An Introduction to Jewish Apocalyptic Literature* (2nd ed.; Grand Rapids, MI, and Cambridge: Eerdmans, 1998); George W. E. Nickelsburg, *Jewish Literature between the Bible and the Mishnah: A Historical and Literary Introduction* (2nd ed.; Minneapolis: Fortress Press, 2005).

20 See Adela Yarbro Collins and John J. Collins, *King and Messiah as Son of God: Divine, Human, and Angelic Messianic Figures in Biblical and Related Literature* (Grand Rapids, MI, and Cambridge: Eerdmans, 2008).

21 See Carlos A. Segovia: *The Quranic Noah and the Making of the Islamic Prophet: A Study of Intertextuality and Religious Identity Formation in Late Antiquity* (JCIT 4; Berlin and Boston: De Gruyter, 2015) 110–13.

22 Segovia: *The Quranic Noah and the Making of the Islamic Prophet*, 37.

23 That is to say, Paul's is strategical (for the non-Jews it is enough to believe that the Messiah has come, so that the nations may join Israel for the sealing and transfiguration of the present eon), whereas the type of Jesus-Christocrentrism established in Nicaea in 325 and ratified in the subsequent councils of the Church is ontological instead (God has sent his Son for the delivery

share a common emphasis on Jesus's role in the economy of salvation – he who manifests (rather than incarnates) himself in Jesus, and through whom Jesus is adopted (rather than created from the start) as God's son, is the eternal Christ (*Christus aeternus*) or supreme archangel (*Archangelus maximus*), i.e. God's Image (Michael, *Quis ut Deus*), who is also God's First Born and the Sustainer of the universe, as well as (simultaneously) God's heavenly Priest and *Verus Propheta* – and hence the Celestial Man whose apparition amounts to that of God's presence and whose return is intensely expected, as he is too the Lord of the future eon, i.e. the Messiah.[24]

It is, to say the least, surprising that this Christological elaboration, which very likely gained prominence in the lands east of the Byzantine empire on the eve of Islam, and against which the earliest quranic Christology stands like in a mirror, has been mostly neglected in study of the Qur'ān's early setting unltil very recently. And somewhat discouraging to see that some scholars interested today in examining afresh, for example, the intertextuality of the Qur'ān – I am thinking here of Gabriel Said Reynolds, for instance – not only ignore it altogether but also remain overall reluctant to the very possibility of rethinking the earliest quranic milieu. Yet as Van Reeth notes[25] apropos the theology of the revelation that one finds in the Qur'ān – I would say instead: in its earliest redactional layers – "[l]a spécificité de la prophétologie coranique s'enracine donc dans la théologie chrétienne, bien qu'elle ne se rattache pas à la doctrine chrétienne nicéenne et chalcédonienne".[26]

Unlike Van Reeth, I am not a Christian, so I have no personal interest whatsoever in approaching the beginnings of Islam to Christianity. Also, I am convinced that Islamic culture is providing today new interesting types of subjectivity that differ – my only quibble is that they do not differ enough! – from the mainstream neoliberal forms of subjectivation, and therefore I have no secular inclination either towards Islamophobia; in my view, Western culture (read: Christianity and, subsequently, capitalism) needs of no defence against its enemies: if it needs

of everyone's sins). On Paul's Jewishness, see now Gabriele Boccaccini and Carlos A. Segovia, eds., *Paul the Jew: Rereading the Apostle as a Figure of Second Temple Judaism* (Minneapolis: Fortress, 2016).

24 See further Corbin, *Le Paradoxe du monothéisme*, 133–44. Also, Richard N. Longenecker, *The Christology of Early Jewish Christianity* (London: SCM, 1970) 26–32; and especially Charles A. Gieschen, *Angelomorphic Christology: Antecedents and Early Evidence* (Leiden and Boston: Brill, 1998).

25 Van Reeth, "Melchisédech le Prophète éternel selon Jean d'Apamée et le monarchianisme musulman," 21–6.

26 Van Reeth, "Melchisédech le Prophète éternel selon Jean d'Apamée et le monarchianisme musulman," 23.

something is to be overcome once and for all – a scenario that the current cosmopolitical crisis may well precipitate in a not-so-distant future. Yet I fully agree with Van Reeth in his analysis. For – going back to the issue at stake here: the clarification of the nature of the Qur'ān's early Christology – the heavenly messenger that speaks directly to mankind with the purpose of instructing it as a prophet would (cf. e.g. Q 75:17–19; 76:3) is also said to be God's co-creator (cf. e.g. 75:4; 76:2). We are now therefore in position, I think, to assign a more precise identity to the heavenly messenger of *sūra*-s 75–93, 95–6, 99–104, and 107 – and to understand the identity between God's descended Word and God's own theophany.[27] Also, we may now better easily understand the insistence of the quranic authors – even after they had the figure of the heavenly messenger subordinated to that of his qualified new human interlocutor, on which see below – that God is "childless" rather than "sonless," i.e. that he has no ولد *walad* or human son (cf. 2:116; 4:171; 6:101; 10:68; 19:88; 21:26; 23:91; 25:2); and hence too their consequent denial of Mary's divinity (in 5:75, 116–17).[28]

27 See further Beck, *Evolution of the Early Qur'ān*, 79–108, 273–334. Interestingly, Beck reads its descent against the background of Syriac theology, providing helpful parallels between the imagery of the Qur'ān's early theology and that of Ephraem, for instance. Furthermore, he interprets the Qur'ān's implicit presentation of the nature of the heavenly messenger as reflecting a sort of extreme Miaphysitism. Without denying a possible Julianist influence e.g. on Q 4:155–9, in my view it is the trace of a non-Chalcedonian, as well as anti-Nicene, angelomorphic Christology that one finds in the earliest "revelations" contained in the Qur'ān; therefore, I roughly concur here with Günter Lüling, *Über den Ur-Qur'ān: Ansätze zur Rekonstruktion vorislamischer christlicher Strophenlieder im Qur'ān*(Erlangen: Lüling, 1974; 2nd ed., 1993); English translation, *A Challenge to Islam for Reformation: The Rediscovery and Reliable Reconstruction of a Comprehensive pre-Islamic Christian Hymnal Hidden in the Koran under Earliest Islamic Reinterpretations* (Delhi: Banarsidass, 2003).

28 In this sense, furthermore, the statement that Jesus is "a word" (3:39, 45) and "a spirit" (4:171) from God may be taken to contradict the paradoxical statement (in 4:171) that he is God's "Word." Yet all these expressions point perhaps to the same notion: he was miraculously created by God's command, and then something from God came to inhabit him. In fact, the biggest contradiction susceptible of being signalled out here is between the early Christology of the Qur'ān and the view that Jesus was miraculously born, inasmuch as this implicitly makes him something more than a normal human being. Still, it is very possible – as I have argued in Chapter 3 – that the Jesus texts come from later stages in the development of the quranic corpus. Likewise, caution is recommendable before 4:155–9, with its allusion to Jesus's death: these verses may be anti-Chalcedonian (God did not suffer on the cross!) or else (less likely in my opinion) express the view that the "Jews" were unable to effectively kill Jesus, who sits next to God and will preside over their judgement (and hence reproduce a very Christian motif after all).

Introducing the Human alongside the Divine (Q 17, 68, 73–4, 81, 87, 88)

The Need of a Human Messenger – Almost Absent from the Earliest Quranic Layers

The notion of a heavenly messenger thus pervades one of the earliest quranic layers. However, in Q 87 and 88 *a human messenger is introduced for the first time alongside the heavenly messenger. If heretofore the latter communicated with the people directly, i.e. without any intermediation, he* (B_1) *now transmits his words to a human messenger whose role is very exactly delimited, in the sense that he is said to be only a reminder to the people; at some point, however, the authority of this human messenger was severely challenged, for which reason* (B_2) *he is*, in Q 68 and 81, *defended, and his mission authenticated against any claim to the contrary by his opponents – of which one* (whom I will call hereinafter his antagonist) *is particularly salient and denounced, moreover, as a liar*. Compared to A, this represents a second move – and entails an "epistemological rupture," as Althusser would have it.

The first two texts of some interest at this juncture are Q 87:1–9 and 88:21–6, i.e. two passages of *sūrat*-s *al-A'lā* ("The Most High") and *al-Ġāšiyya* ("The Overwhelming") in which the quranic prophet – introduced there *ex novo* – is specifically presented as "one who reminds" (مذكّر *muḏakkar*; cf. 87:9; 88:21) – and whose authority is limited, furthermore, to such role (88:22):

($B_{1.1}$) **Q 87:1–9**

سَبِّحِ اسْمَ رَبِّكَ الْأَعْلَى 87:1
الَّذِي خَلَقَ فَسَوَّىٰ 2
وَالَّذِي قَدَّرَ فَهَدَىٰ 3
وَالَّذِي أَخْرَجَ الْمَرْعَىٰ 4
فَجَعَلَهُ غُثَاءً أَحْوَىٰ 5
سَنُقْرِئُكَ فَلَا تَنْسَىٰ 6
إِلَّا مَا شَاءَ اللَّهُ ۚ إِنَّهُ يَعْلَمُ الْجَهْرَ وَمَا يَخْفَىٰ 7
وَنُيَسِّرُكَ لِلْيُسْرَىٰ 8
فَذَكِّرْ إِنْ نَفَعَتِ الذِّكْرَىٰ 9

87:1 Glorify the name of your Lord, the Most High,
2 who creates and fashions,
3 who measures and guides,

4 who brings forth the pasture
5 and then makes it dark stubble!
6 *We shall make you recite so that you do not forget,*
7 save what God wishes – for he knows what is publicly spoken and what is hidden;
8 *we shall make it easy for you.*
9 *So remind* [them], *if the reminder benefits* [them]!

(B1.2) **Q 88:21–6**

فَذَكِّرْ إِنَّمَا أَنْتَ مُذَكِّرٌ 88:21
لَسْتَ عَلَيْهِمْ بِمُصَيْطِرٍ 22
إِلَّا مَنْ تَوَلَّىٰ وَكَفَرَ 23
فَيُعَذِّبُهُ اللَّهُ الْعَذَابَ الْأَكْبَرَ 24
إِنَّ إِلَيْنَا إِيَابَهُمْ 25
ثُمَّ إِنَّ عَلَيْنَا حِسَابَهُمْ 26

88:21 *So remind* [them] – *you are only a reminder* [for them],
22 *you are not their supervisor!*
23 As for whoever turns away and disbelieves,
24 God will punish him with the greatest punishment.
25 For it is certain that *to us is their return,*
26 *and hence on us depends their reckoning.*

Notice, too, how the human qualities of the human messenger are hinted at in 87:8: "We shall make it [namely, the recitation alluded to in 87:6] easy for you." Additionally, it should also be observed that in both cases the human messenger receives his revelations from the heavenly messenger (cf. the "We" speeches in 87:8; 88:25–6).

In contrast, 81:22–8 (which once more stress, in v. 27, that the human messenger is but a reminder) explicitly defend him against his opponents, who presumably had accused him of being possessed (v. 22) by an accursed Satan (v. 25) and of keeping divine secrets for himself (v. 24):

(B2.1) **Q 81:22–8**

وَمَا صَاحِبُكُمْ بِمَجْنُونٍ 81:22
وَلَقَدْ رَآهُ بِالْأُفُقِ الْمُبِينِ 23
وَمَا هُوَ عَلَى الْغَيْبِ بِضَنِينٍ 24
وَمَا هُوَ بِقَوْلِ شَيْطَانٍ رَجِيمٍ 25
فَأَيْنَ تَذْهَبُونَ 26
إِنْ هُوَ إِلَّا ذِكْرٌ لِلْعَالَمِينَ 27
لِمَنْ شَاءَ مِنْكُمْ أَنْ يَسْتَقِيمَ 28

81:22 *Your companion is not possessed.*
23 *He certainly saw him* on the clear horizon.
24 *He is not a withholder of the unseen.*
25 *Nor are his words words those of an accursed Satan.*
26 So which side will you take?
27 This is but a reminder to all peoples –
28 to whoever of you wishes to go straight!

V. 23 echoes *Sūra* 53 (*al-Nağm*, "The Star"), on which see below. It is then possible that it was incorporated into Q 81's *Grundshrift* at a later redactional stage. Besides, the identity of the speaker is this time difficult to establish, though v. 27 closely resembles 87:9 and 88:21. Interestingly too, in vv. 22, 26, 28–9 the heavenly messenger directly addresses the people, like in 77:14, 20, 27, 38–9; 78:18, 30; 79:15, 27, 33; 82:9–10, 12, 17–18; 84:6, 24; 85:12–17; 89:6, 17–20, 27–8; 90:2, 12; 92:14; 93:3–9; 94:1–4; 96:1, 3, 9–13, 19; 99:5; 101:10; 102:1–8; 105:1; 107:1; 108:1–3; 109:1–6; 110:2–3.

We now need to look into what appears to me to be an altogether different redactional layer or layers; more precisely, into *sūra*-s 68, 73–4, and 17.[29] Some connection with the preceding passages is however discernible. Thus, for example, in *Sūratal-Qalam* (Q 68, "The Pen") the defence of the human messenger is undertaken in some depth:

(B2.2) **Q 68:2–16**

مَا أَنتَ بِنِعْمَةِ رَبِّكَ بِمَجْنُونٍ 68:2
وَإِنَّ لَكَ لَأَجْرًا غَيْرَ مَمْنُونٍ 3
وَإِنَّكَ لَعَلَىٰ خُلُقٍ عَظِيمٍ 4
فَسَتُبْصِرُ وَيُبْصِرُونَ 5
بِأَييِّكُمُ الْمَفْتُونُ 6
إِنَّ رَبَّكَ هُوَ أَعْلَمُ بِمَن ضَلَّ عَن سَبِيلِهِ وَهُوَ أَعْلَمُ بِالْمُهْتَدِينَ 7
فَلَا تُطِعِ الْمُكَذِّبِينَ 8

29 Like Q 75–6, 79, 81, 87–8, *sūra*-s 17, 68, 73–4 – as also *sūra*-s 53, 55, 69 – are usually ascribed to the "Meccan I" group (see n.6 above). On my reading, however, we have here five different redactional layers: no. 1 consisting of Q 75–6, 79, 81 (save vv. 22–9), plus Q 77–8, 80, 82–6, 89–96, 99–104, 107; no. 2 consisting of Q 87–8 (unless these two were earlier and hence edited to match the new view that there is a human messenger alongside the heavenly one); no. 3 consisting of Q 68, 73–4, and perhaps 17; no. 4 consisting of Q 53, 55, 69, 81:22–9, and maybe 17; and no. 5 consisting of Q 17 (if the latter does not belong to layer no. 3 or 4, that is). I base this chronology in the sequential development of the "human-messenger" motif, as presented in this study. As for Q 52, 56 (on which see again n.6 above), they could be included in any of these groups.

وَدُّوا لَوْ تُدْهِنُ فَيُدْهِنُونَ 9
وَلَا تُطِعْ كُلَّ حَلَّافٍ مَهِينٍ 10
هَمَّازٍ مَشَّاءٍ بِنَمِيمٍ 11
مَنَّاعٍ لِلْخَيْرِ مُعْتَدٍ أَثِيمٍ 12
عُتُلٍّ بَعْدَ ذَٰلِكَ زَنِيمٍ 13
أَنْ كَانَ ذَا مَالٍ وَبَنِينَ 14
إِذَا تُتْلَىٰ عَلَيْهِ آيَاتُنَا قَالَ أَسَاطِيرُ الْأَوَّلِينَ 15
سَنَسِمُهُ عَلَى الْخُرْطُومِ 16

68:2 *You are not, by the grace of your Lord, possessed.*
3 *Surely there is for you a reward without end,*
4 *for you are a great character.*
5 *So you will see, and they* [too] *will see*
6 *which of you is the afflicted one.*
7 Certainly your Lord knows who goes astray from his path and who are the [rightly] guided ones.
8 So do not obey not the deniers!
9 They want you to compromise, so that they can compromise [too].
10 And do not obey [he who is but] a worthless swearer,
11 a defamer going about with gossip,
12 a hinderer of the good, a transgressor [and] a sinner,
13 [someone] vulgar and, moreover, a bastard,
14 just because he has wealth and sons.
15 When our signs are recited to him, he says, "[These are but] old tales!"
16 We shall brand him on the snout!

(Notice here too the contrast between the third person that corresponds to God in v. 7 and the "We" speech in vv. 15–16.)

The Exaltation of the Human Messenger

Next move. Suddenly, *the human messenger* introduced in Q 68, 81, 87 and 88[30] *seems to capture all the attention of the quranic authors: first,* (C_1) *we get a glimpse*

30 Does this means that *sūra*-s 75–93, 95–6, 99–104, and 107 are pre-"Muhamadan"? It is difficult to tell. It could be that the introduction of a human messenger was contemporary with the appearance of a human prophet, but it could also be – more plausibly perhaps – that the latter was there from the very beginning and that he remained in, say, a secondary position until an appointed time in which he acquired a more central role. On the possibility that the Qur'ān contains pre-Muhamadan materials, see Lüling, *Über den Ur-Qur'ān*; see now too Claude Gilliot, "Des indices d'un proto-lectionnaire dans le « Lectionnaire Arabe » dit Coran," in *Les Origins*

to how he prepares himself to receive his revelations from the heavenly messenger, who thoughtfully comforts him and uses very hard words against his antagonist; then (C_2) *he is "praised"* (محمود *maḥmūd*, an expression from which one may easily derive two other terms that would become the proper names of the quranic prophet: محمّد *muḥammad* ["praised one"] and أحمد *aḥmad* ["most praised"]) *and conferred "divine authority."* Q 73–4 and 17 (unless one considers Q 17 to belong to a later stratum) illustrate this third move.

Therefore, the second motif that we come across in this layer is the description of how the human messenger physically prepares himself to receive the revelation. Thus vv. 1–14 of *Sūrat al-Muzzammil* (Q 73, "The Enwrapped One") read:

($C_{1.1}$) **Q 73:1–14**

يَا أَيُّهَا الْمُزَّمِّلُ 73:1
قُمِ اللَّيْلَ إِلَّا قَلِيلًا 2
نِصْفَهُ أَوِ انْقُصْ مِنْهُ قَلِيلًا 3
أَوْ زِدْ عَلَيْهِ وَرَتِّلِ الْقُرْآنَ تَرْتِيلًا 4
إِنَّا سَنُلْقِي عَلَيْكَ قَوْلًا ثَقِيلً 5
إِنَّ نَاشِئَةَ اللَّيْلِ هِيَ أَشَدُّ وَطْئًا وَأَقْوَمُ قِيلًا 6
إِنَّ لَكَ فِي النَّهَارِ سَبْحًا طَوِيلً 7
وَاذْكُرِ اسْمَ رَبِّكَ وَتَبَتَّلْ إِلَيْهِ تَبْتِيلًا 8
رَبُّ الْمَشْرِقِ وَالْمَغْرِبِ لَا إِلَٰهَ إِلَّا هُوَ فَاتَّخِذْهُ وَكِيلًا 9
وَاصْبِرْ عَلَىٰ مَا يَقُولُونَ وَاهْجُرْهُمْ هَجْرًا جَمِيلًا 10
وَذَرْنِي وَالْمُكَذِّبِينَ أُولِي النَّعْمَةِ وَمَهِّلْهُمْ قَلِيلًا 11
إِنَّ لَدَيْنَا أَنْكَالًا وَجَحِيمًا 12
وَطَعَامًا ذَا غُصَّةٍ وَعَذَابًا أَلِيمًا 13
يَوْمَ تَرْجُفُ الْأَرْضُ وَالْجِبَالُ وَكَانَتِ الْجِبَالُ كَثِيبًا مَهِيلًا 14

73:1 *O you, enwrapped one!*
2 *Stay up through the night – except for a little while,*
3 [be it] *half of it, or a little less,*
4 *or a little more – and arrange the recitation carefully,*
5 [for] *we shall cast upon you an onerous word!*
6 *The first part of the night surely is more effective and suitable for* [our] *word* [to descend upon you],
7 *as during the day you have protracted business* [to attend] –

---

du Coran, le Coran des origines, ed. François Déroche, Christian-Julien Robin, and Michel Zink (Paris: AIBL, 2015) 297–314.

8 *nevertheless, remember your Lord's name and devote yourself to him completely!*
9 Lord of the East and the West, there is no God but him, so *take him as* [your] *guardian*
10 and *be patient with what they say and forsake them graciously.*
11 Let me deal with the deniers – those who are prosperous – and allow them a little respite!
12 Surely we have chains and a Furnace [for them],
13 and food that chokes and a painful punishment
14 on the Day when the earth and the mountains will quake and the mountains become a ridge of drifting sand.

As I have already remarked, Beck has aptly underlined the similarities that this description presents, in terms of imagery, with a number of Syriac Christian texts that focus on the way in which God's word descends to the world.[31] It should also be observed that, in the following verse (v. 15) it is still the heavenly messenger who introduces the human messenger to the people – like in 81:22–9, and therefore unlike 87:1–9 and 88:21–6, where he is addressed by the heavenly messenger alone. (Notice too the shift from "I" to "We" speech in vv. 11–12, as well as the reference to God as him in vv. 8–9.)

As for *Sūrat al-Muddaṯṯir* (Q 74, "The Cloaked One"), it abounds in the same notion displayed in Q 73 but additionally defends the human messenger, like Q 68:2–16 and 81:22–5:

(C1.2) **Q 74:1–26**

يَا أَيُّهَا الْمُدَّثِّرُ 74:1
قُمْ فَأَنْذِرِ 2
وَرَبَّكَ فَكَبِّرْ 3
وَثِيَابَكَ فَطَهِّرْ 4
وَالرُّجْزَ فَاهْجُرْ 5
وَلَا تَمْنُنْ تَسْتَكْثِرُ 6
وَلِرَبِّكَ فَاصْبِرْ 7
فَإِذَا نُقِرَ فِي النَّاقُورِ 8
فَذَٰلِكَ يَوْمَئِذٍ يَوْمٌ عَسِيرٌ 9
عَلَى الْكَافِرِينَ غَيْرُ يَسِيرٍ 10
ذَرْنِي وَمَنْ خَلَقْتُ وَحِيدًا 11
وَجَعَلْتُ لَهُ مَالًا مَمْدُودًا 12
وَبَنِينَ شُهُودًا 13
وَمَهَّدْتُ لَهُ تَمْهِيدًا 14

31 Beck, *Evolution of the Early Qur'ān*, 273–334.

إِنَّا أَرْسَلْنَا إِلَيْكُمْ رَسُولًا شَاهِدًا عَلَيْكُمْ كَمَا أَرْسَلْنَا إِلَىٰ فِرْعَوْنَ رَسُولًا 15
فَعَصَىٰ فِرْعَوْنُ الرَّسُولَ فَأَخَذْنَاهُ أَخْذًا وَبِيلًا 16
فَكَيْفَ تَتَّقُونَ إِنْ كَفَرْتُمْ يَوْمًا يَجْعَلُ الْوِلْدَانَ شِيبًا 17
السَّمَاءُ مُنْفَطِرٌ بِهِ ۚ كَانَ وَعْدُهُ مَفْعُولًا 18
إِنَّ هَٰذِهِ تَذْكِرَةٌ ۖ فَمَنْ شَاءَ اتَّخَذَ إِلَىٰ رَبِّهِ سَبِيلًا 19
ثُمَّ قُتِلَ كَيْفَ قَدَّرَ 20
ثُمَّ نَظَرَ 21
ثُمَّ عَبَسَ وَبَسَرَ 22
ثُمَّ أَدْبَرَ وَاسْتَكْبَرَ 23
فَقَالَ إِنْ هَٰذَا إِلَّا سِحْرٌ يُؤْثَرُ 24
إِنْ هَٰذَا إِلَّا قَوْلُ الْبَشَرِ 25
سَأُصْلِيهِ سَقَرَ 26

74:1 *O you who cloaks himself!*[32]
2 *Stand up and warn* [in the name of your Lord]!
3 Magnify your Lord
4 and *purify your clothes*
5 *and flee from* [all] *defilement*
6 *Do not make a favour to gain* [yourself] *more*
7 *and be patient before your Lord.*
8 Then when the trumpet is blown –
9 that Day will be a hard Day;
10 not [an] easy [one] for the disbelievers!
11 *Let me deal with him whom I have created alone,*
12 *to whom I have given abundant wealth*
13 *and sons as witnesses,*
14 *and for whom I have made everything easy!*
15 *He is eager that I should do more* [for him].
16 *By no means! He is stubborn before our signs.*
17 *I shall burden him with a climb.*
18 *Surely he has thought and made his decision –*
19 *may he perish then* [for] *what he has decided.*
20 *Again, may he perish then* [for] *what he has decided.*
21 He looked;
22 then he frown and scowled,
23 [and] then he turned back and became arrogant
24 and said, “This is but ordinary magic –
25 Nothing but human word[s]!”
26 *Soon I shall burn him in Hell!*[33]

32 Lit., “cloaked one.”

33 Mentioned here as سقر Saqar.

In turn, vv. 79–80 in *Sūrat al-Isrā'* (Q 17 "The Journey") dignify the human messenger by affirming that he may be raised to a "praised" position and given "divine authority":

(C_2) **Q 17:79–80**

وَمِنَ اللَّيْلِ فَتَهَجَّدْ بِهِ نَافِلَةً لَكَ عَسَى أَنْ يَبْعَثَكَ رَبُّكَ مَقَامًا مَحْمُودًا 17:79
وَقُلْ رَبِّ أَدْخِلْنِي مُدْخَلَ صِدْقٍ وَأَخْرِجْنِي مُخْرَجَ صِدْقٍ وَاجْعَلْ لِي مِنْ لَدُنْكَ سُلْطَانًا نَصِيرًا 80

17:79 And in the night, do arise for prayer – for this is a gift for you. It may be that your Lord [then] raises you to *a praised position* (*maqām*^{an} *maḥmūd*^{an}).

80 And say, "My Lord, have me enter a truthful entrance and have me exit a truthful exit, and help me granting me *authority from yourself* (*min ladunka sulṭān*^{an} *naṣīr*^{an})."

He is in this way exalted, and thereby the foundations of a new *kerygma* are laid – one that turns around a qualified human prophet who will be named Aḥmad (in 61:6) and Muḥammad (in 3:144; 33:40; 47:2; 48:29) in accordance with his *maḥmūd*-status.

Substituting the Heavenly Messenger by a Human Messenger: The Beginnings of the Muhamadan *Kerygma* (Q 53, 55, 69)

A Dual Farewell to the Heavenly Messenger

And yet this increasing concentration on the human messenger may be said to reach its climax in Q 69, where (D_1) *the heavenly messenger is substituted by the human messenger, who now happens to be described with exactly the same terms earlier used to depict the former* (in 81:19–21). Moreover, this audacious fourth move – in which the defence of the human messenger against those who deny him is once more at stake – somehow relegates the heavenly messenger to a subordinated (i.e. lower) position: as the angel of revelation, he will keep communicating with the human messenger, but it looks as though it is upon the latter upon whom the stress will fall; and *it would even seem that* (D_2) *the human messenger can present himself before God directly, and receive directly from him his inspired words*. Additionally, at a later stage in the development of the corpus (E) the role of the human messenger vis-à-vis the "People of the Book" (a polysemic expression that most likely means here the "Christians" alone) is established as convenient.

The aforementioned replacement (D_1) takes place in vv. 40–6 of *Sūrat al-Ḥāqqa* (Q 69, "That Which Is Due"):

(D_1) **Q 69:38–52**

فَلَا أُقْسِمُ بِمَا تُبْصِرُونَ 69:38
وَمَا لَا تُبْصِرُونَ 39
إِنَّهُ لَقَوْلُ رَسُولٍ كَرِيمٍ 40
وَمَا هُوَ بِقَوْلِ شَاعِرٍ ۚ قَلِيلًا مَا تُؤْمِنُونَ 41
وَلَا بِقَوْلِ كَاهِنٍ ۚ قَلِيلًا مَا تَذَكَّرُونَ 42
تَنْزِيلٌ مِنْ رَبِّ الْعَالَمِينَ 43
وَلَوْ تَقَوَّلَ عَلَيْنَا بَعْضَ الْأَقَاوِيلِ 44
لَأَخَذْنَا مِنْهُ بِالْيَمِينِ 45
ثُمَّ لَقَطَعْنَا مِنْهُ الْوَتِينَ 46
فَمَا مِنْكُمْ مِنْ أَحَدٍ عَنْهُ حَاجِزِينَ 47
وَإِنَّهُ لَتَذْكِرَةٌ لِلْمُتَّقِينَ 48
وَإِنَّا لَنَعْلَمُ أَنَّ مِنْكُمْ مُكَذِّبِينَ 49
وَإِنَّهُ لَحَسْرَةٌ عَلَى الْكَافِرِينَ 50
وَإِنَّهُ لَحَقُّ الْيَقِينِ 51
فَسَبِّحْ بِاسْمِ رَبِّكَ الْعَظِيمِ 52

69:38 Nay! I swear by what you see
39 and what you do not see!
40 *Certainly this is the speech of a noble messenger*
41 *and not the speech of a poet* – how little you believe!,
42 *nor is it the speech of a soothsayer* – how little you mind!
43 It is a revelation[34] from the Lord of all men.
44 *If he had forged any* [false] *words against us,*
45 *we would have surely seized him by the right* [hand]
46 *and then cut his main artery,*
47 and none of you could have prevented it!
48 Surely this is a reminder for those who fear [God],
49 though we know there are deniers among you –
50 so it will be a [cause of] regret for the disbelievers.
51 For it is indeed the certain truth –
52 so glorify the name of your Lord, the Almighty!

34 Lit., "a sending down (*tanzīl*^{un})."

Again, vv. 41–52 defend the quranic prophet against those who deny him, thus echoing the crisis of authority already mentioned apropos Q 68:2–16; 74; and 81:22–5; whereas v. 49 has once more the heavenly messenger speaking directly to the people, like 77:14, 20, 27, 38–9; 78:18, 30; 79:15, 27, 33; 81:22, 26, 28–9; 82:6–10, 12, 17–18; 84:6, 24; 85:12–17; 89:6, 17–20, 27–8; 90:2, 12; 92:14; 93:3–9; 94:1–4; 96:1, 3, 9–13, 19; 99:5; 101:10; 102:1–8; 105:1; 107:1; 108:1–3; 109:1–6; 110:2–3.

In turn, *Sūrat al-Nağm* (Q 53) expands the motif in 81:23, especially in vv. 5–10:

($D_{2.1}$) **Q 53:1–18**

وَالنَّجْمِ إِذَا هَوَىٰ 53:1
مَا ضَلَّ صَاحِبُكُمْ وَمَا غَوَىٰ 2
وَمَا يَنْطِقُ عَنِ الْهَوَىٰ 3
إِنْ هُوَ إِلَّا وَحْيٌ يُوحَىٰ 4
عَلَّمَهُ شَدِيدُ الْقُوَىٰ 5
ذُو مِرَّةٍ فَاسْتَوَىٰ 6
وَهُوَ بِالْأُفُقِ الْأَعْلَىٰ 7
ثُمَّ دَنَا فَتَدَلَّىٰ 8
فَكَانَ قَابَ قَوْسَيْنِ أَوْ أَدْنَىٰ 9
فَأَوْحَىٰ إِلَىٰ عَبْدِهِ مَا أَوْحَىٰ 10
مَا كَذَبَ الْفُؤَادُ مَا رَأَىٰ 11
أَفَتُمَارُونَهُ عَلَىٰ مَا يَرَىٰ 12
وَلَقَدْ رَآهُ نَزْلَةً أُخْرَىٰ 13
عِنْدَ سِدْرَةِ الْمُنْتَهَىٰ 14
عِنْدَهَا جَنَّةُ الْمَأْوَىٰ 15
إِذْ يَغْشَى السِّدْرَةَ مَا يَغْشَىٰ 16
مَا زَاغَ الْبَصَرُ وَمَا طَغَىٰ 17
لَقَدْ رَأَىٰ مِنْ آيَاتِ رَبِّهِ الْكُبْرَىٰ 18

53:1 By the star when it goes down!
2 Your companion has not gone astray, nor has he erred,
3 nor does he speak whimfully.
4 [What he speaks] is an inspired inspiration.
5 *One full of power has taught him,*
6 *one full of strength!*
7 *He rose while he was at the Highest Horizon,*
8 *then he drew near and came down –*
9 *he was two bow-lengths away or nearer*
10 *when he inspired his servant* [with] *what he inspired him* [with].

11 His heart did not lie about what he saw! –
12 will you dispute with him about it?
13 Certainly he saw him at a second descent
14 by the Lote Tree in the Utmost Boundary,
15 close to the Garden of the Refuge,
16 when the Lote Tree was covered with what covers it;
17 his sight did not turn aside, nor did it [arrogantly] trespass [any limit].
18 Certainly he saw one of the greatest signs of his Lord.

The quranic prophet thus encounters God twice, first "at the Highest Horizon" (v. 7) and then "at a second descent" (v. 13) "by the Lote Tree in the Utmost Boundary" (v. 14). At first, the identity of "he" (vv. 7–10, 13) whom the prophet encounters is anything but clear: the referent in v. 5 ("one mighty in power") is elusive, and the very same can be said of v. 9 (which mentions his astounding physical proportions without further qualifying him); as for vv. 10 and 18, they imply that the prophet – whose defence is undertaken again in vv. 2–12 – is his "servant," while he is the prophet's "Lord." Cf. however the wording in v. 5 and vv. 1–2 in *Sūrat al-Raḥmān* (Q 55, "The Merciful"):

($D_{2.2}$) **Q 55:1–4**

الرَّحْمَٰنُ 55:1
عَلَّمَ الْقُرْآنَ 2

55:1 The *Merciful*
2 has taught [him] the recitation.

In short, the prophet now receives his revelation directly from God. Accordingly, the first two verses in *Sūrat al-Bayyina* (Q 98) portray him as a "clear sign" (بيّنة *bayyina*) from God:

(E) **Q 98:1–3**

لَمْ يَكُنِ الَّذِينَ كَفَرُوا مِنْ أَهْلِ الْكِتَابِ وَالْمُشْرِكِينَ مُنْفَكِّينَ حَتَّىٰ تَأْتِيَهُمُ الْبَيِّنَةُ 98:1
رَسُولٌ مِنَ اللَّهِ يَتْلُو صُحُفًا مُطَهَّرَةً 2
فِيهَا كُتُبٌ قَيِّمَةٌ 3

98:1 The disbelievers among the People of the Book and the idolaters were not to be set free until the *clear sign* [from God] had come to them –
2 a *messenger* from God reciting purified pages
3 that contain true writings.

Re-imagining Jesus as a New John the Baptist

The final move consists in (F) *presenting Jesus as foretelling the coming of the human messenger, which is now declared to be not just "praised"* (محمود *maḥmūd*, as in Q 17:79–80) *but the "most praised" one* (أحمد *aḥmad*), *or else* – in Ubayy's recension – the *"last prophet"*:

(F) **Q 61:6**

وَإِذْ قَالَ عِيسَى ابْنُ مَرْيَمَ يَا بَنِي إِسْرَائِيلَ إِنِّي رَسُولُ اللَّهِ إِلَيْكُمْ مُصَدِّقًا لِمَا بَيْنَ يَدَيَّ مِنَ التَّوْرَاةِ
وَمُبَشِّرًا بِرَسُولٍ يَأْتِي مِنْ بَعْدِي اسْمُهُ أَحْمَدُ فَلَمَّا جَاءَهُمْ بِالْبَيِّنَاتِ قَالُوا هَٰذَا سِحْرٌ مُبِينٌ 61:6

61:6 [Remember] when Jesus, son of Mary, said, "Sons of Israel! I am God's messenger to you, confirming the Torah [given to you] before me and giving you good tidings of a messenger to come after me, whose name will be Aḥmad." But when he brought them clear signs, they said "This is nothing but magic!"

Since *aḥmad* represents an oblique allusion to John's "Paraclete,"[35] the effect of this fifth move proves a little bit awkward, as *he who is originally sent in the Fourth Gospel to provide comfort before the second coming of the Messiah (i.e. during his absence) reaches here, instead, an exalted position above the Messiah himself.*

Excursus 2: Contesting the Exclusiveness of the Muhamadan *Kerygma*, or Reimagining Proto-Shite Christology vis-à-vis the Making of a Tribal- and Supra-Tribal Religion

This latter view therefore posits a major structural problem that makes the whole picture stumble. My contention is that it was contested for coherence's sake on two simultaneous fronts. First, the subordination of the Messiah to the Comforter proved unacceptable for those who identified the Messiah as the central figure of the whole edifice and thereby awaited his return. Who was the human prophet to claim any superiority over him? Secondly, they could neither accept the disempowerment of the heavenly messenger, i.e. his transformation into God's mere speaker. For if the function of the heavenly messenger was limited to such communicative role, how could he manifest himself in the Messiah and return on day to judge the world? Moreover, if the end of the world was somehow imminent, introducing such changes looked like the last think one would be willing to do…

35 See Chapter 2 above.

I have presented the voice of those opponents as an existing one, and yet it is silent – so much so that we can only fancy it. But we need to take the risk and do so, as it is still possible to recognise its tone in between the lines of certain extra-quranic sectarian texts. Those, I would suggest, in which Muḥammad is presented as pointing to 'Alī b. Abī Ṭālib and attributed the following words – which are quite relevant to the purpose or this book: "There is something in you ['Alī] that resembles Jesus, son of Maryam. Had I not to fear that some of our companions may affirm about you what the Christians affirm concerning Jesus, I would have revealed something about you that would have make the people clean your path of all dust to receive your blessing." This well-known *ḥadīth* compiled by the 9th-to-10th-century Shiite scholar al-Kulaynī – in his book *al-Rawḍa min al-Kāfī* – is quoted by Amir-Moezzi in an excellent recent study of his[36] to underline the ongoing connection made in the learned Shiite circles between Alī and Jesus.[37] As Amir-Moezzi writes,

> 'Alī n'est pas une réincarnation de Jésus. Son identification avec le fils de Marie est expliquée dans le shi'isme ancien par la doctrine de la transmission du Legs sacré (*al-waṣiyya*), de la lumière de l'Alliance ou de l'Amitié divine (*nūr al-walāya*), de la parcelle divine (*juz' ilāhī*) ou encore de la « métemphotose » («le déplacement de la lumière » ... *tanāsukh*). Il s'agit du passage, de l'inhérence d'une force divine lumineuse dans les membres d'une longue chaîne de saints initiés, faisant d'eux des inspirés capables de communiquer avec Dieu afin de transmettre au hommes les messages d'En-Haut et même, dans certains cas, les transformant en lieu de manifestation de Dieu (*maẓhar, majlā*)... .
>
> La nature messianique de 'Alī, en tant que Sauveur, résurrecteur et juge de la fin des temps, est illustrée de manière claire dans de nombreuses sentences de quelques prônes (*khuṭba*) attribués à celui-ci où un guide éternel, parlant par la bouche du 'Alī historique, déclare haut et fort sa réalité théophanique.[38]

It is this "Eternal Guide" that interests me here. For, once more, it looks as though we are dealing with the notion of an eternal Christ that repeatedly manifests himself as both teacher – of which the Manichaean, and later Islamic, notion of a prophetical cycle is in turn reminiscent – and Messiah. No matter how late these

---

36 Mohammad Ali Amir-Moezzi, "Muḥammad le Paraclete et 'Alī le Messie. Nouvelles remarques sur les origines de l'islam et de l'imamologie shi'ite," in *L'Ésotérisme Shi'ite. Ses racines et ses prolongements / Shi'i Esotericism: Its Roots and Developments*, ed. Mohammad Ali Amir-Moezzi, with Maria De Cillis, Daniel De Smet, and Orkhan Mir-Kasimov (BEHESR 177; Turnhout, BE: Brepols and The Institute of Ismaili Studies, 2016) 19–54, p. 41 (my translation). The *ḥadīth* in question makes no. 18 of Kulaynī's collection.

37 See also the 10th-century Ismaili text quoted by Amir-Moezzi in pp. 42–3 of his article, in which 'Alī "himself" proclaims his full identity with Jesus.

38 Amir-Moezzi, "Muḥammad le Paraclete et 'Alī le Messie," 43.

sources are, they arguably bear witness to the influence an ancient belief whose preservation makes far more sense than its eventual invention in medieval times, when Christianity was, for the Shiites, already a distant reality; and whose supporters, I would venture, resisted the de-eschatologisation implied, therefore, in the counter-making of the Muhamadan *kerygma*.

By way of conclusion: Perhaps it is no coincidence that 'Alī and his followers established themselves in Iraq, where eschatological and soteriological ideas circulated freely due to the region's peripheral location.[39] What can surely not be a coincidence is that 'Alī's followers developed a religion centred around the figure of the Imām, in his quality of divine guide, instead of Muḥammad;[40] a religion in which the sequence of the earthly Imām-s is to reach its apex with the future coming of the last Imām in his role of Messiah.[41] If it can be argued that, due to its synthesis of East-Diphysite, Manichaean, and perhaps Julianist Christologies,[42] the early Christology of the Qur'ān represented a peripheral innovative response to Chalcedonian theology, and hence to the ideology of the Byzantine empire, it can also be argued that the development of a specifically Muhamadan *kerygma* transformed its premises and content into those of a tribal religion centred around the figure of a charismatic human leader. Now, if one assumes that the quranic prophet was one out of several leaders who shared similar religious views but opposed one another in tribal and political matters – as a careful rereading of the *ridda* literature seems to imply – and furthermore regards his victory over his rivals as the achievement of a temporary supremacy that, fostered perhaps by the 622 anti-Sasanian Byzantine campaign,[43] would be repeatedly contested until the 690s – as the *fitna* literature suggests in turn – then one has good reasons to understand that 'Abd al-Malik (r. 692–705), in his effort to unify the three groups that had sprung in the Ḥiǧāz, Syria, and Iraq, and in order to proclaim himself their undisputed leader once he had defeated his opponents, implemented a twofold integrationist policy: on the one hand, he married his generals to the daughters of the Iraqi (Alid) elite;[44] on the other hand, he incorporated into the Qur'ān, which quite possibly he collected for the

39 See the precedent chapter.
40 Amir-Moezzi, "Muḥammad le Paraclete et 'Alī le Messie," 54.
41 Although led by their desire to place Muḥammad above Jesus, a number of early Muslims might have viewed him instead of 'Alī as the Messiah, as I hypothesised in my book on the quranic Noah (*pace*Amir-Moezzi, "Muḥammad le Paraclete et 'Alī le Messie," 37, n.52).
42 See the previous chapter.
43 See Ch. 3, n.46 above.
44 See Chase F. Robinson, *'Abd al-Malik* (MMW; Oxford: Oneworld, 2005) 48.

very first time,[45] the views, and eventually the texts, of the group that had kept the memory of the quranic prophet as their distinctive insignia: the Hijazi party around 'Abd al-Zubayr, thus allowing for the transition to a supra-tribal religion whose pre-tribal components, apparently, only the Alid faction managed to preserve.

45 See Alfred-Louis de Prémare, "'Abd al-Malik b. Marwān and the Process of the Qur'ān's Composition," in *The Hidden Origins of Islam: New Research into Its Early History*, ed. Karl-Heinz Ohlig and Gerd-R. Puin (Armherst, NY: Prometheus Books, 2010) 189–221.

Afterword

And so it seems that this book demands to end with a reference to the great Umayyad ruler, ʿAbd al-Malik b. Marwān (r. 692–705). ʿAbd al-Malik inscriptions on the octagonal arcade of the Dome of the Rock in Jerusalem bear witness indeed to the final *consolidation* of what I have labelled in the precedent pages the Muhamadan *kerygma* – but interestingly enough they also betray the theological *adjustment* that had to be made in this respect. Thus their relative ambiguity but their immense interest. Let us briefly examine them before moving on to a provisional conclusion – or, better, to a final problem with whose delimitation I would like to put an end to the present study.

The Kufic inscription on the outer face of the octogonal arcade (hereinafter Inscription A) reads as follows:[1]

- (A1) In the name of God, the Merciful, the Compassionate. | There is no god but God alone. He has no associate. | {112} Say, "He is God, the One! – God, Indivisible!" He does not beget nor was he begotten, and no one is equal in rank to him.
- (A2) Muḥammad is the messenger of God. | {*33:56} May God bless him.
- (A3) In the name of God, the Merciful, the Compassionate. | There is no god but God alone. He has no associate.
- (A4) Muḥammad is the messenger of God. | {33:56} God and his angels bless the prophet. O you who believe, implore [God's] blessing and peace upon him! | God bless him, and may [God's] peace and mercy be upon him.
- (A5) {17:111} Say, "Praise belongs to God, who has no child nor partner in his rule. He is not so weak as to need a protector. Proclaim his limitless greatness!"
- (A6) Muḥammad is the messenger of God. | {*33:56} May God bless him, as well as his angels and messengers, and may God's peace and mercy be upon him.
- (A7) In the name of God, the Merciful, the Compassionate. | There is no god but God alone. He has no associate. | {*64:1 + 57:2} To him [belongs all] sovereignty and to him [belongs all] praise. He gives life and makes [people] die. He is almighty.
- (A8) Muḥammad is the messenger of God. | {*33:56} May God bless him. | And accept his intercession for his community.
- (A9) In the name of God, the Merciful, the Compassionate. | There is no god but God alone. He has no associate.

1 For the sake of clarity I will divide its content into eleven sections (A1–11), each containing an uneven number of meaningful sentences or groups of sentences differentiated by a vertical bar (|). I give the quranic cross-references in curly brackets ({}), preceded by * when the wording slightly differs from the canonical quranic wording of the passage in question.

https://doi.org/10.1515/9783110599688-006

- (A10) Muḥammad is the messenger of God. | {*33:56} May God bless him.
- (A11) This dome was built by God's servant [[al-Ma'mūn]] in the year [a.H.] 72.[2] May God accept it from him and be pleased with him. Amen, Lord of all men. The will is God's.

This inscription therefore consists of four more-or-less-homogeneous thematic sections:

AI	A1, A3, A7, A9
AII	A2, A4, A6, A8, A10
AIII	A1 + A5
AIV	A11

Certainly there are some unique elements in it, like the mention of a "prophet" in A4 and the concluding sentence in A8. Yet if we leave aside A11, which merely provides information on the building of the Dome itself, we have an almost symmetrical scheme with A5 at its core:

A1(a)	A2(b)	A3(a)	A4(b)	**A5**	A6(b)	A7(a)	A8(b)	A9(a)	+ A10
→	→	→	→		←	←	←	←	

or in a more dynamic fashion:

1	**2**	**3**
A1↪		
	↩A2	
A3↪		
	A4↪	
		A5
	A6 ↩	
A7 ↩		
	↪A8	
A9↩		
	+ A10	

for A1 and A5 are clearly related.

2 I.e. 692. Yet al-Ma'mūn (r. 813–33) later had his name inscribed instead of ʿAbd al-Malik's.

Now, it is certainly possible to read AI and AII as a double *šahāda*. But should we? As Christoph Luxenberg notices,[3] محمد *mḥmd* (i.e. *muḥammad*) in A2, A4, A6, A8, and A10 can be read as a gerundial passive participle meaning "praised be."[4] This, of course, would make problematic, and ultimately turn unclear, the referent of the title "messenger" (رسول *rasūl*) in A2, A4, A6, A8, and A10, as well as that of "prophet" (نبي *nabī*) in A4. But, as we shall see, *rasūl* is three times explicitly applied to Jesus on Inscription B (cf. B2, B3, B5) – in addition to "servant" (عبد *'abd*), which interestingly enough is appended in B2 to the formula displayed in A2, A4, A6, A8, and A10 ("Muḥammad/Praised be the servant of God and his messenger"), thus rendering even more problematic its referent! This obviously makes Luxenberg's argument not so overarched as it could a priori seem. In short, the rhetoric is ambiguous at best. Besides, if, as I have suggested, A5 is the core of the message contained in this first inscription (which Inscription B in turn expands, see below), the whole text can then be said to be about Jesus – or, a polemical text whose purpose is to question Jesus's divine sonship. Notice that this does not necessarily imply, however, that the referent of the titles "servant," "prophet," and "messenger" in A2, A4, A6, A8, and A10 should be the quranic prophet: it could well be Jesus without affecting that polemical intent.

In turn, the inscription on the inner face of the octagonal arcade (hereinafter Inscription B) may be divided into seven sections (B1–7):

- (B1) In the name of God, the Merciful, the Compassionate. | There is no god but God alone. He has no associate. | {*64:1 + 57:2} To him [belongs all] sovereignty and to him [belongs all] praise. He gives life and makes [people] die. He is almighty.
- (B2) Muḥammad is the servant of God and his messenger. | {33:56} God and his angels bless the prophet. O you who believe, implore [God's] blessing and grace/peace upon him! | God bless him, and may [God's] peace and mercy be upon him.
- (B3) {4:171} O people of the Scripture, do not ∴ exaggerate // err ∴ in your religion/judgement[5] and do not say about God save the truth. The Messiah, Jesus

3 Christoph Luxenberg, "A New Interpretation of the Arabic Inscription in Jerusalem's Dome of the Rock," in *The Hidden Origins of Islam*, ed. Karl-Heinz Ohlig and Gerd-R. Puin (Amherst, NY: Prometheus Books, 2010) 125–51, p. 130.

4 Cf. the analogous {Predicate} + {Subject} structure of Psalm 118:26 and Matthew 21:9 in the Arabic New Testament: *mubārak^{un} al-atī bi-smi r-rabb*, on which see Luxenberg, "A New Interpretation of the Arabic Inscription in Jerusalem's Dome of the Rock," 130.

5 Luxenberg, "A New Interpretation of the Arabic Inscription in Jerusalem's Dome of the Rock," 137, convincingly argues that *l' tglw' fy dynkm* in B3 can also be read *l't'lw' fy dynkm*, as the consonantal skeleton lacks the diacritical dot over the the second letter of the second word, which

son of Mary, is but the messenger of God and his Word, which he conveyed to Mary, and a spirit from him. So believe in God and his messengers and do not say "Three!"; cease [doing that], it is better for you. God is but one God – may he be praised! How could he have a child? To him belongs all there is in the heavens and on the earth. God is sufficient as a helper [to mankind].

- (B4) {4:172} The Messiah does not disdain to be a servant of God, nor do the angels, who are near [to God]. Whoever disdains his service and becomes arrogant – he [= God] will gather them towards him, all of them.
- (B5) O God, bless your messenger and servant Jesus son of Mary! | {19:33–6} Grace/peace [be] upon him on the day when he was born, on the day when he will die, and on the day when he will be resurrected. Such is Jesus, son of Mary, the word of truth about whom you fight with one another. Why would God have a child – may he be praised! When he decides something, he only needs to say "Be!" – and it comes into being. | {*43:64 &5:117} God is my lord and your lord, so serve him – this is a straight path.
- (B6) God is witness that there is no god besides him. | And the angels as well as the learned people confirm [according the truth]: There is no god besides Him, the Powerful, the Wise!
- (B7) The right religion/judgement[6] is agreement/conformity[7] [with this truth]. Those to whom the Scripture was given fell [into disagreement] after receiving knowledge, [thus] disputing amongst themselves. | Whoever denies the signs of God, [let her/him know that] God is swift in reckoning!

Therefore, the thematic division of this second inscription is somewhat simpler, as it consists of two instead of four major sections:

BI	B1, B2
BII	B3, B4, B5, B6, B7

BII, i.e. the longest one, is up to B5 an expansion of A5, as I have already pointed out, while I reproduces the double "*šahāda*" in AI and AII (on which see above). Yet one may additionally divide BII into two complementary subsections:

thus can be rendered as either ʿ or *g*; and *l'tʿlw' fy dynkm*, therefore, as a crypto-Syriac expression meaning "do not err in your judgement.".

6 دين *dīn*.

7 إسلم *'slm* (sic!) = *islām*.

BIIa	B3, B4, B5
BIIb	B6, B7

with BIIa being the expansion of the "Christological" text in A5, and BIIb drawing a few supplementary coda ("God has [therefore] warned that there is no god besides him", "The right religion/judgement is agreement/conformity [with this truth]) on the message displayed on it. Thus we have:

B1(a)	+ B2(b) →	**B3**	**B4**	**B5**	+ B6	+ B7

or (again) in a more dynamic fashion:

1	**2**	**3**	**4**
B1 ↪			
	B2 ↪		
		B3	
		B4	
		B5	
			↪ B6
			B7

Thus the largest part of this second inscription and its thematic core is once more (like A5) a polemical text (B3–5) which purpose is, again, to question Jesus's divine status (notice especially the thematic parallels between A1, A5, and B5).

Additionally, there are two other elements worth of commenting in BII:

First, it is Jesus himself who bears the titles of "messenger" in B3 and B5, and "servant" in B4 and B5, which, as I have earlier underlined (see above my concluding comments on the elusive referent of such titles in A2, A4, A6, A8, and A10), complicates their plain attribution to Muḥammad – and the same applies to the title "prophet" in A4 and B2.

Secondly, even if trinitarianism is explicitly rejected in B3, this does not imply that دين *dīn* ought to be read as "religion" rather than "judgement" therein and in B7. Likewise, the final reference to a judgement (again, *dyn*) in conformity to the truth that Jesus is not to be seen as God's son (let alone as God) does not make of the word إسلم *'slm* = *islām* a noun that denotes (the foundation of) a new "religion" (Islam).

Therefore both inscriptions, while implicitly witnessing to the official promotion of a new confessional creed centred around the figure of Muḥammad as God's servant, prophet, and messenger – and hence to the official inscription of a new religious identity based upon a somewhat innovative confessional symbol[8] – show that the time in which those very same titles were rather applied to Jesus was not distant enough to avoid some very significant conceptual ambivalences. In other words, they evince a moment of *transition* in the process of identity making instead of representing the official sanction of an already existing identity or a clear-cut new start within that process. And this matches the view that the Muhammadan *kerygma* was still on the making in ʿAbd al-Malik's times.

The *ḥadīṯ nabawī* (i.e. the prophetic *ḥadīṯ*) that opens the present essay: وَإِذَا آمَنَ بِعِيسَى ثُمَّ آمَنَ بِي ، فَلَهُ أَجْرَانِ , "Whoever believes in Jesus and *then* believes in me, he will get a double reward,"[9] bear witness to this, as well. Yet the interpretation of this *ḥadīṯ* proves particularly difficult: should we understand that, in order to get a double reward, the believer had to change her/his belief in Jesus into an altogether different one?, or should the two beliefs complement one another?; and if so, in which precise way should they relate? Let us suppose that Jesus was the "Messiah," and Muḥammad God's "last prophet" (Q 33:40) whose sending as *aḥmad*, furthermore, Jesus had fortold (61:6). Does this mean that Muḥammad was the "comforter" sent by God until Jesus's second coming?; but if so, why should he then become the very axis of a new religion? Or is it that by announcing Muḥammad's sending *qua aḥmad* (i.e. as being "more praised" than Jesus) Jesus himself is implicitly transformed into a new John the Baptist, and hence his status lowered before that of Muḥammad himself?; but then, why keep calling Jesus the "Messiah" and Muḥammad the "last prophet," which instead would seem to require the *opposite* subordination?

While obviously not affecting the Muslim faith this apparent contradiction must not be deemed irrelevant for the history of religions, as it betrays a tension not entirely solved in the canonical text of the Qur'ān.

The more we can say then, is that the making of the Muhamadan *kerygma* followed a two-stage process. First, it was promoted to engage in internal identity shaping against a competing, yet perhaps more original, understanding of the new revelation – one that emphasised the divine nature of the heavenly messenger communicating it and the coincidence between his past, present, and future messianic manifestations. Secondly, it was consolidated in terms of external

---

8 Which is only documented prior to ʿAbd al-Malik's rule in a Arab-Sassanian coin minted by the Zubayrid governor of Bīšāpūr in the 680s. On epigraphy, numismatics, and formative Islam, see once more Jeremy Johns, "Archaeology and the History of Early Islam: The First Seventy Years," *JESHO* 46. 4 (2003): 411–36; Robert G. Hoyland, "New Documentary Texts and the Early Islamic State," *BSOAS* 69.3 (2006): 395–416.

9 *Saḥīḥ al-Buḫārī* (5 vols.; Beirut: Dar al-Fikr, 1421/2001) 2:849, no. 3446 (my emphasis).

identity shaping against the rival Christian worldview once the foundations of the new Arab state were effectively laid. Thus the making of the Muhamadan *kerygma* echoes twice the very notion of "apologetics" – or rather reflects the *two* possible forms that apologetic discourse may adopt: "one developing as a response to competing interpretations within one's own worldview and held to be incompatible with it . . . and the other prompted by the existence of a competing worldview."[10] While the first of such uses implies the elaboration, distribution, and identification of such terms as "orthodoxy," "heterodoxy," and "heresy," the latter implies the constitution and the very definition of "religions" themselves as autonomous entities.

---

10 Anders Klostergaard Petersen, "Apologetics," in *Dictionary for the Study of Religions*, ed. Robert A. Segal and Kocku von Stuckrad (3 vols.; Leiden and Boston: Brill, 2015) 1:110–14, p. 113. See further idem, "The Diversity of Apologetics: From Genre to a Mode of Thinking," in *Critique and Apologetics: Jews, Christians and Pagans in Antiquity*, ed. Jörg Ulrich, David Brakke, and Anders-Christian Jacobsen (ECCA; Frankfurt am Main: Peter Lang, 2009) 15–41.

Bibliography

Ahmad, Basharat. *Birth of Jesus in the Light of the Quran and in the Light of the Gospels.* Lahore, India: Dar-ul-Kutib-i-Islam, ca. 1929.

Akyol, Mustafa. *The Islamic Jesus: How the King of the Jews Became a Prophet of the Muslims.* New York: St. Martin's Press, 2017.

Althusser, Louis, in collaboration with Étienne Balibar, Roger Establet, Pierre Macherey, and Jacques Rancière. *Lire le Capital.* TQ. Paris: Maspero, 1965. English translation by Ben Brewster, *Reading Capital.* London: New Left Books, 1970.

Amir-Moezzi, Mohammad Ali. "Muḥammad le Paraclete et 'Alī le Messie. Nouvelles remarques sur les origines de l'islam et de l'imamologie shi'ite." In *L'Ésotérisme Shi'ite. Ses racines et ses prolongements/Shi'i Esotericism: Its Roots and Developments*, ed. Mohammad Ali Amir-Moezzi, with Maria De Cillis, Daniel De Smet, and Orkhan Mir-Kasimov, 19–54. BEHESR 177. Turnhout, BE: Brepols and The Institute of Ismaili Studies, 2016.

Anderson, Gary A. "The Exaltation of Adam and the Fall of Satan." In *Literature on Adam and Eve: Collected Essays*, ed. Gary A. Anderson, Michael E. Stone, Johannes Tromp, 83–110. SVTP 15. Leiden and Boston: Brill, 2000.

Andrae, Tor. *Der Ursprung des Islams und das Christentum.* Uppsala: Almqvist and Wiksells, 1926.

Arbel, Daphna, Robert J. Cousland, and Dietmar Neufeld. *And So They Went Out: The Lives of Adam and Eve as Cultural Transformative Story.* London and New York: T&T Clark, 2010.

Arnaldez, Roger. *Jésus, fils de Marie, prophète de l'Islam.* Paris: Desclée, 1980.

Avni, Gideon. *The Byzantine–Islamic Transition in Palestine: An Archaeological Approach.* OSB. Oxford and New York: Oxford University Press, 2014.

Azaiez, Mehdi, Gabriel Said Reynolds, Tommaso Tesei, and Hamza M. Zafer, eds. *The Qur'an Seminar Commentary/Le Qur'an Seminar: A Collaborative Study of 59 Qur'an Passages/Commentaires collaborative de 50 passages coraniques.* Berlin and Boston: De Gruyter, 2016.

El-Badawi, Emran Iqbal. "From 'Clergy' to 'Celibacy': The Development of *Rahbānīyya* between the Qur'ān, Ḥadīth and Church Canon." *Al-Bayān* 11.1 (2013): 1–14.

El-Badawi, Emran Iqbal. *The Qur'ān and the Aramaic Gospel Traditions.* RSQ. London and New York: Routledge, 2014.

von Balthasar, Hans Urs. *Katolisch. Aspekte des Mysteriums.* Einsiedeln: Johannes Verlag, 1975.

Basetti-Sani, Giulio. *Il Corano nella luce di Cristo: saggio per una reinterpretazione cristiana del libro sacro de l'Islam.* Bologna: Editrice Missionaria Italiana, 1972. English translation by W. Russell Carroll and Bede Dauphinee, *The Koran in the Light of Christ.* Chicago: Franciscan Herald Press, 1977.

Beaumont, I. Mark. *Christology in Dialogue with Muslims: A Critical Analysis of Christian Presentations of Christ for Muslims from the Ninth and Twentieth Centuries.* Foreword by David Thomas. Carlisle, UK: Paternoster, 2005.

Beck, Daniel A. *Evolution of the Early Qur'ān*: From Anonymous Apocalypse to Charismatic Prophet. ACDE 2. New York and Bern: Peter Lang, 2018.

Beck, Daniel. "The Astral Messenger, The Lunar Redemption, The Solar Salvation: Manichaean Cosmic Soteriology in the Qur'ān's Archaic Surahs (Q 84, Q 75, Q 54)." Forthcoming in *Remapping Emergent Islam: Texts, Social Contexts, and Ideological Trajectories*, ed. Carlos A. Segovia. SWLAEMA. Amsterdam: Amsterdam University Press.

https://doi.org/10.1515/9783110599688-007

Beck, Edmund M. "Die Gestalt des Abraham am Wendepunkt der Entwicklung Muhammeds: Analyse von Sure 2, 118 (124)–135 (141)." *Le Muséon* 65 (1952): 73–94. Reprinted in *Der Koran*, ed. Rudi Paret, 111–33. Darmstadt: Wissenschaftliche Buchgesellschaft, 1975.

Becker, Adam H. "Beyond the Spatial and Temporal *Limes*: Questioning the 'Parting of the Ways' Outside the Roman Empire." In *The Ways that Never Parted: Jews and Christians in Late Antiquity and the Early Middle Ages*, ed. Annette Yoshiko Reed and Adam H. Becker, 373–92. TSAJ 95. Tübingen: Mohr Siebeck, 2003.

Beeston, Alfred F. L. "Abraha." In *EI*, 1:105–6. Leiden: Brill, and Paris: A. Maisonneuve, 1960.

Beeston, Alfred F. L. "Foreign Loanwords in Sabaic." In *Arabia Felix. Beiträge zur Sprache und Kultur des vorislamischen Arabien. Festschrift Walter M. Müller zum 60. Geburtstag*, ed. Norbert Nebes, 39–45. Wiesbaden: Harrassowitz, 1994.

Bell, Richard. *The Origin of Islam in Its Christian Environment*. London: Macmillan, 1926; reprinted in London and New York: Routledge, 2012.

Bellamy, James A. "Some Proposed Emendations to the Text of the Koran." JAOS 113.4 (1993): 570–1. Reprinted in *What the Koran Really Says: Language, Text, and Commentary*, ed. Ibn Warraq, 503–5. Amherst, NY: Prometheus Books, 2002.

Bellamy, James A. "Textual Criticism." In *Encyclopaedia of the Qur'ān*, ed. Jane Dammen McAuliffe, 5:237–52. 6 vols. Leiden and Boston: Brill, 2001–6.

Berg, Herbert. "Context: Muḥammad." In *The Blackwell Companion to the Qur'ān*, ed. Andrew Rippin, 187–204. Oxford: Blackwell, 2006.

Berg, Herbert. "The Needle in the Haystack: Islamic Origins and the Nature of the Early Sources." In *The Coming of the Comforter: When, Where, and to Whom? Studies on the Rise of Islam and Various Other Topics in Memory of John Wansbrough*, ed. Carlos A. Segovia and Basil Lourié, 271–302. OJC 3. Piscataway, NJ: Gorgias Press, 2012.

Bernard, Dominique. *Les disciples juifs de Jésus du Ier siècle à Mahomet: Recherches sur le mouvement ébionite*. Paris: Cerf, 2017.

Biale, David. "Counter-History and Jewish Polemics against Christianity: The *Sefer Toldot Yeshu* and the *Sefer Zerubavel*." *JSS* 6 (1999): 130–45.

Blachère, Regis. "Compte rendu de Denise Masson, *Le Coran et la Révélation judéo-chrétienne, études comparées*, Paris (A. Maisonneuve) 1958." *Arabica* 7.1 (1960): 93–5.

van Bladel, Kevin. "The Alexander Legend in the Qur'ān 18:83–102." In *The Qur'ān in Its Historical Context*, ed. Gabriel Said Reynolds, 175–203. RSQ; London and New York: Routledge, 2008.

Blanks, David R. "Western Views of Islam in the Premodern Period: A Brief History of Past Approaches." In *Western Views of Islam in Medieval and Early Modern Europe: Perception of Other*, ed. David R. Blanks and Michael Frassetto, 24–5. New York: St. Martin's Press, 1999.

Bleuchot, Hervé. "Compte rendu de Denise Masson, *Monothéisme coranique et monothéisme biblique. Doctrines comparées*, [Paris,] Desclée de Brouwer, 1976." *ROMM* 24.1 (1977): 281–85.

Block, Jonn. *The Qur'ān in Christian-Muslim Dialogue: Historical and Modern Interpretations*. RSQ. London and New York: Routledge, 2014.

de Blois, François. "*Naṣrānī* (Ναζωραῖος) and *Ḥanīf* (Ἐθνικός): Studies on the Religious Vocabulary of Christianity and of Islam." *BSOAS* 65.1 (2002): 1–30;

Boccaccini, Gabriele. *Beyond the Essene Hypothesis: The Parting of the Ways between Qumran and Enochic Judaism*. Grand Rapids, MI, and Cambridge: Eerdmans, 1998.

Boccaccini, Gabriele. *Roots of Rabbinic Judaism: An Intellectual History, from Ezekiel to Daniel*. Grand Rapids, MI, and Cambridge: Eerdmans, 2002.

Boccaccini, Gabriele, ed. *Enoch and the Messiah Son of Man: Revisiting the Book of Parables*. Grand Rapids, MI, and Cambridge: Eerdmans, 2007.
Boccaccini, Gabriele, and Carlos A. Segovia, eds. *Paul the Jew: Rethinking the Apostle as a Figure of Second Temple Judaism*. Minneapolis: Fortress, 2016.
Bock, Darrell L. and James H. Charlesworth, eds. *Parables of Enoch: A Paradigm Shift*. London and New York: Bloomsbury, 2013.
Boisliveau, Anne-Sylvie. *Le Coran par lui-même. Vocabulaire et argumentation du discours coranique autoréférentiel*. Leiden and Boston: Brill, 2014.
Booth, Phil. *Crisis of Empire: Doctrine and Dissent at the End of Late Antiquity*. Berkeley and London: University of California Press, 2014.
Borrmans, Maurice.Jésus et les Musulmans d'*aujourd'hui*. Paris: Desclée, 1996.
Bowersock, Glen W. *Empires in Collision in Late Antiquity*. Waltham, MA: Brandeis University Press and Historical Society of Israel, 2012.
Bowman, John. "The Debt of Islam to Monophysite Syrian Christianity," *NTT* 19 (1964–5): 177–201.
Boyarin, Daniel. "The Gospel of the *Memra*: Jewish Binitarianism and the Prologue to John." *HTR* 94.3 (2001): 243–85.
Boyarin, Daniel. *Border Lines: The Partition of Judaeo-Christianity*. DRLAR. Philadelphia: University of Pennsylvania Press, 2004.
Boyarin, Daniel. "Rethinking Jewish Christianity: An Argument for Dismantling a Dubious Category (to which is Appended a Correction of my Border Lines)." *JQR* 99.1 (2009): 7–36.
Boyarin, Daniel. *The Jewish Gospels: The Story of the Jewish Christ*, with a Foreword by Jack Miles. New York: The New Press, 2012.
Brock, Sebastian P. "The Christology of the Church of the East in the Synods of the Fifth to Early Seventh Centuries." In *Aksum-Thyateira: A Festschrift for Archbishop of Thyateira and Great Britain*, ed. George D. Dragas, 125–42. London: Thyateira House 1985.
Brock, Sebastian P. "The Church of the East Up to the Sixth Century and Its Absence from Councils in the Roman Empire." In *Syriac Dialogue: The First Non-Official Consultation on Dialogue within the Syrian Tradition, with Focus on the Theology of the Church of the East*, ed. Alfred Stirnemann and Gerhard Wilflinger, 68–85. Vienna: Pro-Oriente, 1996.
Brock, Sebastian P. "The 'Nestorian' Church: A Lamentable Misnomer." *BJRL* 78.3 [1996]: 23–35.
al-Buḫārī. *Ṣaḥīḥ al-Buḫārī*. 5 vols. Beirut: Dar al-Fikr, 1421/2001.
Burkitt, F. Crawford. *Evangelion da-Mepharreshe: The Curetonian Version of the Four Gospels, with the readings of the Sinai Palimpsest*. 2 vols. Cambridge: Cambridge University Press, 1904.
Camplani, Alberto. "The Revival of Persian Monasticism (Sixth to Seventh Centuries): Church Structures, Theological Academy, and Reformed Monks." In *Foundations of Power and Conflicts of Authority in Late-Antique Monasticism*, ed. A. Camplani and G. Filoramo, 277–95. OLA 157. Leuven: Peeters, 2007.
Caquot, André. "Compte rendu de Denise Masson, *Le Coran et la Révélation judéo-chrétienne. Études comparées*, Paris, A. Maisonneuve, 1958." *RHR* 157.1 (1960): 107–8.
Cereti, Carlo. "Zaehner, Robert Charles." *EnIr*, online edition, 2015. Available at http://www.iranicaonline.org/articles/zaehner-robert.
Champion, Renée. "Masson, Denise," in *Dictionnaire des orientalistes de la langue française*, ed. François Pouillon, 704. Paris: IISMM–Karthala, 2012.
Chandler, Paul-Gordon. *Pilgrims of Christ on the Muslim Road: Exploring a New Path between Two Faiths*. Lanham, MD, and Plymouth, UK: Rowman and Littlefield, 2007.

Charles, Henri. *Le christianisme des arabes nomads sur le limes et dans le désert syro-*mésopotamien aux alentours de l'*hégire*. BEHE; Paris: Leroux, 1936.
Cheikho, Louis. *Le christianisme et la littérature chrétienne en Arabie avant l'islam*. 3 vols. Beirut: Imprimerie Catholique, 1912–23. 2nd ed., Beirut: Dar el-Machreq, 1989.
Collins, John J. *The Apocalyptic Imagination: An Introduction to Jewish Apocalyptic Literature*. 2nd ed. Grand Rapids, MI, and Cambridge: Eerdmans, 1998.
Corbin, Henry. *Le Paradoxe du monothéisme*. Paris: L'Herne, 1981.
Courtieu, Gilles. "La *threskeia* des Ismaélites Etude de la première définition synthétique de l'islam par Jean de Damas." In *Hérésies: une construction d'identités religieuses*, ed. Christian Brouwer, Guillaume Dye, and Anja van Rompaey, 105–260. Brussels: Éditions de l'Université de Bruxelles, 2015.
Courtieu, Gilles and Carlos A. Segovia. "Bābil, Makka and Ṭā'if, or (always) Ctesiphon(-Seleucia)? New Insights into the Iranian Setting of the Earliest Quranic Milieu." (Provisional title.) Paper to be presented to the 3rd Nangeroni Meeting of the Early Islamic Studies Seminar, Milan June 2019.
Crone, Patricia, and Michael Cook, *Hagarism: The Making of the Islamic Word*. Cambridge: Cambridge University Press, 1977.
Crone, Patricia, and Michael Cook. "Among the Believers." *Tablet*, August 10, 2010, http://www.tabletmag.com/jewish-news-and-politics/42023/amongst-the-believers.
Debié, Muriel. "Les controverses miaphysites en Arabie et le Coran." In *Les controverses religieuses en syriaque*, ed. Flavia Ruani, 137–56. ES 13. Paris: Geuthner, 2015.
Déroche, François. "Recensions coraniques." In *Dictionnaire du Coran*, ed. Mohammad Ali Amir-Moezzi, 733–5. Paris: Laffont, 2007.
Déroche, François. *La transmission écrite du Coran dans les débuts de l'islam: Le codex Parisinopetropolitanus*. Leiden and Boston: Brill, 2009.
Donner, Fred M. "From Believers to Muslims: Confessional Self-identity in the Early Islamic Community." *Al-Abhath* 50–1 (2002–2003): 9–53.
Donner, Fred M. *Muhammad and the Believers: At the Origins of Islam*. Cambridge, MA, and London: Harvard University Press, 2010.
Drijvers, Han J. V. *Bardaiṣān of Edessa*. SSN 6. Assen: Van Gorkum & Co., 1966. Reprinted in Piscataway, NJ: Gorgias Press, 2012.
Droge, Arthur J. *The Qur'ān: A New Annotated Translation*. Sheffield, UK, and Bristol, CT: Equinox, 2013.
Dubuisson, Daniel. *The Western Construction of Religion: Myths, Knowledge, and Ideology*, translated by William Sayers. Baltimore, MD, and London: John Hopkins University Press, 2003.
Dunn, James D. G. *Christology in the Making: A New Testament Inquiry into the Origins of there Doctrine of the Incarnation*. 2nd ed. Grand Rapids, MI, and Cambridge, UK, 1989.
Dye, Guillaume. "Lieux saints communs, partagés ou confisqués : aux sources de quelques péricopes coraniques (Q 19 : 16–33)." In *Partage du sacré: transferts, dévotions mixtes, rivalités interconfessionnelles*, ed. Isabelle Depret and Guillaume Dye, 55–121. Bruxelles-Fernelmont: EME, 2012.
Dye, Guillaume. "Pourquoi et comment se fait un texte canonique. Quelques réflexions sur l'histoire du Coran." In *Hérésies: une construction d'identités religieuses*, ed. Christian Brouwer, Guillaume Dye, and Anja van Rompaey, 55–104. PHR. Brussels: Éditions de l'Université de Bruxelles, 2015.
Dye, Guillaume. "The Qur'ān and its Hypertextuality in Light of Redaction Criticism." Forthcoming in *Early Islam: The Religious Milieu of Late Antiquity*, ed. Guillaume Dye. LAMINE; Chicago: Chicago Oriental Institute.

Dye, Guillaume and Manfred Kropp, "Le nom de Jésus ('Īsā) dans le Coran, et quelques autres noms bibliques: remarques sur l'onomastique coranique." In *Figures bibliques en islam*, ed. Guillaume Dye and Fabien Nobilio, 171–98. Brussels-Fernelmont: EME, 2011.

Fedeli, Alba. "Is the Dating of Qur'ānic Manuscripts still a Problem?" Forthcoming in *Early Islam: The Religious Milieu of Late Antiquity*, ed. Guillaume Dye. LAMINE; Chicago: Chicago Oriental Institute.

Fisher, Greg. *Between Empires: Arabs, Romans, and Sassanians in Late Antiquity*. Oxford and New York: Oxford University Press, 2011.

Fisher, Greg and Philip Wood, with contributions from George Bevan, Geoffrey Greatrex, Basema Hamarneh, Peter Schadler, and Walter D. Ward. "Arabs and Christianity." In *Arabs and Empires before Islam*, ed. Greg Fisher, 276–372. Oxford and New York: Oxford University Press, 2015.

Fisher, Greg and Philip Wood. "Writing the History of the 'Persian Arabs': The Pre-Islamic Perspective on the 'Naṣrids' of al-Ḥīrah." *IS* 49.2 (2016): 247–90.

Fletcher-Louis, Crispin H. T. *All the Glory of Adam: Liturgical Anthropology in the Dead Sea Scrolls*. STDJ 42. Leiden and Boston: Brill, 2002.

Fossum, Jarl E. *The Name of God and the Angel of the Lord: Samaritan and Jewish Concepts of Intermediation and the Origins of Gnosticism*. WUNT 36. Tübingen: Mohr Siebeck, 1985.

Gajda, Iwona. *Le royaume de Ḥimyar à l'époque monothéiste. L'histoire de l'Arabie du Sud ancienne de la fin du IVe siècle de l'ère chrétienne jusqu'a l'avènement de l'Islam*. MAIBL 40. Paris: Académie des Inscriptions et Belles-Lettres, 2009.

Gallez, Édouard-Marie. *Le messie et son prophète. Aux origines de l'islam*. 2 vols. Versailles: Éditions de Paris, 2005.

Gallez,Édouard-Marie. "'Gens du Livre' et Nazaréens dans le Coran: qui sont les premiers et à quel titre les seconds en font-ils partie?" *OC* 92 (2008): 174–86.

Geiger, Abraham. *Was hat Mohammed aus dem Judenthume aufgenommen?* Bonn: Baaden, 1833. English translation by F. M. Young, *Judaism and Islam: A Prize Essay*. Madras: MDCSPCK Press, 1898.

Gerock, C. F. *Versuch einer Darstellung der Christologie des Koran*. Hamburg: Perthes, 1839.

Gieschen, Charles A. *Angelomorphic Christology: Antecedents and Early Evidence*. Leiden and Boston: Brill, 1998.

Gilliot, Claude. "Des indices d'un proto-lectionnaire dans le « Lectionnaire Arabe » dit Coran." In *Les Origins du Coran, le Coran des origines*, ed. François Déroche, Christian-Julien Robin, and Michel Zink, 297–314. Paris: AIBL, 2015.

Gnilka, Joachim. *Die Nazarener und der Koran: eine Spurensuche*. Freiburg: Herder, 2007.

Guiraud, Morgan. "Adam." in *Dictionnaire du Coran*, ed. Amir-Moezzi, 22–26. Paris: Laffont, 2007.

Gobillot, Geneviève. "Hanîf," in *Dictionnaire du Coran*, ed. Mohammad Ali Amir-Moezzi, 381–4. Paris: Laffont, 2007.

Goldsack, William. *Christ in Islam: The Testimony of the Quran to Christ*. London: Christian Literature Society, 1905.

Grabbe, Lester L. "'Son of Man': Its Origin and Meaning in Second Temple Judaism." In *Enoch and the Synoptic Gospels: Reminiscences, Allusions, Intertextuality*, ed. Loren T. Stuckenbruck and Gabriele Boccaccini, 169–98. Atlanta, GA: SBL, 2016.

Griffith, Sidney H. "Christians and Christianity [in the Qur'ān]." In *Encyclopaedia of the Qur'ān*, ed. Jane Dammen McAuliffe, 1:307–16.6 vols. Leiden and Boston: Brill, 2001–6.

Griffith, Sidney H. "Monasticism and Monks." In *Encyclopaedia of the Qur'ān*, ed. Jane Damen McAuliffe, 3:406. 6 vols. Leiden and Boston: Brill, 2001–6.

Griffith, Sidney H. "Christian Lore and the Arabic Qur'ān: The 'Companions of the Cave' in *Sūrat al-Kahf* and in Syriac Christian Tradition." In *The Qur'ān in Its Historical Context*, ed. Gabriel Said Reynolds, 109–37. RSQ; London and New York: Routledge, 2008.

Grillmeier, Alois. *Christ in Christian Tradition*, English translation by O. C. Dean Jr. 2 vols. Louisville, KY: Westminster John Knox, 1975–96.

Havenith, Alfred. *Les arabes chrétiens nomads au temps de Mohammed*, Préface de Julien Ries. CCL. Louvain-la-Neuve: Centre d'Histoire des Religions, 1988.

Hawting, Gerald R. *The Idea of Idolatry and the Emergence of Islam: From Polemic to History*. Cambridge and New York: Cambridge University Press, 1999.

Heal, Kristian. "Cave of Treasures." In *The Routledge Encyclopedia of Ancient Mediterranean Religions*, ed. Eric Orlin, Lisbeth S. Fried, Jennifer Wright Knust, Michael L. Satlow, and Michael E. Pregill, 172. London and New York: Routledge, 2015.

Heinthaler, Theresia. *Christliche Araber vor dem Islam: Verbreitung und konfessionelle Zugehörigkeit: eine Hinführung*. ECS 7. Leuven: Peeters, 2007.

Henninger, Josef. "Christentum im vorislamischen Arabien." *NZM* 4 (1948): 222–4.

Henninger, Josef. *Spuren christlicher Glaubenswahrheiten im Koran*. Schöneck: ANZM, 1951.

El-Hibri, Tayeb. *Parable and Politics in Early Islamic History: The Rashidun Caliphs*. New York and Chichester, UK: Columbia University Press, 2010.

Horn, Cornelia B. "A Chapter in the Pre-History of the Christological Controversies in Arabic: Readings from the Works of John Rufus." *POr* 30 (2005): 133–56.

Horn, Cornelia B. *Asceticism and Christological Controversy in Fifth-Century Palestine: The Career of Peter the Iberian*. OECS; Oxford and New York: Oxford University Press, 2006.

Horowitz, Elliot S. *Reckless Rites: Purim and the Legacy of Jewish Violence*. Princeton, NJ: Princeton University Press, 2006.

Hoyland, Robert G. "New Documentary Texts and the Early Islamic State." *BSOAS* 69.3 (2006): 395–416.

Hoyland, Robert G. *In God's Path: The Arab Conquests and the Creation of an Islamic Empire*. Oxford and New York: Oxford University Press, 2015.

Humphreys, R. Stephen. *Mu'awiya ibn Abi Sufyan: From Arabia to Empire*. Oxford: Oneworld, 2006.

Jackson, Roy. *Fifty Key Figures in Islam*. London and New York: Routledge, 2006.

Jackson-McCabe, Matt. "What's in a Name? The Problem of 'Jewish Christianity'." In *Jewish Christianity Reconsidered: Rethinking Ancient Groups and Texts*, ed. Matt Jackson-McCabe, 7–38. Minneapolis: Fortress, 2007.

al-Jallad, Ahmad. "The Arabic of the Islamic Conquests: Notes on Phonology and Morphology based on the Greek Transcriptions of the First Islamic Century." *BSOAS* 80.3 (2017): 419–39.

Jeffery, Arthur. *Materials for the History of the Text of the Qur'ān: The Old Codices*. Leiden and Boston: Brill, 1970.

Johns, Jeremy. "Archaeology and the History of Early Islam: The First Seventy Years." *JESHO* 46.4 (2003): 411–36.

de Jong, Marinus and Johannes Tromp. *The Life of Adam and Eve and Related Literature*. Sheffield, UK: Sheffield Academic Press, 1997.

Jongeneel, Jan A. B., with the assistance of Robert T. Coote. *Jesus Christ in World History: His Presence and Representation in Cyclical and Linear Settings*. Frankfurt: Peter Lang, 2008.

Kaplony, Andreas. “The Ortography and Pronunciation of Arabic Names and Terms in the Greek Petra, Nessana, Qurra and Senouthios Letters (Six to Eight Centuries ce).” *MLR* 22 (2015): 1–81.
Khalidi, Tarif. *The Muslim Jesus: Sayings and Stories in Islamic Literature*. Cambridge, MA, and London: Harvard University Press, 2001.
Kister, Meir Jacob. *Concepts and Ideas at the Dawn of Islam*. VCS. Aldershot, IK: Ashgate/ Variorum, 1997.
Kofsky, Aryeh. “Peter the Inerian: Pilgrimage, Monasticism, and Ecclesiastical Politics in Byzantine Palestine.” *LA* 47 (1997): 209–22.
Kohen, Elli. *History of the Byzantine Jews: A Microcosmos in the Thousand Year Empire*. Lanham, MD: University Press of America, 2007.
Kreeft, Peter, and Ronald K. Tacelli. *Handbook of Christian Apologetics: Hundred of Answers to Crucial Questions*. IVP Academic; Downers Grove, IL: InterVarsity Press, 2009.
Kropp, Manfred. “Der äthiopische Satan = šayṭān und seine koranischen Ausläufer; mit einer Bemerkung über verbales Steinigen.” *OC* 89 (1995): 93–102.
Kropp, Manfred. “Beyond Single Words: Māʾida – Shayṭān – jibt and ṭāghūt. Mechanisms of transmission into the Ethiopic (Gəʿəz) Bible and the Qurʾānic text.” In *The Qurʾān in Its Historical Context*, ed. Gabriel Said Reynolds, 204–16. RSQ; London and New York: Routledge, 2008.
Kropp, Manfred. “Tripartite, but Anti-Trinitarian Formulas in the Qurʾānic Corpus, Possibly Pre-Qurʾānic.” In *New Perspectives on the Qurʾān: The Qurʾān in Its Historical Context 2*, ed. Gabriel Said Reynolds, 247–64. RSQ. London & New York: Routledge, 2011.
Kropp, Manfred. “»Im Namen Gottes, (d. i.) des gnädigen (und) B/(b)armherzigen«. Die muslimische Basmala: Neue Ansätze zu ihrer Erklärung.” *OC* 97 (2013–14): 190–201.
Lawson, Todd. “The Crucifixion of Jesus in the Qurʾān and Quranic Commentary: A Historical Survey, Part I.” *BHMIIS* 10.2 (1991): 34–62.
Lawson, Todd. “The Crucifixion of Jesus in the Qurʾān and Quranic Commentary: A Historical Survey, Part II.” *BHMIIS* 10.3 (1991): 6–40.
Lawson, Todd. *The Crucifixion and the Qurʾan: A Study in the History of Muslim Thought*. Oxford: Oneworld, 2009.
Lecker, Michael. “Were the Ghassānids and the Byzantines behind Muḥammad’s Hijra.” In *Les Jafnides. Des rois arabes au service de Byzance (VIe siècle de l’ère chrétienne) – Actes du colloque de Paris, 24–25 novembre 2008*, ed. Denis Genequand and Christian Julien Robin, 277–93. OM 17. Paris: de Boccard, 2015.
Leehmuis, Frederik. “Codices of the Qurʾān.” In *Encycopledia of the Qurʾān*, ed. J. D. McAuliffe, 1:347–51. 6 vols. Leiden and Boston: Brill, 2001.
Leirvik, Oddbjørn. *Images of Jesus Christ in Islam*. London and New York: Continuum, 1999. 2nd ed., 2010.
Leslau, Wolf. *Comparative Dictionary of Geʿez (Classical Ethiopic), Geʿez-English/English-Geʿez, with an index of the Semitic Roots*. Wiesbaden: Harrassowitz, 2006.
Lieu, Judith M. *Marcion and the Making of a Heretic: God and Scripture in the Second Century*. Cambridge and New York: Cambridge University Press, 2015.
Lory, Pierre “ʿImrân et sa famille.” in *Dictionnaire du Coran*, ed. Mohammad Ali Amir-Moezzi, 417–9. Paris: Laffont, 2007.
O’Loughlin, Thomas. *Adomnán and the Holy Places: The Perceptions of an Insular Monk on the Locations of the Biblical Drama*. London and New York: T & T Clark, 2007.
Lüling, Günter. Über den Ur-Qurʾān: Ansätze zur Rekonstruktion vorislamischer christlicher Strophenlieder im Qurʾān. Erlangen: Lüling, 1974. 2nd ed., 1993. English translation,

A Challenge to Islam for Reformation: The Rediscovery and Reliable Reconstruction of a Comprehensive pre-Islamic Christian Hymnal Hidden in the Koran under Earliest Islamic Reinterpretations. Delhi: Banarsidass, 2003.

Luxenberg, Christoph. *Die syro-aramäische Lesart des Koran: Ein Beitrag zur Entschlüsselung der Koransprache The Syro-Aramaic Reading of the Koran*. Berlin: Schiler, 2000. 3rd ed., 2003. English translation, *The Syro-Aramaic Reading of the Koran: A Contribution to the Decoding of the Language of the Koran*. Berlin: Schiler, 2007.

Luxenberg, Christoph. "A New Interpretation of the Arabic Inscription in Jerusalem's Dome of the Rock." In *The Hidden Origins of Islam: New research into Its Early History*, ed. Karl-Heinz Ohlig and Gerd-R. Puin, 125–51. Amherst, NY: Prometheus Books, 2010.

Macherey, Pierre. *Pour une théorie de la production littéraire*. Paris: Maspero, 1966. English translation by Geoffrey Wall, *A Theory of Literary Production*. London: Routledge and Kegan Paul, 1978.

Madigan, Daniel A. The *Qur'ān's Self-image*. Princeton, NJ: Princeton University Press, 2001.

Madigan, Daniel A. "The Limits of Self-referentiality in the Qur'ān." In *Self-referentiality in the Qur'ān*, ed. Stefan Wild. 59–69 DA 11. Wiesbaden: Harrassowitz, 2007.

Makin, Al. *Representing the Enemy: Musaylima in Muslim Literature*. EUS 106. Frankfurt and New York: Peter Lang, 2008.

Makin, Al. "Sharing the Concept of God among Trading Prophets: Reading the Poems Attributed to Umayya b. Abī Ṣalt." In *Religions and Trade: Religious Formation, Transformation and Cross-Cultural Exchange between East and West*, ed. Peter Wick and Volker Rabens, 283–305. DHR 5. Leiden and Boston: Brill, 2014.

Maneval, J.-P. *La Christologie du Coran*. PhD dissertation, Faculté de théologie protestante de Montauban; Toulouse, France: Chauvin, 1867.

Marshall, David. "Christianity in the Qur'ān," in *Islamic Interpretations of Christianity*, ed. Lloyd Ridgeon, 3–29. London and New York: Routledge, 2001.

Masson, Denise. *Le Coran et la Rév*élation judéo-*chr*étienne. Études comparées. 2 vols.; Paris: Maisonneuve, 1958. Reedited in 1976 as *Monoth*éisme coranique et monothéisme biblique. *Doctrines comparées*. Paris: Desclée.

Mazuz, Haggai. "Christians in the Qur'ān: Some Insights Derived from the Classical Exegetical Approach." *SO* 112 (2012): 41–53.

McAuliffe, Jane Dammen. *Qur'ānic Christians: An Analysis of Classical and Modern Exegesis*. Cambridge and New York: Cambridge University Press, 2007.

McCurdy, J. Frederic, Kaufmann Kohler, and Richard Gottheil. "Adam." In *The Jewish Encyclopedia*, ed. Isidore Singer *et al.*, 1:177–8. 12 vols. New York: Funk and Wagnalls, 1906–12.

Meerson, Michael and Peter Schäfer, in collaboration with Yaakov Deutsch, David Grossberg, Abigail Manekin, and Adina Yoffie. *Toledot Yeshu: The Life Story of Jesus*. 2 vols. TSAJ 159. Tübingen: Mohr Siebeck, 2014.

Merad, Ali. "Le Christ selon le Coran," *ROMM* 5 (1968): 79–94. English translation: "Christ According to the Qur'ān." *Encounters* 69 (1980): 2–17.

Meyer, Nicholas A. *Adam's Dust and Adam's Glory in the Hodayot and the Letters of Paul: Rethinking Anthropogony and Theology*. SNT 168. Leiden and Boston: Brill, 2016.

Michaud, Henri. *Jésus salon le Coran*. CTh 46; Neuchatel: Delachaux et Niestlé, 1960.

Micheau, Françoise. *Les débuts de l'islam. Jalons pour one nouvelle histoire*. Paris: Téraèdre, 2012.

Mimouni, Simon Claude. *Le jud*éo-christianisme ancien. *Essays historiques*, Préface par André Caquot. Patrimoines; Paris: Cerf, 1998.

Mingana, Alphonse. "Syriac Influence on the Style of the Ḳur'ān." *BJRL* 11 (1927): 77–98.
Mourad, Suleiman A. "The Qur'ān and Jesus' Crucifixion and Death," in *New Perspectives on the Qur'ān: The Qur'ān in Its Historical Context 2*, ed. Gabriel Said Reynolds, 349–57. RSQ; London and New York: Routledge, 2011.
Nau, François. *Les arabes chrétiens de Mésopotamie et de Syrie du vi*[e] *au vii*[e] *siècle*. CSA; Paris: Imprimerie National, 1933.
Neusner, Jacob. *A History of the Jews in Babylonia, V: Later Sasanian Times*. Leiden: Brill, 1970. Reprinted in Eugene, OR: Wipf and Stock, 2008.
Neuwirth, Angelika. "The House of Abraham and the House of Amram: Genealogy, Patriarchal Authority, and Exegetical Professionalism." In *The Qur'ān in Context: Historical and Literary Investigations into the Qur'ānic Milieu*, ed. Angelika Neuwirth, Nicolai Sinai, and Michael Marx, 499–531. Leiden and Boston: Brill, 2010.
Nevo, Yehuda D. and Judith Koren, *Crossroads to Islam: The Origins of the Arab Religion and the Arab State*. Amherst, NY: Prometheus Books, 2003.
Newby, Gordon D. *The Making of the Last Prophet: A Reconstruction of the Earliest Biography of Muhammad*. Columbia: University of South Carolina Press, 1989.
Nickelsburg, George W. E. *Jewish Literature between the Bible and the Mishnah: A Historical and Literary Introduction.*2nd ed. Minneapolis: Fortress Press, 2005.
Nickelsburg, George W. E. and James C. VanderKam. *1 Enoch 2: A Commentary on the Book of 1 Enoch, Chapters 37–82*, ed. Klaus Baltzer. Hermeneia; Minneapolis: Fortress, 2012.
Nöldeke, Theodor. *Geschichte des Qorāns*. Göttingen: Dieterich, 1860.
Nöldeke, Theodor. *Neue Beiträge* zur Semitischen Sprachwissenschaft. Strassburg: Trüber, 1910. Partial English translation, "On the Language of the Koran." In *Which Koran: Variants, Manuscripts, Linguistics*, ed. Ibn Warraq, 1–30. Amherst, NY: Prometheus Books, 2011.
Nöldeke, Theodor and Friedrich Schwally. *Geschichte des Qorāns*. 2nd ed. 2 vols. Leipzig: Weicher, 1909–19.
Ohlig, Karl-Heinz and Gerd R. Puin, eds. *The Hidden Origins of Islam: New Research into Its Early History*. Amherst, NY: Prometheus Books, 2010.
Pallathupurayidam, James. *The Second Vatican Council and Islam: Change in the Catholic Attitude* (Ph.D. dissertation, McGill University, 1981.
Parrinder, Geoffrey. *Jesus in the Qur'ān*. London: Faber and Faber, 1965. 2nd ed., Oxford: Oneworld, 1995.
Parrinder, Geoffrey. "Robert Charles Zaehner (1913–1974)." *HR* 16 (1976): 66–74.
Pelikan, Jaroslav. *The Christian Tradition: A History of the Development of Doctrine*. 2 vols. Chicago and London: University of Chicago Press, 1971–4.
Penn, Michael Philip. *When Christians First Met Muslims: A Sourcebook of the Earliest Syriac Writings on Islam*. Berkeley and Los Angeles: University of California Press, 2015.
Petersen, Anders Klostergaard. "The Diversity of Apologetics: From Genre to a Mode of Thinking." In *Critique and Apologetics: Jews, Christians and Pagans in Antiquity*, ed. Jörg Ulrich, David Brakke, and Anders-Christian Jacobsen, 15–41. ECCA. Frankfurt am Main: Peter Lang, 2009.
Petersen, Anders Klostergaard. "Apologetics." In *Vocabulary for the Study of Religion*, ed. Robert Segal and Kocku von Stuckrad, 1:110–14. 3 vols.; Leiden and Boston: Brill, 2015.
Pettipiece, Timothy. "Manichaeism at the Crossroads of Jewish, Christian and Muslim Traditions." In *Patristic Studies in the Twenty-First Century: Proceedings of an International*

Conference to Mark the 50th Anniversary of the International Association of Patristic Studies, ed. Brouria Bitton-Ashkelony, Theodore de Bruyn, and Carol Harrison, 299–313. Turnhout, BE: Breopols, 2015.
Pohlmann, Karl-Friedrich. *Die Entstehung des Korans: Neue Erkenntnisse aus Sicht der historisch-kritischen Bibelwissenschaft*. 3rd ed. Darmstadt: WBG, 2015.
Pörksen, Martin. *Jesus in der Bibel und im Koran*. Bad Salzuflen, Germany: MBK, 1964.
Powers, David. *Muḥammad Is Not the Father of Any of Your Men: The Making of the Last Prophet*. DRLAR. Philadelphia: University of Pennsylvania Press, 2011.
de Prémare, Alfred-Louis. *Les fondations de l'islam. Entre écriture et histoire* . Paris: Seuil, 2002.
de Prémare, Alfred-Louis. *Aux origines du Coran: questions d'hier, approaches d'aujourd'hui*. Paris: Téraèdre, 2004.
de Prémare, Alfred-Louis. "Le Coran ou la fabrication de l'incréé." *Medium* 2.3 (2005): 3–30.
de Prémare, Alfred-Louis. "'Il voulut détruire le Temple'. L'attaque de la Ka'ba par les rois yéménites avant l'islam: Abḫār et Histoire." *JA* 288 (2000): 261–7.
de Prémare, Alfred-Louis. "'Abd al-Malik b. Marwān and the Process of the Qur'ān's Composition." In *The Hidden Origins of Islam: New Research into Its Early History*, ed. Karl-Heinz Ohlig and Gerd-R. Puin, 189–221. Armherst, NY: Prometheus Books, 2010.
Radscheit, Matthias. "Table." In *Encyclopaedia of the Qur'ān*, ed. Jane Dammen McAuliffe, . 5:188–91. 6 vols. Leiden and Boston: Brill, 2001–6.
Räisänen, Heikki. *Das Koranische Jesusbild: Ein Beitrag zur Theologie des Korans*. SFGMO 20. Helsinki: Finnischen Gesellschaft für Missiologie und Ökumenik, 1971.
Räisänen, Heikki. "The Portrait of Jesus in the Qur'ān: Reflections from a Biblical Scholar." *MW* 70 (1980): 122–33.
Van Reeth, Jan M. F. "L'Évangile du prophète." In *al-Kitāb: La sacralité* du texte dans le monde de l'*Islam. Actes du Symposium international tenu* à Leuven et *Louvain-la-Neuve du 29 mai au 1 juin 2002*, ed. Daniel De Smet, Godefroy Callatay, and Jan M. F. van Reeth, 155–74. Brussels: SBEO, 2004.
Van Reeth, Jan M. F. "Melchisédech le Prophète éternel selon Jean d'Apamée et le monarchianisme musulman." *OC* 96 (2012): 8–46.
Reeves, John C. "Sefer Zerubbabel: The prophetic Vision of Zerubbabel ben Shealtiel." In *Old Testament Pseudepigrapha: More Noncanonical Scriptures*, ed. Richard Bauckham, James R. Davila, and Alexander Payanotov, 448–66. Grand Rapids, MI, and Cambridge: Eerdmans, 2013.
Reinik, Gerrit J. "Tradition and the Formation of the 'Nestorian' Identity in Sixth- to Seventh-Century Iraq." In *Religious Origins of Nations? The Christian Communities of the Middle East*, ed. R. Bas ter Haar Romeny, 217–50. Leiden and Boston: Brill, 2010.
Retsö, Jan. *The Arabs in Antiquity: Their History from the Assyrians to the Umayyads*. London and New York: RoutledgeCurzon, 2003.
Retsö, Jan. "Arabs and Arabic in the Age of the Prophet." In *The Qur'ān in Context: Historical and Literary Investigations into the Qur'ānic Milieu*, ed. Angelika Neuwirth, Nicolai Sinai, and Michael Marx, 281–92. TSQ 6; Leiden and Boston: Brill, 2010.
Reynolds, Gabriel Said. "The Muslim Jesus: Dead or Alive?" *BSOAS* 72.2 [2009]: 237–58.
Reynolds, Gabriel Said. "On the Qur'anic Accusation of Scriptural Falsification (*taḥrīf*) and Christian Anti-Jewish Polemic." *JAOS* 130.2 (2010): 189–202.
Reynolds, Gabriel Said. *The Qur'ān and Its Biblical Subtext*. RSQ. London and New York: Routledge, 2010.

Reynolds, Gabriel Said. "On the Presentation of Christianity in the Qur'ān and the Many Aspects of Qur'anic Rhetoric." *BJQHS* 12 (2014): 42–54.
Risse, Günther. *"Gott ist Christus, der Sohn der Maria": Eine Studie zum Christusbild im Koran.* Bonn: Borengässer, 1989.
Rizzardi, Giuseppe. *Il problema della cristologia coranica: storia dell'ermeneutica cristiana.* Milan: Istituto Propaganda Libraria, 1982.
Robin, Christian Julien. "Le royaume Ḥujride, dit « royaume de Kinda », entre Ḥimyar et Byzance." *CRSAIBL* 140.2 (1996): 665–714.
Robin, Christian Julien. "Abraha et la reconquête de l'Arabie déserte: un réexamen de l'inscription Ryckmans 506 = Murayghan 1." *JSAI* 39 (2012): 1–93.
Robin, Christian Julien. "Arabia and Ethiopia." In *The Oxford Handbook of Late Antiquity*, ed. Scott Fitzgerald Johnson, 247–332. Oxford and New York: Oxford University Press, 2012.
Robin, Christian Julien. "Note d'information. Soixante-dix ans avant l'islam: L'Arabie toute entière dominée par un roi chrétien." *CRAI* 2012.1 (2012): 525–53.
Robin, Christian Julien. "À propos de Ymnt et Ymn : « nord » et « sud », « droite » et « gauche », dans les inscriptions de l'Arabie antique." in *Entre Carthage et l'Arabie heureuse. Mélanges offerts à François Bron*, ed. Françoise Briquel-Chatonnet, Catherine Fauveaud, and Iwona Gajda, 119–40. OM 12. Paris: De Boccard, 2013.
Robinson, Chase F. *'Abd al-Malik*. MMW. Oxford: Oneworld, 2005.
Robinson, Neal. *Christ in Islam and Christianity*. Albany, NY: State University of New York Press, 1991.
Robinson, Neal. "Christian and Muslim Perspectives on Jesus in the Qur'ān." In *Fundamentalism and Tolerance: An Agenda for Theology and Society*, ed. Andrew Linzey and Peter J. Wexler, 92–105, 171–172. London: Bellew, 1991.
Robinson, Neal. "Jesus." In *Encycopledia of the Qur'ān*, ed. J. D. McAuliffe, 3:17–20. 6 vols. Leiden and Boston: Brill, 2001–6.
Sadeghi, Behnam and Mohsen Goudarzi. "Ṣan'ā' 1 and the Origins of the Qur'ān." *IJHCME* 87 (2012): 1–129.
Schäfer, Peter. *The History of the Jews in the Greco-Roman World*. London and New York: Routledge, 2003.
Schäfer, Peter, Michael Meerson, and Yaakov Deutsch, eds. *Toledot Yeshu ("The Life Story of Jesus") Revisited: A Princeton Conference*. TSAJ 143. Tübingen: Mohr Siebeck, 2011.
Schaff, Philip, ed. *Nicene- and Post-Nicene Fathers*. First Series. 14 vols. London and New York: T & T Clark, 1886–1900.
Schedl, Claus. *Muhammad und Jesus: Die christologisch relevanten Texte des Korans, neu übersetz und erlärkt*. Vienna, Freiburg, and Basel: Herder, 1978.
Schedl, Claus. "Die 114 Suren des Koran und die 114 Logien Jesu im Thomas-Evangelium." *Der Islam* 64.2 (1987): 261–4.
Schick, Robert. *The Christian Communities of Palestine from Byzantine to Islamic Rule: A Historical and Archaeological Study*. SLAEI; Princeton, NJ: Darwin, 1995.
Schmitz, Bertram. "Das Spannungsverhältnis zwischen Judentum und Christentum als Grundlage des Entstehungsprozesses des Islams in der Interpretation von Vers 124 bis 141 der zweiten Sure." In *Der Koran und sein religiöses und kulturelles Umfeld*, ed. Tilman Nagel, 217–38. Munich: Oldenbourg, 2010.
Schöck, Cornelia. "Adam and Eve." In *Encyclopaedia of the Qur'ān*, ed. Jane Dammen McAuliffe, 1:22–6. 6 vols.. Leiden and Boston: Brill, 2001–6.

Schwartz, Seth. *The Ancient Jews from Alexander to Muhammad*. KTAH. Cambridge and New York: Cambridge University Press, 2014.

Segovia, Carlos A. "Noah as Eschatological Mediator Transposed: From 2 Enoch 71–72 to the Christological Echoes of 1 Enoch 106:3 in the Qur'ān." *Henoch* 33.1 (2011): 130–45.

Segovia, Carlos A. "Thematic and Structural Affinities between 1 Enoch and the Qur'ān: A Contribution to the Study of the Judaeo-Christian Apocalyptic Setting of the Early Islamic Faith." In *The Coming of the Comforter: When, Where, and to Whom? Studies on the Rise of Islam and Various Other Topics in Memory of John Wansbrough*, ed. Carlos A. Segovia and Basil Lourié, 231–67. OJC 3. Piscataway, NJ: Gorgias Press, 2012.

Segovia, Carlos A. "Abraha's Christological Formula *RḤMNN W-MAS1Ḥ-HW* and Its Relevance for the Study of Islam's Origins." *OC* 98 (2015): 52–63.

Segovia, Carlos A. *The Quranic Noah and the Making of the Islamic Prophet: A Study of Intertextuality and Religious Identity Formation in Late Antiquity*. JCIT 4. Berlin and Boston: De Gruyter, 2015.

Segovia, Carlos A. "Discussing/subverting Paul: Polemical Re-readings and Competitive Supersessionist Misreadings of Pauline Inclusivism in Late Antiquity: A Case Study on the Apocalypse of Abraham, Justin Martyr, and the Qur'ān." In *Paul the Jew: A Conversation between Pauline and Second Temple Scholars*, ed. Gabriele Boccaccini and Carlos A. Segovia, 341–61. Minneapolis: Fortress, 2016.

Segovia, Carlos A. "'Those on the Right' and 'Those on the Left': Rereading Qur'ān 56:1–56 (and the Founding Myth of Islam) in Light of Apocalypse of Abraham 21–2." *OC* 100 (2017): 197–211.

Segovia, Carlos A. "An Encrypted Adamic Christology in the Qur'ān? New Insights on 15:29; 21:91; 38:72; 66:12." In *The Embroidered Bible: Studies in Biblical Apocrypha and Pseudepigrapha in Honour of Michael E. Stone*, ed. William Adler, Lorenzo DiTommaso, and Matthias Henze, 913–27. SVTP. Leiden and Boston: Brill, 2018.

Segovia, Carlos A. "The Jews and Christians of Pre-Islamic Yemen (Ḥimyar) and the Elusive Matrix of the Qur'ān's Christology" In *Jewish Christianity and Islamic Origins: Papers presented at the Eighth Annual ASMEA Conference (Washington DC, October 29–31, 2015)*, ed. Francisco del Río Sánchez, 91–104. JAOC. Turnhout, BE: Brepols, 2018.

Segovia, Carlos A. "Identity Politics and Scholarship in the Study of Islamic Origins: The Inscriptions of the Dome of the Rock as a Test Case." Forthcoming in *Identity, Politics and the Study of Islam: Current Dilemmas in the Study of Religions*, ed. Matt Sheddy, 98–117. CESIF. Sheffield, UK, and Bristol, CT: Equinox, 2018.

Segovia, Carlos A. "Friends, Enemies, or Hoped-for New Rulers? Reassessing the Early Jewish Sources Mentioning the Rise of Islam." Forthcoming in *Jews and Judaism in Northern Arabia*, ed. Haggai Mazuz. BRLJ. Leiden and Boston: Brill, forthcoming.

Segovia, Carlos A. "Messalianism, Binitarianism, and the East-Syrian Bacground of the Qur'ān." Forthcoming in *Remapping Emergent Islam: Texts, Social Contexts, and Ideological Trajectories*, ed. Carlos A. Segovia. SWLAEMA. Amsterdam: Amsterdam University Press, forthcoming.

Segovia, Carlos A. "A Messianic Controversy behind the Making of Muḥammad as the Last Prophet?" Forthcoming in *Early Islam: The Religious Milieu of Late Antiquity*, ed. Guillaume Dye. LAMINE; Chicago: Chicago Oriental Institute, forthcoming.

Segovia, Carlos A. "Asceticism and the Early Quranic Milieu: A Symptomatic Reading of Q 17:79, 43:36, 73:1–8, 74:43, 76:26, and 108." Forthcoming.

Segovia, Carlos A. "Social Theory, Conceptual Imagination, and The Study of Pre-State Societies: From Lévi-Strauss to Pierre Clastres." Forthcoming in *Anarchist Studies*.

Shepardson, Christine. *Anti-Judaism and Christian Orthodoxy: Ephrem's Hymns in Fourth-Century Syria*. NAPSPMS 20. Washington, DC: Catholic University of America Press, 2008.

Shahîd, Irfan. "Byzantium in South Arabia." *DOP* 33 (1979): 23–94.

Shahîd, Irfan. *Byzantium and the Arabs in the Sixth Century*. 2 vols. DORLC. Washington DC: Dumbarton Oaks, 1995–2002.

Shahîd, Irfan. "Islam and *Oriens Christianus*: Makka 610–622 ad." In *The Encounter of Eastern Christianity with Early Islam*, ed. Emmanouela Grypeou, Mark N. Swanson, and David Thomas, 9–31. Leiden and Boston: Brill. 2006.

Shoemaker, Stephen J. "Christmas in the Qur'ān: The Qur'ānic Account of Jesus' Nativity and Palestinian Local Tradition." *JSAI* 28 (2003): 11–39.

Shoemaker, Stephen J. *The Death of a Prophet: The End of Muhammad's Life and the Beginnings of Islam*. DRLAR. Philadelphia: University of Pennsylvania Press, 2012.

Siddiqui, Mona. *Christians, Muslims, and Jesus*. New Haven, CT, and London: Yale University Press, 2013.

Sirry, Mun'im. *Scriptural Polemics: The Qur'ān and Other Religions*. Oxford and New York: Oxford University Press, 2014.

von Sivers, Peter. "Christology and Prophetology in the Umayyad Arab Empire." In *Die Entstehung einer Weltreligion III*, ed. Markus Groß and Karl-Heinz Ohlig, 255–85. Berlin: Hans Schiler, 2014.

Sivertsev, Alexei. *Judaism and Imperial Ideology in Late Antiquity*. Cambridge and New York: Cambridge University Press, 2011.

Skottki, Kristin. "Medieval Western Perceptions of Islam and the Scholars: What Went Wrong?" In *Cultural Transfers in Dispute: Representations in Asia, Europe and the Arab World since the Middle Ages*, ed. Jörg Feuchter, Friedhelm Hoffmann, and Bee Yun, 107–34. Frankfurt and New York: Campus Verlag, 2011.

Smith, Mark S. *The Early History of God: Yahweh and the Other Deities in Ancient Israel*. 2nd ed. Grand Rapids, MI, and Cambridge: Eerdmans, 2001.

Stead, Christopher. *Philosophy in Christian Antiquity*. Cambridge and New York: Cambridge University Press, 1994.

Steppa, Jan-Eric. *John Rufus and the World Vision of Anti-Chalcedonian Culture*. GDACS 1. Piscataway, NJ: Gorgias Press, 2002.

Stone, Michael E. *A History of the Literature of Adam and Eve*. SBLEJL 3. Atlanta, GA: Scholars Press, 1992.

Stone, Michael E. "The Fall of Satan and Adam's Penance: Three Notes on *The Books of Adam and Eve*." In *Literature on Adam and Eve: Collected Essays*, ed. Gary A. Anderson, Michael E. Stone, Johannes Tromp, 43–56. SVTP 15. Leiden and Boston: Brill, 2000.

Stone, Michael E. and Gary A. Anderson. *A Synopsis of the Books of Adam and Eve*. SBLEJL 17. 2nd revised ed. Atlanta, GA: Scholars Press, 1999.

Stroumsa, Guy G. "Jewish Christianity and Islamic Origins." In *Islamic Cultures, Islamic Contexts: Essays in Honor of Professor Patricia Crone*, ed. Behnam Sadeghi, Asad Q. Ahmed, Adam Silverstein, and Robert G. Hoyland, 72–96. Leiden and Boston: Brill, 2015.

Sundermann, Werner. "CHRISTIANITY v. Christ in Manicheism." In *Encyclopædia Iranica*, 5.5 (1991): 335–39; available online at http://www.iranicaonline.org/articles/christianity-v.

al-Ṭabarī. *Tārīḫ al-Rusul wa-l-Mulūk*, ed. Muḥammad Abū l-Faḍl Ibrāhim. 10 vols. Cairo: Dār al-Ma'ārif, 1960–9.

Tardieu, Michel. *Le Manichéism*. Paris: Presses Universities de France, 1981. English translation by M. B. DeBevoise, with an Introduction by Paul Mirecki, *Manichaeism*. Chicago: University of Illinois Press, 2008.

Tardieu, Michel. "L'arrivée des Manichéens à Al-Hîra." In *La Syrie de Byzance à l'Islam. VIIe–VIIIe siècles*, ed. Pierre Canivet and Jean-Paul Rey-Coquais, 15–24. Damascus: IFD, 1992.

Tesei, Tommaso. "The Prophecy of Ḏū-l-Qarnayn and the Origins of the Qur'ānic Corpus." *MA* (2013–14): 273–90.

Tesei, Tommaso. "The Qur'ān(s) in Context(s)." Unpublished. Available online at https://www.academia.edu/s/435c3a5a16/the-qur'ans-in-contexts

Thurston, John. "Symptomatic Reading." In *Encyclopedia of Contemporary Literary Theory: Approaches, Scholars, Terms*, ed. Irena R. Makaryk, 638. Toronto, Buffalo, and London: University of Toronto Press, 1993.

Toral-Niehoff, Isabel. "The 'Ibād of al-Ḥīra: An Arab Christian Community in Late Antique Iraq." In *The Qur'ān in Context: Historical and Literary Investigations into the Qur'ānic Milieu*, ed. Angelika Neuwirth, Nicolai Sinai, and Michael Marx, 323–47. Leiden and Boston: Brill, 2010.

Toral-Niehoff, Isabel. "Late Antique Iran and the Arabs: The Case of al-Hira." *JPS* 6 (2013): 115–26.

Tottoli, Roberto. *I profeti biblici nella tradizione islamica*. Brescia: Paideia, 1999. English translation by Michael Robertson, *Biblical Prophets in the Qur'ān and Muslim Literature*. RSQ. London and New York: Routledge, 2002.

Tottoli, Roberto. "'Imrān." In *Encyclopaedia of the Qur'ān*, ed. Jane Dammen McAuliffe, 2:509. 6 vols. Leiden and Boston: Brill, 2001–6.

Trimingham, J. Spencer. *Christianity among the Arabs in pre-Islamic Times*. London: Longman; Beirut: Librairie du Liban, 1979.

Van der Velden, Frank. "Kotexte im Konvergenzstrang – die Bedeutung textkritischer Varianten und christlicher Bezugstexte für die Redaktion von Sure 61 und Sure 5, 110–119." *OC* 92 (2008): 130–73.

Van der Velden, Frank. "Die Felsendominschrift als Ende einer christologischen Konvergenztextökumene im Koran." *Oriens Christianus* 95 (2011): 213–46.

Van Voorst, Robert E. *Jesus Outside the New Testament: An Introduction to Ancient Evidence*. Grand Rapids, MI, and Cambridge: Eerdmans, 2000.

Wansbrough, John. *Quranic Studies: Sources and Methods of Scriptural Interpretation*. LOS; Oxford: Oxford University Press, 1977. Reprinted with a Foreword, Translations, and Expanded Notes by Andrew Rippin in Amherst, NY: Prometheus Books, 2004.

Wansbrough, John. *The Sectarian Milieu: Contents and Composition of Islamic Salvation History*. Oxford and New York: Oxford University Press, 1978. Reprinted with a foreword, translation, and expanded notes by Gerald R. Hawting in Amherst, NY: Prometheus Books, 2006.

Ward, Walter D. *The Mirage of the Saracen: Christians and Nomads in the Sinai Peninsula in Late Antiquity*. TCH 54. Oakland: University of California Press, 2015.

Wenzel, Catherina. "'Und als Ibrāhīm und Ismāʿīl die FunDammente des Hauses (der Ka'ba) legten' (Sure 2, 127): Abrahamsrezeption und Legitimät im Koran." *ZR* 45.3 (2002): 193–209.

Wheeler, Brannon. "Adam," in *The Qur'an: An Encyclopedia*, ed. Oliver Leaman, 11–12. London and New York: Routledge, 2006.

Wild, Stefan, ed. *Self-referentiality in the Qur'ān*. DA 11. Wiesbaden: Harrassowitz, 2007.

Winkler, Dietmar W. "The Age of the Sassanians (until 651)," In *The Church of the East: A Concise History*, ed. Wilhelm Baum and Dietmar W. Winkler, 7–41. London and New York: RoutledgeCurzon, 2000.
Wismer, Donald. *The Islamic Jesus: An Annotated Bibliography of Sources in English and French*. New York: Garland, 1977. Reprinted in London and New York: Routledge, 2016.
Witztum, Joseph. "The Foundation of the House (Q 2:127)." *BSOAS* 72.1 (2009): 25–40.
Witztum, Joseph. "Joseph among the Ishmaelites: Q 12 in Light of Syriac Sources," in *New Perspectives on the Qur'ān: The Qur'ān in Its Historical Context 2*, ed. Gabriel Said Reynolds, 425–48. RSQ. London and New York: Routledge, 2011.
Witztum, Joseph. "The Syriac Milieu of the Qur'ān: *The Recasting of Biblical Narratives*." PhD dissertation, Princeton University, 2011.
Wood, Philip. *The Chronicle of Seert: Christian Historical Imagination in Late Antique Iraq*. OECS. Oxford and New York: Oxford University Press, 2013.
Wood, Philip. "Christianity in the Arabian Peninsula." Forthcoming in *Early Islam: The Sectarian Milieu of Late Antiquity*, ed. Guillaume Dye. LAMINE; Chicago: Chicago Oriental Institute.
Yarbro Collins, Adela and John J. Collins. *King and Messiah as Son of God: Divine, Human, and Angelic Messianic Figures in Biblical and Related Literature*. Grand Rapids, MI, and Cambridge: Eerdmans, 2008.
Zaehner, R. C. "Islam and Christ." *DR* (1957): 271–88.
Zaehner, R. C. *At Sundry Times: An Essay in the Comparison of Religions*. London: Faber and Faber, 1958. 2nd ed., Westport, CT: Greenwood, 1977.
Zellentin, Holger M. *The Qur'ān's Legal Culture: The Didascalia Apostolorum as a Point of Departure* (Tübingen: Mohr Siebeck, 2013).
Zellentin, Holger M. "*Aḥbār* and *Ruhbān*: Religious Leaders in the Qur'ān in Dialogue with Christian and Rabbinic Literature." In *Qur'ānic Studies Today*, ed. Angelika Neuwirth and Michael A. Sells, 258–89. RSQ. London and New York: R outledge, 2016.
Zilio-Grandi, Ida. "Satan." in *Dictionnaire du Coran*, ed. Mohammad Ali Amir-Moezzi, 790–3. Paris: Laffont, 2007.
Zwemer, Samuel M. *The Moslem Christ: An Essay on the Life, Character, and Teachings of Jesus Christ according to the Koran and Orthodox Tradition*. Edinburgh and London: Oliphant, Anderson, and Ferrier, 1912.
Zwemer, Samuel M. "The Worship of Adam by Angels." *MW* 27 (1937): 115–27.

Index of Ancient Sources

Hebrew Bible

Apocrypha and Pseudepigrapha

Dead Sea Scrolls

Greek New Testament

https://doi.org/10.1515/9783110599688-008

Syriac New Testament

Early Christian Literature

NT Apocrypha

Pre-Islamic South-Arabian Inscriptions

Islamic and Related Literature

Qur'ān

Islamic Inscriptions

Other Muslim Texts

Index of Ancient and Modern Authors

Establet, Roger 23 n.129
Ephraem the Syrian 23, 67, 83 n.83, 98, 128 n.27
Epiphanius of Salamis 57 n.4
Eusebius of Nicomedia 97 n.32

Fedeli, Alba 87 n.91
Fisher, Greg 19, 19 n.115, 73 n.45 104 n.57
Fletcher-Louis, Crispin H. T. 76 n.52
Fossum, Jarl E. 103 n.54

Gajda, Iwona 90, 90 nn.7–8, 91 nn.10–11, 92 nn.14–15, 21, 95 n.22, 96, 96 nn.26–97
Gallez, Édouard-Marie 16, 17 n.90, 61, 61 nn.14, 17
Geiger, Abraham 79, 79 n.68
Gerock, Carl Friedrich 2, 2 n.3
Gieschen, Charles 103 n.54, 127 n.24
Gilliot, Claude 84 n.83, 132 n.30
Gnilka, Joachim 86 n.89
Gobillot, Geneviève 62 n.18
Goldsack, William 2, 2 n.5
González Ferrín, Emilio x
Goudarzi, Mohsen 115 n.85
Grabbe, Lester L. 67 n.27
Griffith, Sidney H. 18, 18 n.106, 83 n.83, 109 n.67
Grillmeier, Alois 97 n.33
Guiraud, Morgan 76 n.54

Havenith, Alfred 18, 18 n.101
Hawting, Gerald R. 74 n.47
Heal, Kristian 80 n.70
Heinthaler, Theresia 18, 18 n.109
Henninger, Josef 3, 3 n.8, 17, 17 n.98
Henze, Matthias x
Horn, Cornelia B. 110 n.75, 111 nn.80–1
Horowitz, Elliot S. 73 n.43
Hoyland, Robert G. 70 n.34, 73 n.46, 87 n.93, 149 n.8
Humphreys, R. Stephen 70 n.35, 71 n.36

Ibn Hišām 13–14, 81 n.75
Ibn Isḥāq 37 n.53, 81 n.75
Isaac of Antioch 67

Jackson, Roy 70 n.35
Jackson-McCabe, Matt 8, 8 n.34
Jeffery, Arthur 53 n.122
John Rufus 110, 110 nn.74–5
Johns, Jeremy 87 n.93, 149 n.8
Jongeneel, Jan A. B. 3 n.7
Jacob of Serugh 67, 83, 83 n.83
Justin Martyr 60

Kaplony, Andreas 73 n.44
Khalidi, Tarif 10, 10 n.46
Kister, Meir Jacob 18, 18 n.103
Kofsky, Aryeh 110 n.75
Kohen, Elli 2, 72 nn.40–1
Kreeft, Peter 4, 4 n.16
Koren, Judith 73 n.46
Kropp, Manfred x, 26 n.1, 31 n.22, 42 n.83, 77 n.61, 91 n.12, 92 n.21, 99, 115 n.86, 120 n.7

Lawson, Todd 16, 16 n.85
Lecker, Michael 73 n.46
Leirvik, Oddbjørn 5, 5 n.21, 7, 10, 10 n.49, 11 n.53, 14, 14 n.72, 17
Leslau, Wolf 108 n.64
Lieu, Judith 102 n.52
Lory, Pierre 35 n.49
Lourié, Basil x, 22, 22 n.125
Lüling, Günter 18, 18 n.99, 84 n.83, 128 n.27, 132 n.30
Luxenberg, Christoph 18, 18 n.105, 26 n.1, 28 n.19, 38 n.54, 48 n.105, 62 n.18, 77 n.61, 78 n.64, 83 n.81, 84 n.83, 86 n.89, 146, 146 nn.3–5

Macherey, Pierre 23 n.129
Madigan, Daniel A. 33 n.35
Makin, Al 99, 99 n.39–41
Maneval, J.-P. 2, 2 n.4
Mani 102, 102 n.52
Marcion of Sinope 102, 102 n.52
Marshall, David 18, 18 n.107, 63 n.21
Marx, Karl 23–4 n.129
Masson, Denise 2, 3, 3 nn.9, 11–12, 4–5, 7, 9, 11, 11 n.56
Mazuz, Haggai x, x n.3, 18, 19 n.112
McAuliffe, Jane Damen 3 n.10, 16, 16 n.88, 18
McCurdy, J. Frederic 76 n.54
Meerson, Michael 85 n.87